GEORGE OPP
AND
THE FATE OF MOD

George Oppen
and
The Fate of Modernism

PETER NICHOLLS

OXFORD
UNIVERSITY PRESS

OXFORD

UNIVERSITY PRESS

Great Clarendon Street, Oxford OX2 6DP

Oxford University Press is a department of the University of Oxford.
It furthers the University's objective of excellence in research, scholarship,
and education by publishing worldwide. Oxford is a registered trade mark of
Oxford University Press in the UK and in certain other countries

First published 2007
First published in paperback 2013

British Library Cataloguing in Publication Data

Data available

Library of Congress Cataloging in Publication Data

Data available

ISBN 978–0–19–921826–4 (Hbk)
ISBN 978–0–19–967846–4 (Pbk)

For Linda Clarke
ὄπταις ἄμμε

Acknowledgements

I owe a particular debt of thanks to Linda Oppen, not only for her generosity in granting me permission to quote from published and unpublished material, but also for her friendship and encouragement. I hope that the result is worthy of her expectations. I am grateful, too, to Richard Godden who read the whole manuscript in several versions and commented on them with his usual insight and generosity. His thoughts have been a constant stimulus to my own. Other friends have also read sections and provided valuable feedback: special thanks to Rachel Blau DuPlessis, Michael Davidson, Alan Golding, Lyn Hejinian, Eric Hoffman, Peter Middleton, Drew Milne, and Marjorie Perloff. For information on various aspects of Oppen's life and work I am grateful to Diana Anhalt, Jean Rouverol Butler, Eric Davin, Susan Drucker, Miles Groth, Michael Heller, Crawford Kilian, Andy (Meyer) Levy, Alexander Mourelatos, Anthony Rudolf, and Jacky Senker. I am also grateful to Lynda Claassen and Gerald Cloud of the Mandeville Special Collections for their help and support. My thanks, too, to the University of Sussex for granting me study leave in which to work on the book and to the Leverhulme Trust for awarding me a Research Fellowship.

Parts of this book have appeared in other publications. I would like to thank the following publishers for granting me permission to quote from my earlier published work:

Blackwell Publishers, for the extracts from 'Modernising Modernism: From Pound to Oppen', in *Critical Quarterly*, 44/2 (Summer 2002);

Cambridge University Press, for the extracts from 'George Oppen in Exile: Mexico and Maritain', in *Journal of American Studies*, 39/1 (Apr. 2005);

Editions Belin, for the extracts from 'George Oppen and the Poetics of Quotation', in *Revue française d'études américaines*, 103 (Feb. 2005);

Indiana University Press, for the extracts from 'George Oppen: The New or the Avant-Garde?', in *Journal of Modern Literature*, 28/4 (Oct. 2005);

The National Poetry Foundation, Orono, Maine, for the extracts from 'George Oppen and "that primitive, Hegel"', in *Paideuma*, 32/1–3 (Summer 2003);

Quotations from Mary Oppen, *Meaning a Life* are copyright Linda Oppen, used by permission;

Quotations from George Oppen, *New Collected Poems* are by kind permission of New Directions Publishing Corp.;

Quotations from the unpublished papers of George Oppen are copyright Linda Oppen, used by permission;

Quotations from *The Selected Letters of George Oppen* are copyright Linda Oppen, used by permission.

All Louis Zukofsky material Copyright Paul Zukofsky; the material may not be reproduced, quoted or used in any manner whatsover without the explicit and specific permission of the copyright holder.

Every effort has been made to trace all copyright holders, but if any have been inadvertently overlooked the publishers will be pleased to make the necessary arrangement at the first opportunity.

Contents

List of Figures

Abbreviations

GOMP   Burton Hatlen (ed.), *George Oppen: Man and Poet* (Orono, Me.: National Poetry Foundation, 1981).

MAL   Mary Oppen, *Meaning a Life: An Autobiography* (Santa Barbara, Calif.: Black Sparrow Press, 1978).

NCP   George Oppen, *New Collected Poems*, ed. Michael Davidson (New York: New Directions, 2008).

SL   *The Selected Letters of George Oppen*, ed. Rachel Blau DuPlessis (Durham, NC: Duke University Press, 1990).

UCSD   George Oppen Papers, the Mandeville Special Collections, University of California at San Diego, MSS 16. Materials are cited by collection number, followed by box and file numbers. The same form of reference is used for the Mary Oppen Papers (MSS 125) and the Linda Oppen Papers (MSS 33).

Note to Reader

This book draws extensively on the papers of George Oppen held in the Mandeville Special Collections at the University of San Diego. Of the thirty-four boxes that comprise the collection, one (19) contains variously bound notebooks that have come to be known as the poet's Daybooks, while a further six boxes (13–18) contain miscellaneous notes and jottings. Much of the material is difficult to date (Oppen frequently revisited and added to earlier notes) and the text is often unpunctuated, mistyped, and sometimes illegible. I have attempted to present as accurate a version as possible when quoting from this material and to this end I have silently corrected typographical errors where these have no special significance. Where possible I have tried to reproduce Oppen's rather idiosyncratic use of dashes and his habit of substituting spaces for points. The reader will gain some sense of the nature of Oppen's unpublished material by looking at the typescript shown below in Figures 4 and 5 and then consulting the pages as transcribed in Appendix B.

Introduction

George Oppen acquired impeccable modernist credentials at the very begin-
ning of his career. Aged 25, he was prime mover in a publishing venture which
issued works by Ezra Pound, William Carlos Williams, and Louis Zukofsky,
and his own first book of poems, *Discrete Series* (1934) announced what
looked like yet another avant-garde tendency, Objectivism. Add to this the
commendatory Preface to the book contributed by Pound which concluded:
'I salute a serious craftsman, a sensibility which is not every man's sensibility
and which has not been got out of any other man's books.'[1] Pound's typically
generous 'salute' to a writer implicitly very different from himself now seems
closer to the mark than Hugh Kenner's claim that Oppen and his fellow
Objectivists were straightforwardly the inheritors of the 'formed tradition' of
Poundian modernism.[2] Indeed, in 1933, the year before the book appeared,
Oppen and his wife Mary had visited Pound in Rapallo, and one brief anecdote
published in Mary's later memoir, *Meaning a Life*, indicates that a distance was
already opening up between the older poet and the admiring but clear-sighted
young couple:

Walking with us on the waterfront, Ezra pointed with a grand gesture of his cape and
his cane in the wrong direction and said, 'From there came the Greek ships.' He was
telling us, 'Read, study the languages, read the poets in their own tongues.'

Our message to him would have been just as clear: 'You are too far away from your
own roots.' But we were twenty and Pound was forty, and respect for him as a poet
forbade our telling him that we lacked respect for his politics and that he should go
home. (MAL, 132)

The characteristic 'grand gesture' is eloquent indeed, a mixture of good sense
and pure bluff which memorably associates the excesses of modernism, as
Oppen saw them, with error (an association that would become increasingly
important to him as his career unfolded). Pound's own reverence for 'roots'
is neatly turned back on him here, for the Oppens were concerned not with

---

[1] Ezra Pound, 'Preface to *Discrete Series*' (1934), repr. *Paideuma*, 10/1 (Spring 1981), 13.
[2] Hugh Kenner, *A Homemade World: The American Modernist Writers* (London: Marion
Boyars, 1977), 169.

the 'roots' in myth and tradition celebrated in the ongoing *Cantos*, but with a more literal 'home' that was now in thrall to the Depression. It was the year in which Hitler became Chancellor of Germany and Roosevelt was installed as American President, a fateful moment indeed in which modernism, at least as that was represented by Pound, seemed to the Oppens remote and untimely. Recalling that visit, Mary clearly discerned in the histrionic play with cape and cane an encoding of disaster to come.

This moment on the Rapallo esplanade powerfully associates two extremes of modernism which Oppen would consistently contest in his own work: on the one hand, traditionalism, on the other, avant-gardism. Somewhere between these, he felt, the poet might discover something truly original—a poetics of being, I have called it—that was not reducible to either a myth of the past or to stylistic experimentation masquerading as politics. Oppen was deeply suspicious of 'art' and 'artists', and, as I shall show, avant-gardism, whether of the twenties or the sixties, seemed to him brutal at worst and fashionable at best, a fulfilment of the 'fate' of modernism as he and Mary had discerned it in that flamboyant gesture of Pound's. Oppen's own work would as a result be conceived as a new beginning, the poems not at all part of a 'formed tradition', but each in its own way seeking to free the mind from thoughts known in advance, a characteristic which would make his work hard to 'place' for literary historians and anthologists.

In fact, there were many kinds of beginnings in Oppen's career. Most dramatically he gave up poetry and returned to it twenty-five years later, a story told in the pages to come. And in highly individual ways, each of the books he published also constituted a new beginning. *Discrete Series*, with its enigmatic and syntactically compacted brevities, looked deliberately out of joint with most of the poetry of its period and remains a problematic work. *The Materials* (1962) quite literally registered Oppen's second try at a literary career and entailed a taking stock of where he had reached after his return to writing, while *This in Which* (1965), a volume seen partly in the 'light of the miraculous', as Oppen put it, announced a poetics of being derived partly from the philosophy of Heidegger, whose own understanding of beginnings underpinned an influential notion of poetic thinking. With the 1968 volume *Of Being Numerous* Oppen began once more to consider questions of singular and collective identity, questions he had previously resolved through political action in the thirties, but which still remained unresolved within his poetry. With *Seascape: Needle's Eye* (1972) Oppen's residency in San Francisco, the city of his adolescence, turned him away from the urban landscape of his previous volume, to the ocean and the 'metaphysical' questions prompted by horizon and space. With *Myth of the Blaze* and *Primitive*, questions of survival and mortality were uppermost in the poet's mind, though even here, confronted with illness and with a palpable sense of ending, Oppen managed again to find that 'first light' in which the world might still be encountered as if for the first time.

In his writings, published and unpublished, Oppen rarely situates these concerns in relation to particular modernist poets and poems; at the same time, though, it is a modernism broadly conceived that provides him with a constant instigation to begin again. The recurring poetic gesture is one of uncertainty and openness, at once scrupulous ('It is part of the function of poetry to serve as a test of truth', he wrote[3]) and pledged to finding new and unanticipated rhythms of attention. Perhaps nothing embodies so well the spirit of Oppen's work as that word 'test' which, for him, entails a search for sincerity in the smallest units of the poem. Indeed, to test is 'To slow down, that is, to isolate the words' (UCSD 16, 16, 11), a procedure alert to the too hasty presumptions of avant-gardism as Oppen saw it and sensitive to the intricacies of the poetic thinking he valued. In this respect, Oppen's poetics has something in common with Nietzsche's conception of philology which 'does not so easily get anything done, it teaches to read *well*, that is to say, to read slowly, deeply, looking cautiously before and aft, with reservations, with doors left open, with delicate eyes and fingers'.[4] For Oppen, it was a similar sense of slowness and the emphasis on 'reading well' that would promise some immunity to what he saw as the fate of modernism.

[3] 'The Mind's Own Place' (1963), repr. in *Selected Poems of George Oppen*, ed. and introd. Robert Creeley (New York: New Directions, 2003), 176.

[4] Friedrich Nietzsche, *Daybreak: Thoughts on the Prejudices of Morality*, trans. R. J. Hollingdale (Cambridge: Cambridge University Press, 1997), 5.

1

Beginning Again

In 1960, George Oppen and his wife Mary settled in New York City after a period of nine years of political exile in Mexico. Oppen was the author of a slim volume of poems entitled *Discrete Series*, published back in 1934 with a then highly desirable preface by Ezra Pound. Only a few of Oppen's contemporaries, however, would now remember him as a poet, a consequence of what he would term in a later interview 'my rejection of poetry for twenty or twenty-five years'.[1] For only at the end of the fifties, at the very end of the period spent in Mexico, had Oppen begun to write again. Success would come to him later in the decade, with the award of the Pulitzer Prize for Poetry, but, for the time being, as Oppen observed of the rather similar case of Basil Bunting, he felt as if he had returned to writing 'as from the dead' (SL, 129).

For the reader of Oppen and for anyone wishing to write about him, this 'silence', lasting almost a quarter of a century, poses some difficult questions. We know, for example, almost nothing about his reading and intellectual interests during this period, the long abandonment of poetry coinciding with an almost complete lack of any other written materials, of notes or correspondence. The editor of his *Selected Letters*, Rachel Blau DuPlessis, observes that there is only 'one extant letter' by Oppen between 1934 and 1958 (SL, 17), and Eliot Weinberger suggests in his preface to the *New Collected Poems* that Oppen 'may never be the subject of a biography, for his life beyond its outline remains a mystery, and for decades left no paper trail' (NCP, p. xvii).

The life that went unrecorded was eventful enough, as we shall see, but what is immediately intriguing about the 'shape' of Oppen's career is its pattern of disjunction and return. What does it mean to go back to poetry in the way that Oppen did? And how do we narrate a literary career which contains a 'silence' of this duration at its centre? The conventionally linear account of a life and works will hardly be adequate to the challenge, since what we have to do with here also entails a complex dialectic of forgetting and remembering which

---

[1] L. S. Dembo, 'The "Objectivist" Poet: Four Interviews', *Contemporary Literature*, 10/2 (Spring 1969), 173–4.

insinuates itself into the deepest recesses of Oppen's theory and practice of poetry. And while, of course, we need a conventional narrative of a continuous, lived temporality to grasp the sequence of events that took the Oppens to Mexico and then to New York, we must also take account of what might be called a psychological time in which different chronologies overlaid and interacted with each other. The difficulty of such a narrative is compounded by the fact that the principal sources from which it must be drawn—Mary Oppen's autobiography, *Meaning a Life*, and the various interviews the couple gave in their later years—are themselves marked by gaps and silences, while at the same time they exhibit compensatory patterns of emphasis and repetition which tend to give certain pivotal events in these lives an almost mythic status. In a note to himself, Oppen once referred to such events as 'ur-scenes' (UCSD 16, 17, 3), a phrase that might recall Freud's concept of the primal scene, and at the least suggests an ambivalence about *origins*—social, familial, and otherwise—which, I shall suggest, is a consistent feature of Oppen's writing.

We make of the biographical record what we can. Oppen was born in 1908 in New Rochelle, New York.[2] His was a wealthy, upper-class Jewish family; Oppen was, he told one correspondent, 'born of a couple of rather millionaire lines' (SL, 207), and elsewhere he described his childhood and adolescence as 'chauffeured, butlered, nurse-maided, and for a brief and absurd period valeted' (UCSD 16, 16, 9). A cosseted childhood, then, but one not unmarked by traumatic events. Oppen's mother killed herself when the boy was 4, and he was to have a deeply troubled relationship with his new stepmother.[3] Later, aged 17, Oppen was involved as driver in a fatal car accident and as a result was expelled from school. Two years after that and following a period travelling in Europe he attended Oregon State University where he was soon expelled again after spending a night out of college with his wife-to-be Mary Colby. Oppen would always remember this night as a decisive turning-point in his life, estranging him finally from his wealthy family and inaugurating a period of bohemian freedoms. 'What happened is that Mary Colby and I walked off,' he recalled, 'Ran off, actually, being under-age at the moment of running' (SL, 297). The next few years were exciting ones as the couple

---

[2] Main sources of biographical information are MAL; Rachel Blau DuPlessis, 'Introduction', to SL; Michael Davidson, 'Introduction', to NCP; Jeffrey Peterson, 'George Oppen', in *Dictionary of Literary Biography: American Poets since World War II*, 4th ser. ed. Joseph Conte et al. (Farmington Mills, Mich.: Gale Research Inc., 1996), 188–206; David McAleavey, 'The Oppens: Remarks towards Biography', *Ironwood*, 26 (Fall 1985), 309–18; Rachel Blau DuPlessis, 'An Oppen Chronology', in *Selected Poems of George Oppen*, ed. and introd. Robert Creeley (New York: New Directions, 2003), 191–8.

[3] See Peterson, 'George Oppen', 189 quoting an unpublished comment by Oppen: 'My father's second marriage opened upon me an attack totally murderous, totally brutal, involving sexual attack, [and] beatings.'

hitchhiked around the States before moving temporarily to France where they set up To Publishers which quickly brought out works by Ezra Pound, William Carlos Williams, and Louis Zukofsky in revolutionary new paperback form.[4] The financial situation was increasingly precarious, however. While Oppen received an inheritance from his mother's estate, the onset of the Depression suddenly reduced his income from it; To Publishers was an inevitable casualty. By 1933 they were back in New York where Oppen formed The Objectivist Press with Williams, Zukofsky, and Charles Reznikoff.

The Press, which would publish Oppen's *Discrete Series* the next year, was named, of course, for a new tendency, Objectivism, to be associated in the future primarily with Zukofsky, Oppen, Reznikoff, Carl Rakosi, Lorine Niedecker, and Basil Bunting. Zukofsky had adopted the term in his manifesto essay 'Sincerity and Objectification' in *Poetry* magazine in 1931, though he had done so rather reluctantly and at editor Harriet Monroe's insistence. The essay itself, which is largely an appreciation of the work of Reznikoff, offers some at first sight fairly unexceptionable principles, and in referring to it in his preface to the anthology, Zukofsky stressed that his interest had been 'in the craft of poetry, NOT in a movement'.[5] Oppen himself seems to have had little stake in any programme as such: later he would recall that 'the theory of objectivism—and there was one—was Zukofsky's' (SL, 46), and the most he would say of shared aspirations was that there had been 'some degree of agreement between us at the time of the anthology' (UCSD 16, 17, 9). Programmatic or not, though, the Objectivists were happy to acknowledge their roots in the modernism of the twenties. Almost thirty years later, in an essay called 'The Mind's Own Place', Oppen would observe that 'Modern American poetry begins with the determination to find the image, the thing encountered, the thing seen each day whose meaning has become the meaning and the color of our lives'.[6] In the work of Pound, Eliot, and Williams, the Objectivists had discovered a new 'visual clarity' and a 'freedom from the art subject' (175). Now they, too, called for 'clarity of image and word-tone' and defined 'the accuracy of detail in writing' as 'sincerity' (Pound's notion of 'technique as a test of man's sincerity' was an obvious touchstone here).[7] A

---

⁴ On the To Publishers venture, see SL, 46, 83, 370 n. 2. According to Zukofsky, *Prepositions* (London: Rapp & Carroll, 1967), 41 the name of the press was his idea—'*To*—as we might say, a health to'. See also Tom Sharp, 'The Objectivists' Publications', *Sagetrieb*, 3/3 (Winter 1984), 41–7.

⁵ Louis Zukofsky (ed.), An *'Objectivists' Anthology* (Le Beausset and New York: To Publishers, 1932), 24–5.

⁶ 'The Mind's Own Place' (1963), repr. in *Selected Poems*, ed. Creeley, 173. Further references will be given in the text.

⁷ Louis Zukofsky, 'Sincerity and Objectification', *Poetry*, 37/5 (Feb. 1931) 272, 280; Ezra Pound, *Literary Essays*, ed. T. S. Eliot (London: Faber and Faber, 1968), 9.

further Poundian image emphasized the importance of verbal concentration, as Zukofsky defined 'An Objective' as 'The lens bringing the rays from an object to a focus'.[8] Most of this was familiar modernist doctrine by 1931, complicated only by the particular spin it gave to the word 'objectivist' which here designated—somewhat paradoxically—a practice of writing which was ultimately concerned less with objects than with what Zukofsky called the 'shape' of the poem and 'the resolving of words and their ideation into structure'.[9] What was objectified was the poem itself; as Zukofsky put it: 'This rested totality may be called objectification—the apprehension satisfied completely as to the appearance of the art form as an object'.[10]

I will return to this idea of the poem as an 'object', but what is initially perhaps most striking about the poems in *Discrete Series* is their attention to everyday urban experience. In 'The Mind's Own Place', Oppen would look back to the pioneers of modernism, observing that

They meant to replace by the data of experience the accepted poetry of their time, a display by the poets of right thinking and right sentiment, a dreary waste of lies. That data was and is the core of what 'modernism' restored to poetry, the sense of the poet's self among things. So much depends upon the red wheelbarrow. The distinction between a poem that shows confidence in itself and in its materials, and on the other hand a performance, a speech by the poet is the distinction between poetry and histrionics. (175–6)

'[T]he sense of the poet's self among *contemporary* things', we might add when applying this 'distinction' to Oppen's own work, for the world of *Discrete Series* contains no wheelbarrows and agricultural implements (or indeed petals and fountains) but elevators, fridges, cars, steam-shovels, and tug boats. There is a fascination with the gritty detail of modern American life which inevitably calls Williams to mind (though there are actually more differences than similarities between their writings, as Oppen would emphasize (SL, 20)), and an early admiration for Sherwood Anderson, Carl Sandburg, and Vachel Lindsay can

---

[8] Zukofsky, 'Sincerity and Objectification', 268.

[9] Ibid. 273, 274. The word would continue to mislead, however, and on several occasions Oppen attempted to make the distinction clear—see e.g. Serge Faucherau, 'Three Oppen Letters with a Note', *Ironwood*, 5 (1975), 79: 'Several dozen commentators and reviewers have by now written on the assumption that the word "Objectivist" indicated the contributors' objective attitude to reality. It meant, of course, the poets' recognition of the necessity of form, the objectification of the poem.' Cf. SL, 47: 'Objectivist meant, not an objective viewpoint, but to objectify the poem, to make the poem an object. Meant form.'

[10] Ibid. 274. For the counter-view, that Zukofsky's practice 'exposes the object-status of the poem as a delusion', see Michael Davidson, 'Dismantling "Mantis": Reification and Objectivist Poetics', *American Literary History*, 3/3 (Fall 1991), 522. I have suggested a qualification to Davidson's argument in 'Lorine Niedecker: Rural Surreal', in Jenny Penberthy (ed.), *Lorine Niedecker: Woman and Poet* (Orono, Me.: National Poetry Foundation, 1996), 199–200.

sometimes be felt in, say, the evocations of 'Town, a town', with its roads
'Inhabited partly by those | Who have been born here' (NCP, 25).[11] The poems
give us snapshots of early Depression America, some of which recall the doc-
umentary photography which was becoming so important at the time,[12] and
while the book offers no overview as such—it is an 'empirical' series[13]—Oppen
deftly evokes the gaping social divisions between 'A man [who] sells post-
cards' on the street (NCP, 30) and the different world of 'Somebody's lawn'
(NCP, 18) and the house which 'flaunts | A family laundry' (NCP, 16).

In presenting these 'data of experience' largely without comment or inflec-
tion, Oppen continues the project of 'modernism' as he would later describe it
in 'The Mind's Own Place'. Yet one can hardly fail to notice that his description
there gives only the most partial account of literary modernism. While his
suspicion of rhetoric and 'histrionics' might seem to resonate with, say, Eliot's
concept of 'impersonality' and Pound's commitment to 'direct presentation',
no attention is paid to the defensive forms of irony which continued to be such
a distinctive feature of first-generation modernism in Britain and America.
And while Oppen commends the modernists' responsiveness to the 'data
of experience', he says nothing here of their investment in tradition, myth,
and forms of literary allusiveness that might be seen to undermine the kind
of immediacy at issue. Indeed, in the very partiality of his reckoning with
modernism we may discern a measure of dissociation from it: 'I did not feel
myself to be inherent in a tradition, to inhere in a tradition,' he recalled, 'I felt
myself to be as I found myself———' (UCSD 16, 15, 12). It is notable that
while Williams famously repudiated Eliot's traditionalism and, in doing so,
proposed an alternative, American version, Oppen characteristically sidesteps
the whole debate. 'I felt myself to be as I found myself', he says, a comment
which demonstrates the kind of independence he felt from a 'nascent canon'
of modernist writings and his related sense that even in his first book he
was striking out in a different direction—a direction shaped, to be sure,
by the larger objectives of modernism, but not constrained by them.[14] In

---

[11] See Rocco Marinaccio, 'George Oppen's "I've Seen America" Book: *Discrete Series* and the
Thirties Road Narrative', *American Literature*, 74/3 (2002), 539–69.

[12] Noted by Andrew Crozier in 'Inaugural and Valedictory: The Early Poetry of George
Oppen', in R. W. Butterfield (ed.), *Modern American Poetry* (New York: Barnes & Noble,
1984), 154. See also Monique Claire Vescia, *Depresssion Glass: Documentary Photography and
the Medium of the Camera Eye in Charles Reznikoff, George Oppen, and William Carlos Williams*
(New York and London: Routledge, 2006).

[13] See e.g. SL, 122: 'Discrete Series——a series in which each term is empirically justified
rather than derived from the preceding term. Which is what the expression means to a
mathematician'.

[14] On the 'nascent canon' of modernist writing, see Tyrus Miller, *Late Modernism: Politics,
Fiction, and the Arts between the World Wars* (Berkeley and Los Angeles: University of California
Press, 1999), 23.

this respect, Hugh Kenner is a little too keen to domesticate Objectivism by assimilating it to an already developed modernist poetics when he argues that 'The Objectivists seem to have been born mature, not to say middle-aged. The quality of their very youthful work is that of men who have inherited a formed tradition'.[15] Oppen and Zukofsky were certainly quieter in going about their business than their modernist predecessors—Zukofsky, as we have seen, didn't even want to name the group—but they were hardly passive inheritors of a 'formed tradition'. Indeed, by the late twenties it would seem that both men felt that modernism risked losing its momentum (Oppen wrote later of 'the liquidation of poetry into the sentimentalism of the American so-called Imagists of the late twenties and early nineteen-thirties'[16]) and the emphatic attention to the poem as 'object' could soon be understood as a way of curbing a subjectivism variously present in the evolving forms of modernism, as much in the 'sentimentalism' of its epigones as in the major works of Pound and Eliot which were increasingly to become vehicles for their authors' political and religious beliefs. None of this was as clear in the early thirties as it would be retrospectively, of course, but the social implications of Oppen's early poems immediately began to raise questions about the poet's stance toward 'the data of experience'. Here Imagism, far from constituting part of a now 'formed tradition', turned out to be of limited importance: 'That lucence, that emotional clarity, the objectivists wanted, and by that they are related to Imagism,' Oppen later reflected, 'But not the falsity of ingenuity, of the posed tableau, in which the poet also, by implication, poses.'[17] The defining strength of Imagism had lain in 'its demand that one actually *look*', he argued, though this had too frequently been compromised by mere 'affectation' and mannerism. Objectivism sought instead 'a realist art in that the poem is concerned with a fact which it did not create'.[18] Zukofsky offered a comparable definition in 'Sincerity and Objectification': 'Writing occurs which is the detail, not mirage, of seeing, of *thinking with the things as they exist*, and of directing them along a line of melody.'[19] Writing, then, is conceived of not as a discourse about things, but rather as one object among others (this is, says Zukofsky, 'writing (audibility in two-dimensional print) which is an object or affects the mind as such'.[20]

---

[15] Hugh Kenner, *A Homemade World: The American Modernist Writers* (London: Marion Boyars, 1977), 169.

[16] Faucherau, 'Three Oppen Letters with a Note', 79.   [17] Ibid. 84.

[18] Ibid.   [19] 'Sincerity and Objectification', 273 (my emphases).

[20] Ibid. 274. It is this which first impressed Williams when he read Zukofsky's 'Poem Beginning "The"': 'It escapes me in analysis (thank God) and strikes against me a thing (thank God). There are not so many things in the world as we commonly imagine. Plenty of debris, plenty of smudges'. *The Selected Letters of William Carlos Williams*, ed. John C. Thirlwall (New York: New Directions, 1957), 94.

With these informal but also rather subtle definitions of what the poem should be—definitions which, as we shall see, entailed more than merely claims for the autonomy of the poem—Oppen and Zukofsky began to adumbrate a poetics which renounced the idealism of the early modernists and the forms of discursive mastery with which it was associated.[21] Everything would flow instead from the poetry's concern with 'a fact which it did not create': materiality would be valued precisely because it offered resistance to the mind's embrace, and not because it might yield perceptions of 'form' and 'pattern', as Pound's Vorticism had proposed, or 'correlatives' for emotional states, as Eliot had suggested.[22] This redistribution of emphasis offered, for Oppen, a way of finally freeing poetry from artificiality and posturing, from 'right thinking and right sentiment', and from the kind of ironic detachment which had traditionally produced the 'art subject'. The lightness of touch and the epigrammatic brevities of some of the poems in *Discrete Series* tend to conceal the extent to which these early works actually contained the germ of a large-scale dissociation of Oppen's own work from modernism broadly conceived. We have to do, then, not with a late expression of a 'formed tradition', but with a sort of reconfiguring of modernism from within, and one that seems the more striking for the low-key way in which it was carried out.

T. W. Adorno has a precise formulation for the kind of shift I am suggesting here when he speaks in an essay on Bach of 'the emancipation of the subject to objectivity in a coherent whole of which subjectivity itself was the origin'.[23] The subject is liberated from an impotent privacy into a world of material beings through the objectified form of the artwork. For the reader, such 'emancipation' derives not from some identification with the poet's feeling, but from the *syntax* of the work, from a particular arrangement of words which, like the conjunction of planes in a painting, produces a sense of a materiality resistant to conventional grammars of thought and design. And, rather like the relation of abstract art to representational art, a language of 'objectification' amounts to a reconfiguring of the semantic field so as to accent particular items in a non-discursive way. Prominent features are inverted word order, indeterminacy or ambiguity attaching to pronouns, the emphatic use of prepositions to substitute for usual narrative markers, heightened attention

---

[21] For this aspect of Anglo-American modernism, see my *Modernisms: A Literary Guide* (Basingstoke: Palgrave Macmillan, 1995), 179–92 and 'Divergences: Modernism, Postmodernism, Jameson and Lyotard', *Critical Quarterly*, 33/3 (1991), 1–18.

[22] See e.g. Pound, 'Vorticism', repr. in *Gaudier-Brzeska: A Memoir* (1916; Hessle: Marvell Press, 1960), 81–94; Eliot, *Selected Essays* (London: Faber and Faber, 1972), 145.

[23] T. W. Adorno, *Prisms*, trans. Samuel and Shierry Weber (Cambridge, Mass.: MIT Press, 1983), 142.

to 'minor' parts of speech such as conjunctions, and a resulting disfigurement of anticipated speech-patterns. Such devices assure us that we are dealing not with 'a performance, a speech by the poet' but rather with 'the poet's self among things' and a 'thinking with the things as they exist'.

In the early poems of both Oppen and Zukofsky, a praxis of perception is defined by thus 'objectifying' the verbal components of the poem, by giving them an opacity in its own way as resistant as the material 'facts' of which they write. Zukofsky's short lyrics, for example, often begin abruptly, leaving the reader looking for hints of syntactical connection:

> Not much more than being,
> Thoughts of isolate, beautiful
> Being at evening, to expect
>   at a river-front:
>
> A shaft dims
> With a turning wheel;[24]

Compare the opening lines of 'Ferry':

> Gleams, a green lamp
> In the fog:
> Murmur, in almost
> A dialogue
>
> Siren and signal
> Siren to signal.
>
> Parts the shore from the fog,
> Rise there, tower on tower,
> Signs of stray light
> And of power.[25]

The syntax throws us off balance, with verbs appearing before their subjects and in some cases the subject remaining ambiguous (as with 'Parts', for example). This, perhaps, is one meaning of 'thinking with the things as they exist', for the poem is 'about' nothing more than the composition of the scene it articulates—the green light moving in the fog, the siren and signal responding to each other—and in this respect we might say that Zukofsky achieves 'objectification' in so far as the poem's syntax becomes inseparable from the relational field of which it speaks.

This kind of opacity or density is also a distinguishing feature of Oppen's *Discrete Series*:

[24] Louis Zukofsky, *All: The Collected Shorter Poems* (New York: Norton, 1971), 24.
[25] Ibid. 27.

> Who comes is occupied
> Toward the chest (in the crowd moving
>   opposite
> Grasp of me)
>   In firm overalls
> The middle-aged man sliding
> Levers in the steam-shovel cab,———
> Lift (running cable) and swung, back
> Remotely respond to the gesture before last
> Of his arms fingers continually———
> Turned with the cab.
>
>   (NCP, 14)

The actions of the man operating the steam-shovel are completely bound up with the unfurling syntax of the poem which is highly elliptical and often dispenses with punctuation altogether. Once again we must distinguish 'Objectification' from the Poundian 'image' (which presents 'an emotional and intellectual complex in an instant of time'[26]): while a poem like 'In a Station of the Metro' may 'record the precise instant when a thing outward and objective transforms itself into a thing inward and subjective',[27] the obstructive syntax of Oppen's poem inhibits the Imagistic move from outer to inner (we note that Pound's originating 'faces in the crowd' are already shaped by the perceiving mind as an 'apparition' and their exteriority reduced accordingly). By way of contrast, 'I was', recalls Oppen, 'even in 1929 (discrete series) consciously attempting to trace, to re-produce, the act of the world upon the consciousness'.[28] In 'Who comes', a series of mechanical shifts and gestures produces a syntax at once indeterminate in its parsing of items and at the same time emphatic in its subordination of the poem's movement to the paradoxical motions of the man and the cab (each moving differently but at the same time in a systematic confusion of the linear and circular). The poem is at once about literal construction—the laying of cable and the complex interaction of physical sinew and mechanical motion—and about the poem itself as an event of making, an event whose syntax carries everywhere the urgent pressure of some kind of resistant otherness. It is 'the act of the world', then, that produces the singularity of the poem, making it an occasion which exceeds conceptualization and paraphrase.[29]

The pleasure we may take in poems such as these, where the subject matter itself may be of only limited interest, lies in their capacity to make us think 'with

---

[26] Pound, *Literary Essays*, ed. T. S. Eliot, 4.   [27] Pound, 'Vorticism' (1914), 89.
[28] 'Selections from George Oppen's *Daybook*', ed. Dennis Young, *Iowa Review*, 18/3 (1988), 30.
[29] Ibid. 11. For a helpful discussion of literary 'singularity', see Timothy Clark, *The Poetics of Singularity* (Edinburgh: Edinburgh University Press, 2005).

the things as they exist', in Zukofsky's valuable phrase. A later unpublished poem captioned 'a single music' seems to speak directly to this aspect of Oppen's writing:

> the most stubborn
> material enters
> the poem
>
> or nothing
> enters
>
> and this is singularity
> the single poem
> single word
>
> and the line
> the single vision
> single music
>
> (UCSD16, 13, 6)

The poem becomes as 'stubborn' as the 'material' it articulates, the 'singularity' of its vision compelling us to accept it on its own terms and to suspend to some extent the work of interpretation to which as readers we are naturally drawn. To put this another way, we might say that 'objectification' clearly does entail much more than just the autonomy of the poem and that it attributes a certain exteriority to the syntax that is felt in the often discordant emphasis attaching to what Oppen would later call 'the little words'.[30] This perhaps explains why so many of the poems in *Discrete Series* display objects in tension with each other or, as in 'Who comes', movements which run counter to each other. For example:

> Tug against the river——
> Motor turning, lights
> In the fast water off the bow-wave:
> Passes slowly.
>
> (NCP, 19)

The motion of the tug-boat works against the 'fast water' to produce the slow, almost stately progress of the final line. Here as in many of the other poems, prepositional markers ('against', 'in') are a means of registering the contiguity of objects perceived, and this 'thinking with the things' entails a generosity of attention which has, as Andrew Crozier suggests, 'the inclusiveness of the photographic image, its inability to state preferences within its visual

---

[30] Dembo, ' "Objectivist" Poet', 162. See also Marjorie Perloff, *Radical Artifice: Writing Poetry in the Age of Media* (Chicago: University of Chicago Press, 1991), 79–85 for an account of Oppen's exploration of 'the possibilities of syntax rather than of image or metaphor' in *Discrete Series* (84).

field'.[31] Hence, perhaps, the importance of connections between parts and whole in these poems—but connections, we note, that are not, finally, mental constructions (like the Poundian image, for example) but that are actually there, in the world. This sense of the text as haunted by a materiality it cannot and does not want wholly to master through discourse is fundamental to Oppen's Objectivism and marks its difference from a modernism that sees aesthetic form as purely the product of some inner necessity. Interestingly, it differs also from Zukofsky's attention to the mind or imagination as a focusing 'lens'. Indeed, Oppen was later to note that even this theory was still caught up in a (modernist) notion of subjective agency: 'Louis's "objectification"—tho he denied it—related back to Kant: the consciousness's *act* of objectification.'[32] It was a just discrimination, since Zukofsky in his 'Preface' to *An 'Objectivists' Anthology* had also spoken in transparently Poundian terms of 'the concentrated locus which is the mind acting creatively upon the facts'.[33]

So we find that connections of a more abstract or hidden kind can also be mapped in Oppen's obstructive syntax:

> Thus
> Hides the
>
> Parts————the prudery
> Of Frigidaire, of
> Soda-jerking————
>
> Thus
>
> Above the
>
> Plane of lunch, of wives
> Removes itself
> (As soda-jerking from
> the private act
>
> Of
> Cracking eggs);
>
> big-Business
>
> (NCP, 7)

The subject matter may once again make us think of Williams, though the mode of presentation here is quite different from the extended structures of some of the poems in *Spring and All*. Where Williams still works largely in terms of recognizable sentence structure, Oppen begins, characteristically,

---

[31] Crozier in 'Inaugural and Valedictory: The Early Poetry of George Oppen', 154.

[32] 'An Adequate Vision: A George Oppen Daybook', ed. Michael Davidson, *Ironwood*, 26 (Fall 1985), 30 (his emphasis).

[33] Zukofsky, *'Objectivists' Anthology*, 22.

in medias res ('Thus hides . . .'), going on to bury the second main verb ('Removes itself') and thus to defer the appearance of its subject ('big-Business') until the poem's final line. The syntactical opacities here aptly accord with Oppen's sense of the habitual tendency of modern capitalism to conceal its own processes beneath extravagant surfaces. A number of the poems thus detail the mystifications of contemporary urban culture, nicely summed up in the vogue for streamlined appliances where style conceals function—'Hides the || Parts' (NCP, 7)—just as the veil drawn over real processes corresponds in that poem to the substitution of the social ritual of 'lunch' for sexual gratification that is the lot of the wives of 'big-Business'.[34] There is again a deliberate awkwardness in the writing which prevents us from 'resolving' the poem into a single image or emotion; this is indeed 'the poet's self among things' rather than the writer situated at a contemplative remove from them (we might again compare Pound's exquisitely formed but discretely distanced 'Petals on a wet black bough' or 'A wet leaf that clings to the threshold'). And while the Frigidaire coyly hides its 'parts', the verbal 'parts' of the poem itself are brazenly displayed, drawing attention to themselves as if to emphasize the difficulty of subordinating them to any single theme or figure (note the studied indeterminacy of the preposition 'Above', for example).

The syntax is, we might say, marked by a kind of opacity which resists the tendency of language to render up the singular—'is-ness', as Oppen calls it (SL, 89)—to the universal. As soon as we tie subject to predicate, as soon as we say that 'x' is 'y', the thing that is becomes something which was already-there. To say, for example, that Oppen is a poet is to insert 'Oppen' into a general category that precedes him; it is not to say how Oppen is—*is being*—a poet. We shall see in another chapter that this particular grammatical issue lay at the centre of Oppen's later concerns, but already in *Discrete Series*, the syntax wants 'is-ness' to register itself not as passive existence but as some kind of emergence in the world. To use one of his favourite words, we might then say that the world is not just passively there but that it *discloses* itself to consciousness and that it is this 'act' that the poem seeks to articulate. 'A new syntax', as Oppen puts it in one of his notebooks, 'is a new cadence of disclosure' (UCSD 16, 17, 2). Another example:

> The mast
> Inaudibly soars; bole-like, tapering:
> Sail flattens from it beneath the wind.
> The limp water holds the boat's round
> > sides. Sun

---

[34] See NCP, 360 for Oppen's association of this poem with ideas of masturbation.

Slants dry light on the deck.
Beneath us glide
Rocks, sand, and unrimmed holes.

(NCP, 12)

A perception such as this is one in which, as Oppen later puts it, 'the world stops, but lights up':[35] mast and sail are caught up together by the wind, while the water 'holds' the boat's sides. Such formal disclosure, which is literally a product of word-order, pace, and emphasis, stands over against inhibiting forms of *en*closure which figure in several of the poems in *Discrete Series*: the room associated with boredom in the opening poem (NCP, 5), for example, the 'Closed car—closed in glass' (NCP, 13), the man in 'the steam-shovel cab' (NCP, 14), and so on. These images give a sense of what Oppen calls elsewhere 'the closed universe, the closed self',[36] and in *Discrete Series* this kind of (en)closure is associated with the superficiality of metropolitan life as Oppen experienced it in the late twenties and with the rigidity of choice he saw as underlying apparent consumer freedoms—the 'Up | Down. Round | Shiny fixed | Alternatives' offered by the fashionable elevators, for example (NCP, 6).[37] The form of these poems, with their frequent lack of punctuation and main verbs, seems to speak for a countervailing openness. And not just openness, for the effect of syntactical disjunction and incompleteness is to make this world strange and unfamiliar: 'Who comes is occupied | Toward the chest' (NCP, 14), and 'Wave in the round of the port-hole | Springs, passing' (NCP, 15)—these oddly contorted locutions reproduce not the effect of things just seen from outside but rather of an event of perception which seems to bring objects into being gradually, as perception unfolds (the elevator poem is perhaps the most stylized example of this). In an interview, Oppen recalled that 'One imagines New York City dwellers involved most of the time with artificial concepts, the game, the definitions. So I did remember the root of my own Objectivism.'[38] On another level, then, *Discrete Series* might be read as an attempt to develop a form of poetic thinking which breaches the fixed boundaries of a 'game' in which all the moves are known in advance.

* * * * *

There were latent philosophical questions here which definitely set Oppen's Objectivism apart from Pound's Imagist concerns, questions to which he

---

[35] Faucherau, 'Three Oppen Letters with a Note', 84.
[36] 'Letters to June Oppen Degnan', *Ironwood*, 26 (Fall 1985), 223.
[37] See SL, 90 on the 'limited alternatives' evoked in the poem.
[38] 'A Conversation with George Oppen, conducted by Charles Amirkhanian and David Gitin, *Ironwood*, 5 (1975), 24.

would return. But no sooner had the Press published *Discrete Series* (1934) than poetry seemed suddenly quite beside the point (recalling this in the sixties, Oppen wrote: '1933———Staggering———It confronts us with an issue, a decision, overdue. Whether we must not recover from the great mish-mashes, the doubtful knowledge of the Pounds, Zukofskys, Olsons' (UCSD 16, 12, 3). New York City was now in the grip of mass poverty and unemployment (by the winter of 1934, 20 million Americans were jobless). Mary remembered the city as having 'an air of disaster' (MAL, 151), and Oppen later explained that 'That Depression almost cost us our reason; we could not bear the sight of what had happened. It threw us into twenty years of political frenzy' (UCSD 16, 19, 4).[39]

It was also a moment of significant redirection for the communist left. Mary recalled that they joined the Party in autumn 1935 'after reading Dimitroff's report & call for United Front with bourgeoisie' (a report given to the Seventh World Congress of the Communist Party).[40] At the same time, the Oppens joined the Workers' Alliance of America (WAA), a nationwide union for the unemployed which had grown out of the Unemployed Councils set up by the communists in 1929 and which from its foundation in 1935 was headed by one David Lasser.[41] The WAA brought together socialists and communists, though its inspiration was originally socialist and it was not until late 1938 that it found itself under attack because of its communist ties (Lasser left the union in 1940 apparently because of the increasing communist involvement).[42] The Alliance quickly became a national presence—by the end of 1936 it had amassed a membership of 600,000 across forty-three states[43]—but it retained a strong local focus: its activities, Mary recalled, 'in every neighbourhood

---

[39] See too the draft of a passage (headed 'Pro Vita') later to be incorporated into 'Return': 'Turning and turning in the broken streets | The hundred million desperate. | What mattered were the hungry. | | So they felt. | Surely verse can be an insolence' (UCSD 16, 20, 46).

[40] For this handwritten note, see the draft chronology made by Rachel Blau DuPlessis, Mary Oppen Papers, UCSD 125, 4, 16. The report was subsequently collected in G. Dimitroff, *The United Front* (New York: International Publishers, 1938).

[41] For the Socialist origins of the WAA, see Francis Fox Piven and Richard A. Cloward, *Poor People's Movements: Why They Succeed, How They Fail* (New York: Pantheon Books, 1977), 69–70. The Communist Party (CP) account of the origins of the Alliance is predictably rather different—see Earl Browder, *The People's Front* (New York: International Publishers, 1938), 48.

[42] See Daniel Bell, 'The Background and Development of Marxian Socialism in the United States', in Donald Drew Egbert and Stow Persons (eds.), *Socialism and American Life*, 2 vols. (Princeton: Princeton University Press, 1952), i. 382. James J. Lorence, *Organizing the Unemployed: Community and Union Activists in the Industrial Heartland* (Albany, NY: SUNY Press, 1996), 272 notes that 'by the time the CP came to dominate its activities [in the mid–1940s], the Alliance had already declined as a militant peoples' movement'. See also Chad Alan Goldberg, 'Haunted by the Specter of Communism: Collective Identity and Resource Mobilization in the Demise of the Workers Alliance of America', *Theory and Society*, 32 (2003), 750–4.

[43] Piven and Cloward, *Poor People's Movements*, 76.

where it existed were the immediate concerns of that neighbourhood' (MAL, 153).[44] Crucially, where the Congress of Industrial Organization concentrated on problems within the Works Progress Administration, the WAA attended to the needs of 'the larger jobless community, including relief recipients, transients, unemployables, and others unreached by government job programs'.[45] The radicalism of the WAA was felt at this level rather than at that of national strategy: indeed, by the autumn of 1938, Alliance locals were actually campaigning to elect New Deal governors and congressmen, just one indication of the fluidity of movements on the left during the Popular Front era.[46]

Perhaps as a result of the Oppens' local involvements, 'The Communist Party', writes Mary, 'remained strange to us; we threaded our way in the organization, and even the vocabulary within the Party was a different vocabulary than I had known' (MAL, 153). They attended several Party training sessions (Mary only after protest at the initial exclusion of women) and one imagines that they familiarized themselves with Party literature. Twenty years later, Oppen would recommend one such publication to his daughter Linda: a *History of the Communist Party of the Soviet Union*, published in English in 1938. This 'Short Course' in dialectics, he recalled, 'really makes sense of history, and so far as I know no one else does'.[47] Yet the accounts we have of the Oppens in New York generally emphasize the practical as opposed to the theoretical (the WAA was known for its promotion of strikes and sit-ins[48]). That they had had literary and artistic aspirations was something they now kept very much to themselves. Oppen wrote later that 'the catastrophe of

---

[44] Cf. Piven and Coward, *Poor People's Movements*, 72–3: 'The movements of the unemployed had originated in local communities, in sporadic street demonstrations, in rent riots, and in the disruption of relief centers. Many of the local organizations were loosely structured, held together more by the periodic demonstrations than by regular and formal affiliations; they gathered momentum from direct action victories which yielded money or food or a halt to evictions.'

[45] Lorence, *Organizing the Unemployed*, 195.

[46] As noted in Roy Rosenzweig, ' "Socialism in Our Time": The Socialist Party and the Unemployed, 1929–1936', *Labor History*, 20 (Fall 1979), 505.

[47] Linda Oppen Papers, UCSD 33, 1, 13 (dated 1958). The book is *History of the Communist Party of the Soviet Union (Bolsheviks): Short Course*, ed. Commission of the CIC of the CPUSA (B) (1938; London: Cobbett Pub. Co., 1943). Oppen refers his daughter specifically to a chapter on Historical Materialism (i.e., 'Dialectical and Historical Materialism', 105–31. In keeping with the period, the emphasis falls squarely on Marxism as a science: 'Hence Socialism is converted from a dream of a better future for humanity into a science' (115).

[48] See Matthew Josephson, *Infidel in the Temple: A Memoir of the Nineteen-Thirties* (New York: Knopf, 1967), 390. Cf. Oppen in Dembo, ' "Objectivist" Poet', 175: 'we wanted to gather crowds of people on the simple principle that the law would have to be changed where it interfered with relief and that settlement laws would have to be unenforceable when they involved somebody's starvation. And we were interested in rioting, as a matter of fact—rioting under political discipline. Disorder, disorder—to make it impossible to allow people to starve. It also involved the hunger march on Washington [1937] as well as local undertakings.' See also the later (1973) rebuke to John Crawford (SL, 255), 'your Marxism is too "scholarly" '.

human lives in the thirties . . . seemed to me to put poetry and the purposes of poetry in question' (SL, 186). In another letter he observed that 'I did not write "Marxist" poetry. I made a choice. Stopped, for the crisis, writing' (SL, 277). It was to be a painfully long 'crisis', as Oppen would note soon after his return from Mexico: 'in fact I wrote no poetry for 25 years. Don't know if I was right. But I was right not to write bad poetry—poetry tied to a moral or a political (same thing) judgment' (SL, 66).[49] Instead, the Oppens immersed themselves in the everyday work of the Alliance, something, Oppen later noted, that his friend Zukofsky was not keen to do: 'Louis Z and the CP—"They wanted me to distribute Leaflets!"' (UCSD 16, 18, 2).[50] Oppen would recall their own work for the Farmers' Union during the New York Milk Strike in Utica and his role as 'the best of the soap-boxers' during the 1936 Kings County election campaign for the Communist Party (SL, 278). Yet they do not seem to have become embroiled in the bureaucratic affairs of the Party. Mary Oppen in a late interview recalled that 'In general, the Communist Party was taking orders from Moscow, but the actual work that we were involved in was doing things which should have been done by liberals, and I think nowadays a "liberal" would pretty much describe what we were then.'[51] 'Liberals' they may have been—hardly 'small Lenins. Or big ones', Oppen joked (SL, 278)—but the couple were active organizers from 1936 to 1941.[52] Predictably, their names began to figure in FBI reports and they were arrested several times, a worrying development with a new daughter, Linda, to look after.

Another war loomed. The Nazi-Soviet pact was signed, and the Oppens, like so many on the left, found themselves politically at sea. Oppen recalled that he was 'Disillusioned with the CP   unable to do *nothing* about the war ———I meant to enter it' (SL, 202). Although exempt from conscription as an employee of an aircraft manufacturer, Oppen moved the family to Detroit 'to obtain qualification as a tool and die maker' (SL, 202). The move made

[49] The matter of choice is crucial and distinguishes the silence of the thirties and forties from that of the fifties in Mexico. However, in *From West to East: California and the Making of the American Mind* (New York: The Free Press, 1998) 285, Stephen Schwartz, in a highly antagonistic presentation of Oppen, argues in line with his 'anti-Stalinist' agenda that the Party ordered silence—'Rather than specifying *what* to write, the party told them not to write at all.' Schwartz's animus against Oppen makes his comments deeply unreliable.

[50] The unpublished note continues: 'Simply, he never was willing to do anything for anyone. He was quite willing that the communists should regard him as a great poet. He offered. That was the extent of his willingness.'

[51] Dennis Young, 'Conversation with Mary Oppen', *Iowa Review*, 18/3 (1987), 39.

[52] Peterson, 'George Oppen', 194. Oppen's FBI file (included in the Register of George Oppen Letters, ed. Rachel Blau DuPlessis, UCSD 205, 4, 2) notes that he was 'registered as affiliated with the Communist Party for the purpose of elections in 1936, and was described as CP Campaign Manager'. The file also refers to an article in the *Daily Worker* (25 Sept. 1936) 'stating subject was a CP Election Campaign Manager at that time'.

him eligible for military service, as he had known it would, and he went on to see action in both the Rhineland and Central Europe campaigns. On 22 April 1945, Oppen was seriously wounded in the Vosges Mountains, south of the Battle of the Bulge, when, as he tersely reported in a letter, '88 mm shell landed in a fox-hole: Three of us were in that fox hole' (SL, 203). Of the three, only Oppen, his body pitted with shrapnel, would live to be haunted by the attack, and haunted, too, by feelings of guilt for his inability to carry a wounded comrade to safety.[53] That experience in the fox-hole was for him, he later noted, the definitive 'ur-scene' (UCSD 16, 17, 3) and it would figure as a commanding presence in his later thinking.

Back with his family in the US, Oppen started a two-man building outfit in Redondo Beach, California, where the family settled into a house of his own construction. The political climate was rapidly moving rightwards, however, and the Oppens' record, along with their involvement in the Henry Wallace presidential campaign, drew the interest of the FBI who paid several visits to the couple.[54] Fearing prosecution under the Smith Act, the Oppens hurriedly removed to Mexico City in June 1950'[55] They had been to Mexico before. In the summer of 1934 they had visited with two friends from Berkeley and had seen 'the ideas of socialism applied in a poverty-stricken nation'. 'We admired Cárdenas, the President of Mexico, and we observed that Mexico was coming

[53] McAleavey, 'The Oppens: Remarks towards Biography', 309 tells of one other soldier in the fox-hole who was more seriously wounded than Oppen: 'George's guilt, which he evidently felt all his life thereafter, centered on the fact that he did not attempt to drag or carry the badly wounded soldier above him to safety or himself attempt to find medical attention, even though either course would have been mortally foolish.'

[54] The extent of the Oppens' party activities at this time is impossible to gauge, though rumours continue to circulate. Schwartz, *From West to East*, 465–7, for example, gives credence to a ridiculous story of Kenneth Rexroth's that Oppen had somehow been involved in the Party's alleged murder of ex-communist Eli Bernard Jacobson. Linda Hamalian, *A Life of Kenneth Rexroth* (New York: W. W. Norton, 1991), 408 dismisses the story as 'absurd', but its continuing currency indicates the extent to which understanding of CP activities has been dogged by rumour and suspicion. Jacobson died in Dec. 1952 when Oppen was, of course, in Mexico. Oppen's friend screenwriter Julian Zimet gives a more plausible account: after settling in Southern California, the Oppens 'gave up full-time political work but continued to be members of a Party chapter in Redondo Beach that George headed'. Zimet adds that the Oppens' removal to Mexico led to George's expulsion from the Party for 'desertion'—see Zimet's memoir in Patrick McGilligan and Paul Buhle (eds.), *Tender Comrades: A Backstory of the Hollywood Blacklist* (New York: St Martin's Grifin, 1999), 727. According to Mary Oppen, however, the couple did not transfer to a local party branch when they settled in California (SL, p. xv). The FBI file observes after a 1949 interview with Oppen that he 'has not been reported to be currently active in Communist Party affairs in the Los Angeles County Communist Party'.

[55] The Oppens' hasty departure from California meant '[we] lost *all* our papers in 1950' (SL, 298). Linda Oppen remembers that 'The Marxist books, after considerable thought, were shoved into the space above the ceiling in hopes the FBI would not find them soon, or before we got out of the country' (personal communication). US nationals had only two options if they wished to leave the country without passports: exile in Mexico or in Canada.

to a new life', recalled Mary in her memoir, going on to describe the vibrant political murals covering many of the walls (MAL, 150).

That sense of colour and promise is markedly absent, however, from her account of their return to Mexico.[56] In a memoir running to just over two hundred pages, she devotes a mere eight pages to their entire period of exile. We hear something of the rather exotic 'old colonial house' they rented in the San Ángel district (MAL, 196), of the schooling they provided for Linda, and of several occasions on which they were subject to police surveillance. Little is said, though, of the social circle in which they moved—'we were friendly with many of the Hollywood exiles' (MAL, 199), Mary notes, but she doesn't elaborate—and there is no real sense of the beauty and strangeness of the then unpolluted city that so impressed other US émigrés and visitors. For during the fifties, Mexico continued to be a magical destination for dissident American writers. William Burroughs was there in the early years of the decade, as was Jack Kerouac. Others came to explore Mayan sites—Allen Ginsberg and Charles Olson, for example—while Norman Mailer spent several summers in Mexico City researching an essay on bullfighting.[57] Both Kerouac and Ginsberg would return intermittently, the latter introducing Peter Orlovsky and Gregory Corso to the country in 1956 during a trip in which they also visited Denise Levertov in Guadalajara. But the Beats' image of Mexico, exemplified in Kerouac's romantic vision of the capital as 'the great wild uninhibited Fellahin-childlike city that we knew we would find at the end of the road', lay quite outside the Oppens' necessarily inhibited existence as involuntary exiles rather than as tourists.[58] And while Mary took more interest

---

[56] Linda Oppen observes (personal communication) that 'The earlier trip in '34 was politically exciting, the Arts Schools, the leftist projects and optimism is what [Mary] reports.' It is also perhaps significant that Rivera's reputation was somewhat on the wane in fifties Mexico—see e.g. George Woodcock, *To the City of the Dead: An Account of Travels in Mexico* (London: Faber and Faber, 1957), 61 for the view that Rivera's 'highly stylized primitivism' 'has helped to confirm in the minds of city Mexicans that their Indian fellow-countrymen are really a race of primeval beings, heavy as the earth they dig and in no way related to those who make up the world of Europeanized Mexico'. During the period of the Oppens' residence, however, Rivera remained a powerful iconic presence and owned a house in their neighbourhood.

[57] Norman Mailer, *The Bullfight: A Photographic Narrative with Text by Norman Mailer* (New York: Macmillan, 1967).

[58] Jack Kerouac, *On the Road* (New York: Viking, 1957), 299. See also the account of literary visitors to Mexico in the fifties in Drewey Wayne Gunn, *American and British Writers in Mexico, 1556–1973* (Austin: University of Texas Press, 1974). Gunn does not, however, mention writers fleeing the blacklist. It was probably easier for the children of the exiles to grasp the magical dimension of Mexico. Crawford Kilian, for example, writes in his unpublished memoir 'Growing Up Blacklisted' (1990), 225: 'I look back on those years in Mexico now, and they seem suffused with a kind of glow: the streets and markets were so beautiful, the people so vivid, the sun so bright and the air so clear that it seems impossibly romantic.' Linda Oppen has similarly remained positive about her Mexico years (personal communication).

Figure 1. Oppen at home in San Ángel, Mexico DF, early 1950s

than George in Mexican archaeology and folklore,[59] her account of these years attends primarily to the couple's feelings of displacement as they were compelled 'to live a bourgeois life . . . because to live as the lower classes live in Mexico is a life fraught with danger due to the lack of hygiene in such a poverty-stricken, undeveloped country' (MAL, 200).

George became a partner in a furniture-making business, though under Mexican law he was supposed to operate only in an executive capacity and not as a craftsman.[60] Perhaps by way of compensation, he studied wood-carving on the GI Bill at the Escuela Esmeralda de Pintura y Escultura. For her part, Mary worked at photography and painting, and the couple lived a kind of bohemian life *manqué*:

[59] Linda Oppen, personal communication.
[60] See Dembo, ' "Objectivist" Poet', 176 where Oppen speaks of his continuing 'sense of being a craftsman, for whatever it's worth, and my sense of not being an executive'.

We were not expatriates by choice, and we were unrelenting in withholding ourselves from becoming exiles forever. We wanted more than anything to return home to the United States. To be artists in these conditions was impossible to us. We needed to be freely in our own country, to have time to assimilate the violent years before turning them into thought and poetry. (MAL, 200)

The stiffness of the prose in this part of the autobiography certainly matches that 'withholding [of] ourselves' which seems to have characterized the couple's time in Mexico. Oppen's own later comments on this period are also sparse and generally negative:

One becomes accustomed to paying bribes everywhere and with the greatest possible tact and skill—a situation of infinite corruption, to begin to tell it, a society, a culture really trapped and not the fault of the people. They are trapped by their culture, by the relation of men and women, by the absolute corruption of government, by the habits of bureaucracy, the habits of people.[61]

In a 1975 interview, for example, he was dismissive of the period of exile, remarking simply that he had been 'in Mexico for quite a long while from which I have very little',[62] and in a letter the next year to his niece, Diane (Andy) Meyer, he described their exile as 'Not an easy time. Very nearly lost each other among other things. Not broke but persecuted. Every now and then in hiding' (SL, 315). To Mary, 'Mexico was a prison for us for ten years',[63] and she recalled that 'we [i.e., the community of exiles] were used a great deal in the newspaper as Communist Jews who were responsible for something that was going on in Mexico, and we would all have to leave town for a few days, weeks'.[64] Linda Oppen has similarly reported that 'the family was even watched while they lived in Mexico, and toward the end of their stay, they fled to Acapulco, fearing that the Mexican government, in collusion with the FBI, would arrest them'.[65]

The Oppens' rather reticent and colourless accounts of their time in Mexico can be fleshed out a little by reference to two recent memoirs of the exile community to which they belonged: Jean Rouverol's *Refugees from Hollywood* (2000) and Diana Anhalt's *A Gathering of Fugitives* (2001).[66] Both authors

---

[61] See Dembo, 177.
[62] 'Interview with George Oppen', conducted by Reinhold Schiffer on 1 May 1975, *Sagetrieb*, 3/3 (Winter 1984), 9.
[63] Mary Oppen Papers, UCSD 125, 1, 32.
[64] Young, 'Conversation with Mary Oppen', 23.
[65] Davidson, 'Introduction', NCP, p. xxxv n. 21. Oppen's FBI file (UCSD 205, 4, 2) records that 'periodic residence checks on a 60 day basis' were made on the family.
[66] Jean Rouverol, *Refugees from Hollywood: A Journal of the Blacklist Years* (Albuquerque: University of New Mexico Press, 2000); Diana Anhalt, *A Gathering of Fugitives: American Political Expatriates in Mexico, 1948–1965* (Santa Maria, Calif.: Archer Books, 2001). Further references to each will be given in the text.

knew the Oppens, and Rouverol (then Jean Butler, Hollywood actress and wife of scriptwriter Hugo Butler) and her family were especially close to them.[67] The two memoirs offer a fuller picture of the Oppens' social circle, which included the families of Hugo Butler, Dalton Trumbo, Ring Lardner Jr., and Ian Hunter (all Hollywood scriptwriters), Conlon Nancarrow (composer), Julian Zimet (novelist and scriptwriter), Charles Humboldt, aka Clarence Weinstock (editor of the Marxist *Mainstream and Masses*), Albert Maltz (novelist and scriptwriter), the painter David Alfaro Siqueiros and his wife Angeles, and Fred Vanderbilt Field (millionaire left-winger and a specialist on China).[68] Luis Buñuel had also been living in Mexico City since 1946, though Oppen seems to have had no close acquaintance with him. Hugo Butler, however, wrote the script for Buñuel's 1954 *Robinson Crusoe* (filmed in Manzanillo in 1952) and it is possible that his talk of work on the movie laid the foundations for Oppen's later allusions to the Crusoe theme in his long poem 'Of Being Numerous' (1968).[69]

This community of political exiles from the US—probably comprising around sixty families, according to Anhalt's estimate—were quite close-knit and generally supported each other in times of trouble.[70] They had had the misfortune to arrive in Mexico at a time when the government was hostile toward the left, and although the climate would improve when Cortines took over from Alemán as President in 1952, there remained the threat of

[67] Anhalt (personal communication) tells me that her parents were not friendly with the Oppens, which is slightly ironic since, according to Linda Oppen (personal communication), when her father met Anhalt's father, Mike Zykofsky, 'he asked if he was related to Louis Zukofsky and was told dismissively, "yes, cousins"'. Diana Anhalt confirms (personal communication) that 'Louis Zukofsky was either my father's first or second cousin.' The families were never close, however.

[68] In her search for information about Humboldt, Diana Anhalt found that 'little or no reference was made to his time in Mexico' (personal communication). An obituary in the left-wing weekly the *National Guardian*, 30 Jan. 1964, e.g., notes only that in 1947 he 'went to Mexico to study Mexican mural painting'. Frederick Vanderbilt Field's *From Right to Left: An Autobiography* (Westport, Conn.: Lawrence Hill and Co., 1983) gives some sense of expatriate life in Mexico. Oppen mentions Field in UCSD 16, 1, 1. Oppen was also responsible for introducing composer Charles Amirkahnian to Nancarrow—see Kyle Gann, *The Music of Conlon Nancarrow* (Cambridge: Cambridge University Press, 1995), 47.

[69] On Butler's career, see Paul Buhle, *Radical Hollywood: The Untold Story behind Hollywood's Favorite Movies* (New York: New Press, 2002). For the making of *Robinson Crusoe*, see also the interview with Jean Rouverol Butler by Paul Buhle and Dave Wagner in *Tender Comrades* 168–9. Buñuel recalls his years in Mexico in *My Last Breath*, trans. Abigail Israel (London: Jonathan Cape, 1984), 197–216.

[70] Field, *From Right to Left*, 275 estimates the number of families as around twenty-five and observes that 'We formed a congenial group. Our problem, socially, was to avoid seeing so much of each other that we would fail to become acquainted with the Mexicans among whom we were living. We solved that problem with varying degrees of success.' Rouverol also emphasizes the close-knit nature of the community. Anhalt is more sceptical, though she does concede that 'we were thrown in each other's company frequently enough to share the same experiences' (89).

sudden kidnap and deportation (the handing over to US authorities in August 1950 of Morton Sobell, friend of Julius Rosenberg, and Gus Hall, one-time General Secretary of the Party, offered a telling reminder of that threat). Not surprisingly, most of the Americans steered well clear of any involvement in Mexican politics and severed connections with the Communist Party. Mary Oppen recalled that 'In Mexico we were utterly, utterly passive politically. I think it was necessary. We had a young child, and we were utterly and most completely uninvolved in whatever went on in Mexico. Interested, yes, and we knew leftists, but we were absolutely just silent.'[71] Diana Anhalt observes similarly that 'Almost without exception the bulk of political expatriates kept away from politics once they left the States' (119). This avoidance of politics was bound up with a necessary secrecy: 'Controversial books were rarely left out in the open,' recalls Anhalt, 'My parents kept theirs in a cardboard box on the upper shelf of the closet' (69). And this secrecy which 'circumscribed their lives' (25) extended to their own political histories. People were not keen to speak of their past even within the safety of their own families: Anhalt remembers that 'Much of what was said in our family—in most families, I suppose—was communicated through silences and evasions: the turned back, a flushed face, the hand tightening into a fist' (13).

The Oppens also had their secrets. George was no longer writing poetry, but he seems to have wanted privately to disown what he had previously written and studiously concealed from his friends and even from his daughter his earlier career as a poet.[72] Jean Rouverol only learned of it in the late fifties when she came across a mention of Oppen as 'an earnest young poet' in William Carlos Williams's *Autobiography*, while others had to wait until news of his Pulitzer reached them in 1969.[73] Oppen's reticence about his early poetic ambitions was characteristic of the kind of reserve that prevailed in the exiled community. Indeed, it was a curious feature of this life in Mexico that their collective reason for being there—commitment to politics, membership of the Party—quickly became the very thing that was never talked about. A certain silence and 'withholding' entailed, then, at once a withdrawal from political expression and a tacit recognition of the all-pervasive, all-constraining political

[71] Young, 'Conversation with Mary Oppen', 22.
[72] Rouverol, *Refugees from Hollywood*, 177: 'But why he concealed from us (even from Linda, she told me later) his former life as a poet, I never learned. I couldn't help feeling aggrieved at the deception.' See also McAleavey, 'The Oppens: Remarks towards Biography', 312 where Oppen remarks: 'I think we deceived her [Linda]. We deceived her as to what we were, and I think she still feels that.' Kilian, 'Growing Up Blacklisted', 226 recalls Oppen as 'a taciturn American carpenter and furniture maker [who] would later win a Pulitzer Prize for poetry'.
[73] Rouverol, *Refugees from Hollywood*, 175. Cf. Anhalt, *Gathering of Fugitives*, 72 n.: 'Oppen kept his identity as a poet a secret from his Mexico City friends who learned of it when they read about his Pulitzer Prize in the newspapers.'

pressures that made such silence necessary. And it was, one might imagine, a difficult silence to keep, especially in view of Khrushchev's revelations at the Twentieth Party Congress in 1956 and the Soviet invasion of Hungary in the same year. Linda Oppen has recalled the effect of these events on her parents, remarking, however, that 'the earlier Stalin-Hitler pact caused them more shock, though they remained Marxists always. The Party was not ideologically or intellectually important to them afterward.'[74] That view would seem to be confirmed by a comment in a 1959 letter from Oppen where he remarks that 'there were only some fifteen years that political loyalties prevented me from writing poetry. After that I had to wait for Linda to grow up' (SL, 30).[75] Yet if the Oppens effectively abandoned the Party when they left the US, there was still plenty to concern them about conditions in the Soviet Union, notably, as Rouverol reports (125), the rumours of rising anti-Semitism there. In Mexico, such anxieties could have no outlet in any kind of action: instead, the general damage done to left-wing hopes, coupled with the news of continuing House Un-American Activities Committee action in the US and the execution of Julius and Ethel Rosenberg, left the Oppens and their fellow exiles in a kind of political suspension. While in the thirties Oppen had at least been able to choose between politics and poetry, now both avenues seemed closed to him.

In this constrained and potentially claustrophobic world, friendships also had to be sustained in a discrete and circumspect way, as Rouverol remembers:

Whatever accommodation each of our various families struggled to arrive at, however, most of us seemed, subconsciously, to reach the same conclusion: *friendships, here in exile, were more important than doctrine.* . . .We didn't want to test the boundaries beyond which disagreement became acrimony. If we differed from each other now in any important way, we didn't want to know. We drew back. We changed the subject. (130; her emphases)

The underlying tension inevitably caused rifts, and while Oppen would remain in contact with Zimet and Humboldt after he left Mexico, the friendship with the Butlers did not survive the period of exile.[76] Those were personal tensions, of course, but they do suggest the extent to which the Oppens' loss of access to a sphere of political activity may have led them to a sense of confinement within a world of purely domestic and 'aesthetic' activities. Rouverol catches something of this in her account of the couple's bohemian lifestyle: 'George

---

[74] Linda Oppen, quoted in Anhalt, *Gathering of Fugitives*, 203. Zimet, *Tender Comrades*, 742 similarly emphasizes the Oppens' disillusionment about the Soviet Union.

[75] Cf. Mary Oppen Papers, UCSD 125, 3, 1: 'In Mexico we said that we were giving Linda the time that she needed, and we tried to make it a good and growing time for her. It was not that for us.'

[76] See Rouverol, *Refugees from Hollywood*, 177–8 for an account of how in 1958 'the distance between ourselves and the Oppens became complete'.

still did a little wood sculpture in addition to his cabinetwork, and Mary was still painting, but they didn't seem to be trying to achieve anything with this work; they merely pursued it because they enjoyed it. It was *living* they were skilled at' (176). Yet neither of the Oppens could sustain a merely hedonistic lifestyle, and the commitment and seriousness they craved could sometimes lead to damaging social confrontations. Rouverol claims, for example, that 'George and Mary had even fallen out with the Hoffmans [Anne and Hans], close friends since their arrival here, over the philosophic point of whether art was or was not therapy, with George, passionately, taking the negative' (176). By 1958, their last full year of exile in Mexico, as it would turn out, things were coming to a head. Mary was, to use her words, 'disturbed', 'suffering anxiety' (200, 201), and looking for psychiatric help. 'My need', she wrote later, 'was finally desperate, and although George was reluctant, I convinced him that I needed help from outside our private world, from which I could not now find my way forward' (200).

That 'private world' was suddenly facing other, outside threats. Toleration of the left under Cortines had come to an abrupt end with the flight from Mexico in July 1957 of two wealthy left-wingers, Alfred and Martha Dodd Stern. The Sterns had been indicted in the US on the charge of conspiracy to commit espionage, a charge carrying the death penalty. The Mexicans refused to deport them and when the couple successfully escaped to Prague on Paraguayan passports America was given the justification it had been seeking to intervene in Mexican affairs. With the deportation of two men in December, a wave of arrests began which would reach its height in September 1958. Oppen told his half-sister June of 'the more or less kidnap-deportation of two foreigners in the last weeks' (UCSD 16, 1, 4), calling this in another letter 'a serious attempt at a grab from far, far right field' (UCSD 16, 1, 5).

* * * * *

The deportations coincided with widespread labour unrest and political agitation, making this (in Diana Anhalt's words) 'the most critical year many would face during their time in Mexico' (172). It was a critical year for the Oppens in yet another respect. Oppen had written no poetry since *Discrete Series* and recalled in a letter to Charles Tomlinson in 1963 that 'I kept nothing of the little I wrote for some twenty five years' (SL, 83).[77] An earlier letter from 1959 gives a vivid instance of the difficulty he had found in contemplating his early work in the light of recent experiences: 'Selma [Wolfman] kept trying to force my book

[77] Rachel Blau DuPlessis, SL, 383 n. 13, rightly cautions against reading this ambiguously worded sentence to imply that Oppen did, in fact, write during the period of 'silence'.

[*Discrete Series*] on me. I couldn't face it. Finally borrowed it and I thought some of the poems were very good, and none of them shameful' (SL, 20).[78] The completeness of Oppen's rejection of his own work up to this point is indicated by the fact that he felt able 'finally' to borrow this copy of his book only after he had actually begun to write again. For early in 1958, when George visited Mary's therapist, he reported to him a dream in which he and his sister were looking through his father's papers after his father's death. In Mary Oppen's words:

In a file marked 'miscellaneous' was a paper entitled 'How to prevent Rust in Copper'. George thought, 'My old man was a little frivolous perhaps, but he certainly knew that copper does not rust.'. . . When he told the doctor the dream, laughing again at its ridiculousness, the doctor stopped him. 'You were dreaming that you don't want to rust,' he said. On the way home George stopped and bought a pad of paper and some pencils and started to write *The Materials* (MAL, 201–2)[79]

Whatever the meaning of this odd dream,[80] Oppen was suddenly writing again, his first new poem called 'To Date' and then retitled, not inaptly, 'Blood from the Stone' (NCP, 52). By January 1959 he was, he said, 'writing steadily—I guess some 8 hours a day, trying to get thru a back log of things I've wanted to say' (SL, 18). This intensity of concentration was matched only by the pressure of experience suddenly available for expression: 'I have twenty five years of life to write about,' he said in another letter, and now, it seemed, *Discrete Series* was no longer an obstacle:

The early poems just have to stand as is—Some of them come up against the limit of my understanding at the time, and sort of break to pieces. Those that stay solidly within what I had grasped seem to me good. But I am starting now as if from scratch to write of things I knew nothing about when I was twenty. I just have to say it as best I can. (SL, 26)

This outburst of energy is also evident in Oppen's letters to his half-sister, June Oppen Degnan, record of which begins with a communication of 26 November 1957. At the time, Oppen was coming to the end of a brief period working for General Electric in the hope of qualifying for the next level of immigration documents. He was now about to try another means to this end

---

[78] Selma Wolfman was a close friend of Mary Oppen and greatly admired George (personal communication from Linda Oppen). She was personal secretary to Lillian Helman from the late fifties on into the sixties.

[79] Slightly varied accounts of the dream are also given in 'Poetry and Politics: A Conversation with George and Mary Oppen', conducted by Burton Hatlen and Tom Mandel, in GOMP, 27–8 and SL, 127 where Oppen seems to date the dream as occurring in 1956. Linda Oppen (personal communication) dates it as 'early in 1958'.

[80] Rachel Blau DuPlessis (SL, p. xvii) speculates on a possible matrix of words (Oppen, communist, poppa) which might imply some lifting of a paternal prohibition after his father's death in 1954.

by becoming treasurer of an import business in Mexico.[81] This first letter is exclusively concerned with financial matters (UCSD 16, 1, 1).[82] In contrast, the second letter, written sometime in 1959, lists nine poems composed between 1958 and 1959 and seeks June's help in intervening on his behalf with the *San Francisco Review* of which she was publisher (UCSD 16, 1, 3).[83] Oppen derived support and encouragement from this correspondence with June, and some of his new poems would first appear in the *San Francisco Review* (in a letter of early February 1959, he wrote that 'it was certainly you forced me to start writing' (UCSD 16, 1, 1)).[84] By February 1959, the correspondence no longer concerned finance at all, concentrating instead on poetic matters, the politics of the thirties, and the threat of the atom bomb.[85]

In part this rush of new concerns—or at least the articulation of them in writing—paralleled the discovery of a way out of that 'private world' which exile had made so constricting. In the summer of 1958, the Supreme Court ruled in the case of artist Rockwell Kent that the right to travel was a basic civil right, and by August the Oppens once again had passports. In November, they left Mexico to visit Linda, now at Sarah Lawrence College, and they also saw the Zukofskys in New York. Autumn 1959 found them taking up residence in Acapulco, though by January they had returned to the US for good, settling for the time being in New York City. Oppen's career as a poet would now begin again in earnest.

---

[81] Linda Oppen, personal communication.

[82] By 8 Jan. 1958 (UCSD 16, 1, 4) Oppen had 'come very reluctantly to the conclusion that I am not willing to appear as treasurer of a corporation in Mexico'.

[83] For a list of the poems written 1958–9, see SL, 373 n. 1.

[84] *This in Which* (1965) was dedicated 'For June || Who first welcomed | me home' and an earlier draft of this dedication was 'To June Who by some miracle of kindness | and of tact has been able to | give to me, in spite of myself, | those things which I needed to | survive' (UCSD 16, 21, 1).

[85] See e.g. UCSD 16, 1, 11.

2

Materials

The Oppens' last few years in Mexico were difficult ones, and it is unwise, perhaps, to attribute George's return to poetry simply to the 'rust and copper dream' which in its partly humorous retellings never quite conveys the sudden focusing of energies at work here. A complex of factors was obviously involved and Mary Oppen once even suggested in interview that in addition to George's dream 'It's significant also that your father had to die. . . . And another thing: Linda had to leave home for either of us to get going again.'[1] It's clear, too, that Oppen's reading during the Mexico years had an important part to play in his return to writing, and the little information that we have about this indicates that philosophical works came high on his agenda. In an interview in 1973, for example, Oppen told Charles Tomlinson that he 'was startled on encountering Heidegger some time ago, 1950' (UCSD 16, 34, 4) and whether or not this date is precise we might conclude that he had read the first of Heidegger's volumes to be translated, *Existence and Being* (1949), at some point during the Mexico years.[2] A letter of 1959 to June also indicates familiarity with unspecified work by Jean-Paul Sartre, and Oppen owned (and annotated) the 1958 imprint of Walter Kaufmann's *Existentialism from Dostoevsky to Sartre.*[3]

Beyond these texts, one other looms large, and Robert Hass suggests that Oppen 'found himself writing poems again in the late fifties when he began to read a book about aesthetics by [Jacques] Maritain'.[4] There is no way of knowing exactly when the Oppens chanced upon Maritain's *Creative Intuition*

---

[1] David McAleavey, 'The Oppens: Remarks towards Biography', *Ironwood*, 26 (Fall 1985), 312. Oppen's father died in May 1954.

[2] Martin Heidegger, *Existence and Being*, ed. and introd. Werner Brock (Chicago: Henry Regnery Co., 1949). Oppen's reading of Heidegger is considered below, Ch. 3 and Appendix A.

[3] See the letter to June Oppen Degnan, quoted below, p. 43; Walter Kaufmann, *From Dostoevsky to Sartre* (1956; New York: Meridian Books, 1958). The only marked passages occur, curiously, in the excerpts from Karl Jaspers.

[4] Introd. to Michael Cuddihy, *Try Ironwood: An Editor Remembers* (Boston: Rowan Tree Press, 1990), p. x. Hass does not develop this suggestion. The book is Jacques Maritain, *Creative Intuition in Art and Poetry* (New York: Meridian Books, 1955); further page references will be given in the text. The Oppens' copy of this edition of the book, with a home-made binding in what seems to be black corduroy, is held in the Mandeville Special Collections. It contains some

in Art and Poetry (1953) though Mary Oppen recalls that 'We discovered that while we were still in Mexico'.[5] The book was, she said, 'very important to us' as an alternative to the 'proscribed reading list' which had overshadowed their years in the Communist Party.[6] An alternative it certainly was, since Maritain was a Thomist philosopher whose appeal to the left-wing Oppens may come as something of a surprise. Maritain was, however, a leading intellectual figure by this time and after moving to Princeton in 1948 he drew the attention of American writers such as Robert Lowell, Allen Tate, Flannery O'Connor, Walker Percy, and Oppen's friend, Thomas Merton.[7] While critics have tended to notice *Creative Intuition* as merely the source for an elusive (mis)quotation which provides the epigraph for Oppen's 1962 collection *The Materials*, it was arguably this text which provided him with many of the core ideas of his mature poetics.[8] Indeed, in another interview, Mary suggested that their discovery of Maritain coincided closely with Oppen's return to writing:

When we were first thinking of approaching coming back to the United States, and George was approaching beginning to write again, we picked up, at I suppose the American Library in Mexico, Maritain's book, and we were immensely impressed and we discussed it a lot.[9]

If *Creative Intuition* was in some sense a catalyst for Oppen, then, the passage which he chose to head *The Materials*—'We awake in the same moment to ourselves and to things' (NCP, [38])—celebrated both a way of being in the world and Oppen's own reawakening to creativity. The fact that Maritain wrote from a scholastic theological position proved no obstacle to Oppen's interest, and as would frequently be the case with his later reading he would mine religious writings (those, for example, of Meister Ekhart, Simone Weil, and Kierkegaard) for insights which he could put to non-transcendental uses.[10] *Creative Intuition*, it would seem, offered Oppen much more than a suggestive epigraph for his new collection, paving the way for his later, developed interest

---

annotations on the inside covers (discussed below), though most are now illegible. The text itself is unmarked.

    [5] 'Poetry and Politics: A conversation with George and Mary Oppen; conducted by Burton Hatlen and Tom Mandel, in GOMP, 35.

    [6] Ibid.

    [7] See e.g. Farrell O'Gorman, 'The Angelic Artist in the Fiction of Flannery O'Connor and Walker Percy', *Renascence*, 53/1 (Fall 2000), 61–81.

    [8] Burton Hatlen in '"Not Altogether Lone in a Lone Universe": George Oppen's *The Materials*', in GOMP, 325–57, is the only critic to have looked beyond the epigraph for the significance of Maritain for Oppen. The focus of his discussion is, however, different from the one offered below.

    [9] Dennis Young, 'Conversation with Mary Oppen', 23.

    [10] See Dembo, '"Objectivist" Poet', 169 where Oppen remarks: 'I don't like his [Maritain's] religious apologetics, though.'

in Heidegger and thereby initiating a meditation on the nature of poetic thinking that would determine the whole shape of his subsequent poetic career.

We can understand the appeal of Maritain's text to Oppen if we think again of the poetics of *Discrete Series* which in some sense it seemed to confirm. In elaborating an aesthetic from the writings of Thomas Aquinas, Maritain sought to recover a sense of being in the face of modern subjectivism. For this task, poetry was better suited than metaphysics since, as commentator John Hittinger notes, in Maritain's view 'poetic knowledge is existential because it must attend to the sensible particulars; it is less apt to be lost in the cloud of abstraction'.[11] Like Heidegger, Maritain began with what he called 'the intuition of being', this providing 'a testimony to the integrity and wholeness of things, the depth of reality that will always elude our final grasp' (206). As Hittinger demonstrates, Maritain drew on 'Thomas' insistence on a nondiscursive moment in intellection. In addition to the complex apparatus of dialectic and abstraction, demonstration and reasoning, the human knower must be said to "see" simply' (206). This 'simple moment of vision' (207) might seem to echo the perceptual frames of *Discrete Series*, where syntactical opacities offer a 'thinking with the things as they exist' which resonates with the idea of 'the connatural knowing of the self and the world' for which Maritain's aesthetic philosophy is best known (209).

As we shall see in the next chapter, Oppen would pursue this poetics of being in his later reading of Heidegger's texts, but it is clear that *Creative Intuition* paved the way for his receptiveness to these. There is evidence, too, in Oppen's unpublished papers that, as Mary suggests, his return to poetry did coincide with his discovery of Maritain's book. One leaf from a *Daybook*, for example, contains a passage in which he seems to take over some of Maritain's terms to develop a personal speculation on what he calls 'the primordial intuition of being'. While this *Daybook* is dated 1963–4 by the Archive, it's almost certain that this particular leaf is a rare survival from notes written in Mexico since a consistent pattern of mistyping regularly produces 'ñ' instead of 'm' and 'l'—the only example I have found of Oppen using a typewriter with Spanish characters.[12] The passage is as follows:

---

[11] John P. Hittinger, *Liberty, Wisdom, and Grace: Thomism and Democratic Theory* (Lanham, Md.: Lexington Books, 2002), 208 (further references will be given in the text).

[12] Linda Oppen (personal communication) tells me: 'I was given a typewriter with a Spanish keyboard to take to college in 1958. George would have had easy access to it until I left in August, and I do remember him using it.' The leaf also contains handwritten comments relating to the assassination of President Kennedy which explains the Archive's dating. Oppen frequently revisited his notes to add further comments, a habit which often makes precise dating very difficult.

Thus the primordial intuition of being is the intuition of the solidity and inexorability of existence; and second, of the death and nothingness to which MY existence is liable. And third, in the sañe flash of intuition, which is but my becoñing aware of the intelligible value of being, I reañize that this solid and inexorable existence, perceived in anything whatsoever, implies—I do not yet know in what form, perhaps in the things theñselves, perhaps separately from them—some absolute, irrefragable existence, completely free from nothingness and death.   these three leaps (UCSD 16, 19, 7)

Underneath this typed passage, there is an autograph annotation, 'Maritain', with an arrow pointing to 'these three leaps'. The 'flash of intuition' certainly echoes Maritain, who uses variations on the phrase repeatedly,[13] but more importantly Oppen's speculative remarks seem to be a deliberate reworking of the following passage toward the end of *Creative Intuition*:

What matters to poetry in a close and direct manner are, I think, certain extremely simple but basic *presences* or existential certainties, assured by the universe of thought which constitutes the vital environment of poetic intuition: for instance a certitude both of the mysterious irrefragable existence and the exigency of intelligibility involved in things; a certitude of the *interiority* of the human being, and its importance; a certitude that between man and the world there is an invisible relationship deeper than any material interconnection; a certitude that the impact of his freedom on his destiny gives his life a movement which is *oriented*, and not lost in the void, and which has to do, in one way or another, with the whole fabric of being. (276)

In reading Maritain, Oppen was, we might conclude, attempting to arrive at his own sense of 'basic presences or existential certainties', and the passage from his *Daybook* negotiates the 'irrefragable' (or incontrovertible) nature of existence, 'solidity' and 'inexorability' compelling an awareness of 'nothingness and death', but at the same time allowing a kind of 'leap' to a perception of a life which is, as Maritain puts it, 'not lost in the void'. In a 1963 letter, Oppen would return to this *Daybook* entry and recast it as follows:

The mystery for me begins where it begins for Aquinas: The individual encounters the world, and by that encounter with something which he recognizes as being outside himself, he becomes aware of himself as an individual, a part of reality. In that same intuition, he registers the existence of what is not himself, what is totally independent of him, can exist without him, as it must have existed before him, as it will exist after him, and is totally free of *nothingness and death*.   (which is, for Aquinas, the intuition of God.   It is at any rate the intuition of the indestructible) (SL, 91–2, my emphases)[14]

---

[13] See e.g. *Creative Intuition*, 203: 'we have an actual flash of knowing—poetic experience, poetic intuition—born through spiritualized emotion, in the preconscious, non-conceptual life of the intellect'.

[14] See also 'Interview with George Oppen', conducted by Reinhold Schiffer, *Sagetrieb*, 3/3 (Winter 1984), 20 where Oppen agrees with the interviewer that he 'got to Aquinas through

Together, the two passages show Oppen attempting to focus what he calls 'the intelligibility of being' through that 'flash of intuition' in which oppressive thoughts of 'nothingness and death' recede. Underlying Maritain's account of 'existential certainties' is the sense of 'an invisible relationship' between man and world which is 'deeper than any material interconnection', and it is the 'certitude' of this bond that for Oppen clearly constitutes the central insight of Maritain's thinking.

Maritain thus proposes in the early pages of *Creative Intuition* that great art, be it of East or West, allows a reciprocal illumination of Self and Things:

at the root of the creative act there must be a quite particular intellectual process, without parallel in logical reason, through which Things and the Self are grasped together by means of a kind of experience or knowledge which has no conceptual expression and is expressed only in the artist's work. . . . in such an experience, creative in nature, Things are grasped in the Self and the Self is grasped in Things, and subjectivity becomes a means of catching obscurely the inner side of Things. (29–30)

Maritain's conception of poetry as an activity of the intelligence which is fundamentally distinct from that of 'logical reason' places its origin in the 'preconscious', a realm of the spiritual or 'musical' which he carefully distinguishes from the 'automatic' or 'Freudian' unconscious, 'the unconscious of blood and flesh, instincts, tendencies, complexes, repressed images and desires, traumatic memories, as constituting a closed or autonomous dynamic whole' (67). Maritain attributes to art the expression of that 'radiance or clarity' (123), generated by the 'illuminating image' (167), which liberates us from the 'autonomous' unconscious which, he says, is 'deaf to the intellect, and structured into a world of its own apart from the intellect' (67). Years after first reading *Creative Intuition*, Oppen would write that 'There is a certain force of clarity, it is | Of what is not autonomous in us', and his meaning there would coincide closely with Maritain's.[15] An unpublished note also shows that he would subsequently find further corroboration of this insight in Heidegger: 'I believe that Heidegger is saying (On the Essence of Truth) that freedom is freedom from the automatism of the organism, that freedom is awareness' (UCSD 16, 17, 1).[16]

For Oppen, as for Maritain, 'clarity' would thus become a key word, denoting that 'fabric of being' in which Self and Things illuminate each other. Such propositions would have significant consequences for his new poetics. Like

Maritain'. A *Daybook* for the same period offers a more abbreviated version of the theme: 'I can see nothing at all except that one encounters the thing. And, it is impossible not to say, encounters oneself' (UCSD 16, 19, 7).

15 The lines occur in 'Route' (NCP, 193), first published in *Of Being Numerous* (1968).
16 'On the Essence of Truth' is included in *Existence and Being*.

Maritain, he would have no time for art forms such as Surrealism which celebrated the random workings of the 'automatic' or 'autonomous' unconscious, nor for the personal and confessional modes of much contemporary American poetry.[17] In *Creative Intuition*, he had discovered a powerful distinction between 'the creative Self and the self-centered ego' (105), the latter being merely 'a neuter subject of predicates and phenomena, a subject as *matter*, marked with the opacity and voracity of matter, like the I of the egoist' (106). Maritain stressed accordingly that poetic emotion was to be understood not as a '*thing* which serves as a kind of matter or material in the making of the work', but as '*form* which, being one with the creative intuition, gives form to the poem, and which is *intentional*, as an idea is, or carries within itself infinitely more than itself' (87). Even more clearly in line with Oppen's early poetics was Maritain's view that 'creative emotion, losing its original state, objectivises itself in some respect' (256). That idea of objectification, resonating, of course, with Oppen's theories during the thirties, is for Maritain a bulwark against mere imitation, on the one hand, and abstraction, on the other. Indeed, the passage from which Oppen's epigraph derives mounts an attack on non-representational art and it does so by emphasizing the instantiating power of 'Things' in a way which would allow Oppen to discern a kind of 'materialism' here to counterbalance the emphasis on the creative consciousness in Maritain's text:

Now if it is true that *creative subjectivity awakens to itself only by simultaneously awakening to Things*, in a single process which is poetic knowledge; and that the way by which the free creativity of the spirit enters into act is essentially poetic intuition, and that poetic intuition is nothing but the grasping of Things and the Self together through connaturality and intentional emotion—then it must be said that in breaking away from the existential world of Nature, from Things and the grasping of Things, nonrepresentative art, by this very fact, condemns itself to fall short of its own dearest purposes and the very ends for the sake of which it came to life. (159–60; my emphases)[18]

---

[17] See Maritain, *Creative Intuition* on 'that element of imposture and quackery which is so deep-rooted in surrealism' (61) and his call for 'a process of relative depersonalization' (256). Cf. 'Selections from George Oppen's *Daybook*', ed. Dennis Young, *Iowa Review*, 18/3 (1988), 1: 'Most and almost the whole of modern art is influenced by surrealism. It means to produce art not out of the experience of things but out of the subjectivity of the artist.'

[18] The italicized phrase provides the closest source of Oppen's epigraph, but in the prelims of his own copy he writes: 'source of my misquotation: page 83' and then quotes and encircles the following italicized passage on that page: 'The poet does not know himself in the light of his own essence. Since man perceives himself only through a repercussion of his knowledge of the world of things, and *remains empty to himself if he does not fill himself with the universe*, the poet knows himself only on the condition that things resound in him, and that in him, at a single wakening, they and he come forth out of sleep.' On the page facing the title page, Oppen has also written: 'Things: that things resound in him and he and they come forth together out of sleep.'

All of Oppen's subsequent speculations about the nature of poetry and the poetic would stem from this process of 'awakening' as a very special kind of 'knowledge', one for which, as Maritain put it, 'there is no goal, no specifying end' (131) and which aspires to the condition of 'ontological simplicity', following the example of the child 'who seems simply astonished *to be*, and condemns all our interests and their futility' (267).

* * * * *

When we look to the poems of *The Materials* (1962) to discern the traces of Oppen's engagement with Maritain's aesthetics we may be surprised to find 'ontological simplicity' of a very different kind from that evoked in *Creative Intutition*. *The Materials* is a troubled and anxious volume, overshadowed by the threat of atomic catastrophe and by the spectre of an alien 'stone universe'. And if Oppen's return to poetry is a sort of working through of hitherto unwritten experience, it is also an oblique engagement with a modernism which now seemed disastrously complicit in the waves of violence which had engulfed the first half of the century. In making his return to poetry at this late stage, Oppen's points of reference still lay in the earlier modernism, but a modernism, of course, whose trajectory was now more readily discernible than it had been in the mid-thirties. Who, though, were for him the main representatives of this modernism? The question arises partly because Oppen, in his published and unpublished writings, so rarely mentions the major poets of the time. As we have already noted, he admires Williams 'for his ability to just go on, to talk along, without becoming strained or mannered', though between this poetry and his own he finds 'hardly a "poetic" similarity at all' (SL, 20). As he notes in another letter, 'we don't sound much alike' and 'the common factor is well defined in Zuk's essay. And surely I envy still Williams' language, Williams' radiance; Rezi's lucidness; and frequently Zukofsky's line-sense' (SL, 83). These fragmentary judgements on other poets come back again and again to Oppen's suspicions of literary posturing—of Zukofsky, for example: 'I stripped myself bare while you, Louis, have hung on yourself every fancy rag you could find' (UCSD 16, 13, 20). Of modernism more generally (he refers in passing to Stravinsky, Picasso, and Pound) he observes rather similarly that 'That extreme sharpening of "taste" is no part of my intention' (UCSD 16, 7, 29). By the mid-sixties, Oppen was thinking of modernism as comprising two major strands: 'one may think of one current of American poetry as deriving primarily from Williams and Pound, and a second stream as deriving from Eliot thru Auden and including—a bit remotely, Stevens, then Bronk is in the current of Eliot and Stevens' (UCSD 16, 12, 4). Stevens's work seems, in fact, not to have occupied him much at all: in a letter of 1963, he alludes to 'Stevens and his little elegances' (SL, 77) though when, two years later, he appraises Carl Rakosi's *Amulet* he detects there 'a rich, imaginative and supple rhetoric' which is comparable to that of Stevens (though Rakosi has 'Not the final depth of Stevens' (SL, 125)). As for Eliot, while his 'early work exists in an agony of agnosticism, the later poems present the world as it is experienced by an established faith. At no time has he attempted to describe the world as most of us would have to describe it' (UCSD 16, 15, 4).[19]

In these sparse comments on modernism, one can determine several main emphases. First, Oppen carefully dissociates his own work from a poetry attuned to the speaking voice: writing to his friend Charles Humboldt about 'Blood from the Stone', the first of his 'new' poems, Oppen wonders 'How did I get to fiddling around like that? To my shame this will sound like an Auden explanation. . . . Of course, I need to make that a totally forthright statement. Shades of Auden———me, the unaudenized and diselioted! I'll rewrite it' (SL, 31).[20] Some years later, when Charles Tomlinson set up a passage from one of Oppen's letters as free verse ('To C. T.', NCP, 158), Oppen wrote to June that 'I would never have made those line divisions. It is the discursive, the conversational' (UCSD 16, 21, 39). Second, Oppen distrusts any dependence on 'established faith', as he finds that in Eliot's work: as he puts it in a note about *Four Quartets*, 'the fire and the rose are one, only in the absolute. Glare of the world is the secret hidden' (UCSD 16, 28, 28). A letter written to June in 1959 brings these various arguments to a focus and helps us to see how some decisions about literary modernism would inform his second volume of poems. 'The modern temper', he writes, 'reacts to a liberal statement as intolerable soap-boxing, and is remarkably tolerant to Yeats' Theosophy, Eliot's Catholicism, Pound's fascism' (SL, 22). These three writers, he continues, are 'reactionary to the point of insanity'; 'add Joyce, Proust, Lawrence for that matter', he goes on, observing that 'being democratic has got to be absolutely non-dogmatic, a-political, unsystematic: whereas system, dogmatism and all the rest is found tolerable in Yeats Pound Eliot' (SL, 22).[21] Not fortuitously, *The Materials* carried

---

[19] Oppen was also sensitive to Eliot's anti-Semitism and his notes include a five-line parody of 'Gerontion': 'An old man not being read to by a boy | Not waiting for rain | I have fought in the rain | I have been bitten by flies, and fought. | I am a jew and squat in my own house' (UCSD 16, 28, 63).

[20] See also a 1962 letter to Williams on his 'Asphodel, That Greeny Flower' (SL, 61): 'The work is so open and so frank and so solid! Like Auden, for whom I acquired a new respect.' For Oppen's sense of failure in *The Materials*, see below, pp. 55–7.

[21] The reference to Joyce is a little unexpected in this context. See SL, 106–8, where Oppen reads the Warren Report through the lens of *Ulysses*.

as an epigraph a version of some dark lines from Yeats's 'Meditations in Time of Civil War':

> We had fed the heart on fantasies,
> The heart's grown brutal from the fare;
> More substance in our enmities
> Than in our love. . . . [22]

In alluding to these lines, Oppen tacitly dissociates himself from this modernism: in his version, '*They* fed their hearts on fantasies | And *their* hearts have become savage' (NCP, [38]), an emphatic shifting of emphasis which gestures toward modernism's fateful indulgence in fantasies of violent transformation at the expense of a humane politics.

In beginning to write again, then, Oppen was mindful of the pitfalls of avant-gardism and deeply sceptical of claims for the political efficacy of poetry. Perhaps for this reason it was his old friend Ezra Pound who, alone amongst the modernists, was a regular point of reference for Oppen in his private conversations with himself. As if to confer symbolic importance upon the connection, Pound's release from St Elizabeths Hospital happened in the same year that Oppen returned to poetry. If Maritain's book had been a prime mover in that return, a discovery compounding the effect of Oppen's famous 'rust and copper' dream, it was in part because it also offered an 'awakening' from what he had increasingly come to see as the bad dream of a modernism he associated primarily with Pound.[23] The Oppens, of course, had published Pound's work and had visited him in Rapallo in 1933. It was Pound, too, who had written the commendatory preface for *Discrete Series* and it may have seemed in 1934 that Objectivism was to be an orderly development from the older poet's Imagism. Yet while Oppen was grateful at the time for Pound's endorsement and could still on occasion speak of him as 'A great poet. A great man' (SL, 194), he also found himself repeatedly interrogating the older poet's errors, remarking the failure of his economic and political theories and the apparent futility of a poetry committed to an ideology of 'knowledge'. 'Pound', he remarked, 'never freed himself from argument, the moving of chess pieces',[24] a game in which 'everything has already been named' (UCSD 16, 16, 9). For Pound 'knew what he thought. The fact ruined much. (but when the wasp takes him by surprise ——)!' (UCSD 16, 24, 15).[25] This subordination of the world to the poet's ideas

---

[22] W. B. Yeats, *The Poems*, ed. Daniel Albright (London: Dent & Sons Ltd, 1990), 251.

[23] For an illuminating discussion of Oppen's relation to Pound, see Rachel Blau DuPlessis, 'Objectivist Poetics and Political Vision', in GOMP, 123–48.

[24] 'Selections from George Oppen's *Daybook*', ed. Young, 5.

[25] For Pound's evocation of the wasp, see *The Cantos* (London: Faber and Faber, 1994), LXXXIII. 546–7: 'and in the warmth after chill sunrise | an infant, green as new grass, | has stuck

marks the crucial point of divergence between Oppen and the modernists, a divergence at once formal and political: 'for me,' he continues, 'the writing of the poem is the process of finding out what I mean, discovering what I mean', a statement which may remind us again of Objectivism's attempt to find the subjective in the objectified form of the poem. In contrast, Oppen now saw Poundian modernism as characterized by 'ego', by an agonistic relation of subject and object, and by a masculinist sense of aesthetic form as something won from struggle with a recalcitrant 'other':[26] 'Pound's ego system, Pound's organisation of the world around a character, a kind of masculine energy, is extremely foreign to me.'[27] And while the Objectivists' commitment to 'sincerity' had taken its cue from Pound's idea of 'technique as a test of a man's sincerity', Oppen was increasingly dubious about Pound's own qualifications in this respect:

When Pound speaks of moments he has himself known he re-creates a world, he gives life. The masks, personae are coarse paint and papier maché, a Punch and a Judy, a baby made of an old sock. (UCSD 16, 17, 3)

For Oppen, *The Cantos* fails because it is dominated precisely by what the poet has *not* known, his Douglasite economics foundering because Pound (unlike Oppen) had never actually been inside a factory.[28] *The Cantos*, in Oppen's view, thus amounts to little more than a repository of fragments—'I read the Cantos in fragments as fragments', he remarked (SL, 250)—and it remains a work partially salvageable only on account of those lapidary moments of illumination in which the poem is true to the world rather than to its own motivating ideologies. So that evocation of the wasp in *The Pisan Cantos* remains, for Oppen, 'the great moment' of the poem, exhibiting a precision and generosity of attention which temporarily undermine the more familiar predominance of 'Pound's ego system'. For Oppen, Pound's blindness to what was happening during the war—he 'didn't speak of the gas chambers' (UCSD 16, 16, 10)—was bound up with a persistent

---

its head or tip | out of Madame La Vespa's bottle'. See also UCSD 16, 13, 20: 'pull down they [*sic*] vanity etc It's a remarkably bombastic ant but the wasp, whose head or tip . . . I think it is the great moment in Pound's writing, the great moment of the cantos.' Even Oppen's admiration for this particular passage did not prevent him from remarking elsewhere 'the brutal theatricality of the green w[orld]' (UCSD 16, 16, 6).

[26] See e.g. SL, 254 on Pound's 'stupid masculine rhetoric' and UCSD 16, 31, 4 on his tendency to 'competitive bullying'.

[27] Dembo, ' "Objectivist" Poet', 170.

[28] 'An Adequate Vision: A George Oppen Daybook', ed. Michael Davidson, *Ironwood*, 26 (Fall 1985), 17: 'and if Pound had walked into a factory a few times the absurdity of Douglas' theory of value, which Pound truculently repeats in the *Cantos*, would have dawned on him'. Cf. UCSD 16, 14, 3: 'he [Pound] understood nothing of *work*, much less of economics'.

modernist tendency to read the political through the lens of an avant-garde aesthetic:

The root of his fascism is remoteness, self hatred   In fact his literariness [has] an operatic quality   a vision of history rooted in no real sense of time and the sense of his own presence on a mineral world, but a swirl of heroes and words in his mind——.[29]

Pound's politics, in other words, was constantly vitiated by its overwhelming literariness: 'He spoke directly of banks and corporations———If he spoke of the people he spoke in antique metaphors: "the stonecutter is kept from the stone——"' (UCSD 16, 28, 7). Subjective, 'literary', remote from actuality, and blind to the world's fundamental ('mineral') otherness: these were failings that Oppen would continue to associate more generally with the avant-garde on his return to poetry. 'The avant-garde', he writes in an unpublished note, 'is not a matter of rushing ahead of everyone——it is a matter of TURNING A CORNER' (UCSD 16, 17, 10). Compare this characteristically urban figure with the grandness of Pound's borrowing in Canto XCIII from the beautiful opening of Dante's *Paradiso*, ii: 'O voi che siete in piccioletta barca', where readers in their 'little bark' follow serenely in the wake of the poet's ship.[30] Such gestures neatly encapsulate the avant-gardist confidence which, in Pound's case, could survive even the debacle of Italy's defeat and his own incarceration. For Oppen, however, the disaster of the war made the sense of failure omnipresent, and even the revival of his own creativity seemed to testify to failure of a kind: 'And I broke off that book [*Discrete Series*] and the writing of poetry for that search once more on the actual ground, and returned to poetry only when we knew that we had failed' (UCSD 16, 17, 4). The failure of a larger dream of social transformation set stark limits to artistic ambition; and where pre-war avant-gardists had sought above all to precipitate crisis, Oppen now saw poetry's obligation as one of *responding* to a crisis far in excess of anything of its own making ('Not invent—just answer—all | That verse attempts', as he put it in 'Blood from the Stone' (NCP, 52)).[31]

He was, of course, reckoning with the potentials—and the limits—of poetry in a period over which the threat of nuclear destruction now cast a long shadow. For Oppen, as for many others, the spectre of 'chain-reaction, the destruction of the world' was something 'just naturally on all our minds ——To such an extent that it makes most of the poetry seem silly' (SL, 18–19). To understand the austerity of some of the new poems included

---

[29] 'Selections from George Oppen's *Daybook*', ed. Young, 11.
[30] Pound, *Cantos*, 645. Pound also alludes to this passage in Canto VII, 26 and Canto CIX, 788.
[31] Probably the first of Oppen's poems on his return to writing; an earlier version is titled 'To Date'.

in *The Materials*, it is important to grasp the sense of emergency which accompanied his new creativity. For Oppen—in contrast to Pound—the value of the aesthetic was never something to be taken for granted; indeed, his own experience had already convinced him that in the face of certain crises the arts only too quickly revealed their inadequacy, irrelevance even. The pleasure Oppen took in his return to writing, then, was shadowed by a troubled awareness of that earlier modernism which had shown itself so unequal to the challenge of modern barbarism. Here his sense of aesthetic failure has less in common with Pound's reaction to the war than it does with European works such as Thomas Mann's *Doctor Faustus* (1947) and Hermann Broch's *The Death of Virgil* (1945), works which share with *The Cantos* a sense of grand design but which seek more directly to reckon with the fate of the arts in a ruined modernity. In fact, Broch's novel offers numerous points of comparison with Pound's *Pisan Cantos*, published three years later. Both texts regard the war as marking a seismic fault-line in history which calls in question the very nature of art's function. On the day before his death, Broch's Virgil dreams of destroying his *Aeneid*, a work he now feels to be somehow inhuman in its sacrifice of ethics to aesthetics and in its misplaced celebration of the Roman state. Like Pound in the death cells at Pisa, Broch had had his own intimations of mortality when imprisoned by the Gestapo, and his novel weighs his sense of human finitude against what he now sees as the failure of art's metaphysical pretensions. Pound was also counting the cost of art's failed engagement with politics, but *The Pisan Cantos*, in contrast to Broch's novel, attributes that failure not to the shortcomings of art but to the politicians who have refused to learn from it. Hence the remarkable stoicism of the sequence and its never wavering belief that a poetic language of 'rectitude', as Pound calls it, might somehow survive the debacle of Mussolini's regime, like a diamond 'torn from its setting', even though its desired political embodiment lies in ruins.[32]

Here, indeed, we have a memorable expression of what Oppen described as Pound's 'remoteness' and in this respect the world of the late Cantos invites comparison with that of another important European novel which sought to reckon with cultural 'disaster', Hermann Hesse's *The Glass Bead Game* (1943). Hesse's novel ironically projects a distant future in which culture has survived only by becoming an elitist, semi-religious game. Like an unimaginably complex form of chess, the game is played with cultural fragments: it might start, says Hesse, 'from a sentence out of Leibnitz or the Upanishads, and from this theme, depending on the intentions and

---

[32] Pound, *Cantos*, 444. For an elaboration of this argument, see my *Ezra Pound: Politics, Economics, and Writing* (Basingstoke: Macmillan, 1984).

talents of the player, it could either further explore the initial motif, or else
enrich its expressiveness by allusion to kindred concepts'.[33] The form of the
game, modelled on fugue and counterpoint, and developing an 'international
language of symbols' akin, says Hesse, to 'the ancient Chinese script', cannot
but remind us of Pound's later Cantos, and uncomfortably so, since the
Glass Bead Game exemplifies not only an ideal of artistic autonomy but
also the social remoteness of the intellectuals who play it and the disastrous
aestheticization of politics which their withdrawal ultimately permits. Witness
to its own redundancy, the avant-garde can stake its claims to the new only
in the realm of the aesthetic which, marked now by closure and solipsism, is
doomed to mirror the totalitarian structures which it had failed adequately to
recognize or to repudiate. This was, finally, the fate of modernism, as Oppen
now saw it.

* * * * *

In light of these ideas of aesthetic 'failure', Maritain's repudiation of 'the self-
centered ego' and his commitment to quite different 'existential certainties'
signalled a necessary break with a modernism which was now felt by Oppen to
be seriously compromised. There was a promise of openness here, a route out
of the confining structures which he associated with both the legacy of high
modernism and the claustrophobic conditions of his own exile in Mexico.
Maritain's conviction that 'in the field of art, the mind does not have to
know, but *make*' (316 n. 14; emphasis in original) may have found a particular
resonance here, for it was not the case that Oppen was about to give up
political thinking for some version of existentialism. As his new poetry would
richly show, it was actually a matter of rediscovering politics, but this time in
the 'existential world' of being and making rather than in that other world
in which 'knowledge' had been devalued to the currency of conspiracy and
surveillance.

Maritain, as Oppen frequently noted, convincingly distinguished 'the brute
ego, the accidents of the ego, from the self which perceives' (SL, 56–7),
perception meaning here not objectification but rather a powerful sense
of the reciprocity of self and world. In this spirit, a later formulation in
one of Oppen's notebooks proposes that 'WHAT THE EYES SEE CONTAINS
US', a pithy corrective to instrumentalist notions of seeing (UCSD 16, 18,
4). Oppen thus tries to conceive of a world neither to be seen from a
distance and appraised merely for its usefulness, nor one fully absorbed by
the avant-garde artwork and read in terms of a primarily formal-subjective

---

[33] Hermann Hesse, *Magister Ludi* (*The Glass Bead Game*), trans. Richard and Clara Winston
(1943; New York: Bantam Books, 1970), 30.

crisis.[34] But what exactly is this world that 'contains us'? In the notes written alongside the poems of the late fifties, Oppen brooded on the problem of materiality, a problem which the threat of nuclear destruction now posed in an existential light rather different from that of the 'stubborn' materiality which underwrites the Objectivism of *Discrete Series*. Increasingly oppressed by a sense of the alienating force of the material world, a world seemingly without any intelligible kinship with the human, Oppen set himself the task of recovering from the sheer facticity of things the kind of 'existential certainties' of which Maritain had spoken. So he explained his title in a 1962 letter to fellow poet William Bronk: 'It's true that I believe in the materials, that they are there. . . . I have little confidence in . . . the revelation of purposes. But a faith in the Thing—tho of course it's a faith.'[35] And 'material' had other obvious implications since, as the title of his 1962 volume would unequivocally announce, a mass of autobiographical experience remained to him as materials to be worked through. Oppen's new volume would thus be concerned at once with specifically historical and political evaluations of the thirties and with what he now began to call 'metaphysical' questions: 'Metaphysics: a language that talks *about* physical fact' (SL, 84; his emphasis) would be his later definition, but a language, we might add, which apprehends 'fact' in its relation to self and to nothingness. Here we can trace an emergent poetics committed to acknowledging the world's materiality but at the same time to making the act of creative perception a defence against what Maritain had called the 'subject as *matter*, marked with the opacity and voracity of matter, like the I of the egoist' (106).

These different but related senses in which the 'material' might be invoked coalesced around Oppen's central idea that the making of the poem would itself articulate the self's encounter with the world. A 1959 letter from Oppen to June shows that he was beginning to explore the mechanism of such encounters in existentialist thought:

I had a lot of remarks scrawled about the fact that we are material bodies, and really born, in a sense, out of the world of matter, which is a closed world to us from the moment of birth, as if we had been born in a locked room, and found ourselves growing up on some door-step with people and things which, since they were in some way our siblings, indicated that we all had a mother in Nature. . . . And the fact that we are not self-contained like a stone, since our consciousness goes out, and therefore as Sartre pretty much said, we are faced all the time with a void. And that since we're not self-contained——I said——we want to be contained——against empty space. (UCSD 16, 1, 1)

---

[34] For further discussion of Oppen's critical view of avant-gardism, see Ch. 5, below.
[35] Unpublished letter, quoted in Burt Kimmelman, *The 'Winter Mind': William Bronk and American Letters* (Madison: Fairleigh Dickinson, 1998), 148.

The reference to Sartre is intriguing, though we can only speculate about the work or works Oppen has in mind. According to his daughter, he frequented bookshops in the city and the used book stalls in Lagunilla. 'Books were cheap,' she remembers, 'no duty into Mexico, European paperbacks abounded in the house. I mention again his francophilia.'[36] Oppen's talk of not being 'self-contained like a stone' certainly recalls Sartre's account of the *en-soi* (in-itself) in *Being and Nothingness* (English translation 1957): 'The in-itself has nothing secret; it is *solid* [*massif*]. . . . The result is evidently that being is isolated in its being and that it does not enter into any connection with what is not itself'.[37] It is perhaps more likely, though, that Oppen had read Sartre's *Nausea*, first translated into English in 1949, where the narrator's awareness of 'existence' begins when he picks up a stone: 'I existed like a stone, a plant or a microbe'.[38] A few years later, Oppen would remark in regard to Simone de Beauvoir's *The Ethics of Ambiguity* that 'She seems unaware of the mineral fact, of which Sartre is so conscious' (UCSD 16, 14, 9), and it is likely that the idea of a 'stone universe' drew something from *Nausea*'s depiction of an inert and 'superfluous [*de trop*]' world of absolute 'contingency':[39] 'The Boulevard Noir is inhuman. Like a mineral. Like a triangle', while the town of Bouville is distinguished eponymously by its 'mud and pebbles'.[40] For Oppen, 'mud' is consistently the sign for hopelessness, recalling the 'terrible ground' of Alsace ('Survival: Infantry', NCP, 81).

Yet while Sartre's Roquentin is doomed to a lonely and meaningless life, Oppen as he composed *The Materials* was finding a rich diversity of experience to write about. By February 1959, he wrote to June that 'the youngish crop of poets . . . have not led lives at all compared to mine. I've been writing as hard and fast as I can of the Infantry, skilled workers, row boats, people in trailer camps, the unemployed movement in the thirties, a family, marital love, children, the old codgers of Southern California, the H Bomb' (SL, 25). At the same time, though, as he noted in a letter to Julian Zimet, one of his new poems, 'Time of the Missile', with its talk of atoms as constituents of both the human body and the bomb, set the tone for the whole volume ('all of the poems are about this same thing' (SL, 30)), and it is as if the multifariousness of his poetry's 'materials' was intended to provide one way of evoking 'human

[36] Linda Oppen, personal communication.

[37] Jean-Paul Sartre, *Being and Nothingness: An Essay on Phenomenological Ontology*, trans. Hazel E. Barnes (1957; London and New York: Routledge, 2003), 22.

[38] Sartre, *Nausea*, trans. Lloyd Alexander (1949; London: Hamish Hamilton, 1962), 20. The 1949 text was first published as *The Diary of Antoine Roquentin*.

[39] See also the unpublished poem 'Man's Time' which ends 'Daughter, our daughter, no child but our child. | Stone universe, but we are not' (UCSD 16, 1, 1).

[40] *Nausea*, 39.

time' against the dead reaches of the 'stone universe'.[41] For Zimet, he provided a further gloss on the poem:

yes, Nature, stone nature and the empty space must be the mother from which we were born since the others are deserted too outside a closed door of nothingness and therefore presumably our brothers. . . . I said the rest of it is just stone, and the enemy. And death, which is a victory of stone. And the mud, and the terrible ground. The half-life ground. (SL, 31–2)

In his letter to June, Oppen had gone on to develop this theme by quoting an early version of lines from 'Time of the Missile':

> . . . look
> To vision's limit anywhere we look; nothingness,
> Viviparous.
> And the closed door where there is no door.

Then he quotes lines from later in the draft:

> . . . Mother,
> Nature! because we find the others
> Deserted like ourselves, and therefore brothers.[42]

Against that last line, June has written 'political', as if to note that the point of the poem lies in its attempt to bring political and metaphysical views into some sort of conjunction. It is as if Oppen is trying to trace the desire for human association back to some primal alienation in face of an impassive 'mineral world', a world whose natural energies have now been lethally harnessed by the atom bomb. The poem as published ends thus:

> My love, my love
> We are endangered
> Totally at last. Look
> Anywhere to the sight's limit: space
> Which is viviparous:
>
> Place of the mind
> And eye. Which can destroy us,
> Re-arrange itself, assert
> Its own stone chain reaction.

(NCP, 70)

This theme of loss of origin, of the mystery of a birth unknown to us, keeps surfacing in *The Materials*. Oppen's suggestion that our collective estrangement from the roots of life is actually the spur to sociality seems

---

[41] See also UCSD 16, 20, 26: 'Atom we are made of | We did not make'.
[42] The lines subsequently became part of the conclusion to 'Blood from the Stone'.

now to cast politics in a deliberately existential perspective. In 'Blood from the Stone', for example, 'we find the others | Deserted like ourselves and therefore brothers' (NCP, 54), while in 'Image of the Engine' we read that 'From lumps, chunks, || We are locked out: like children, seeking love | At last among each other' (NCP, 42).[43] In passages like these, Oppen seems at once to ground politics in a primal desire for association—'that we can somehow add each to each other' ('Blood from the Stone', NCP, 52)—and to hint at something unknowable which governs this desire (the lines from 'Image of the Engine' are preceded by a quotation from Ecclesiastes 3: 11, '*Also he has set the world* | *In their hearts*' which continues: 'so that no man can find out the work that God maketh from the beginning to the end'). The unknowability of our origin—an unremembered moment out of human time, as it were, in which we are imagined as part of the universe, 'spring[ing] | From the ground together' ('Return', NCP, 47)—prompts a tangle of feelings, eliding loss and hope in a way that is reflected in Oppen's ambivalence toward the crowd. At times, 'we are | A crowd, a population, those | Born, those not yet dead' ('Population', NCP, 43), and the crowd is 'the living, that other | Marvel among the mineral' ('Tourist Eye', NCP, 65). Yet this same crowd 'can become a fist | Having menace, the power of menace' ('Tourist Eye', NCP, 66), and a number of poems lament the loss of that 'morality | Of hope' that had brought people together in the thirties but whose 'metaphysic' has now degenerated into the possessive individualism of 'small lawns of home' ('From Disaster', NCP, 50). To identify oneself with the crowd or with 'humanity' is highly problematic—Oppen will explore this further in 'Of Being Numerous'—and in *The Materials* identification with others beyond the immediate family tends to be with other 'makers', the workers of 'The Men of Sheepshead', for example ('Who is not at home | Among these men?' (NCP, 71)), the machine workers of 'Debt' (NCP, 68), the carpenter of 'Workman' (NCP, 62), the labourers building Grand Central Station ('Where we built . . .' ('Antique', NCP, 72)), and the masons who crafted Chartres Cathedral (NCP, 77), or else it is with the poet's fellow soldiers in wartime ('Survival: Infantry' (NCP, 81)).

The ambiguities that cluster around the concept of 'humanity' had already been mooted in 'Party on Shipboard' in *Discrete Series*, the last composed poem in the sequence and, as Oppen put it in 1959, 'a statement, and a very clear one, of what I was going in search of when I quit writing' (SL, 20). The

---

[43] Cf. SL, 248: 'Being . . . The lumps, the chunks, that which one cannot not see . . .'. The image of the locked room continued to haunt Oppen and recurs in 'Penobscot' in *This in Which*: 'Children of the early | Countryside || Talk on the back stoops | Of that locked room | Of their birth || Which they cannot remember' (NCP, 123).

Figure 2. Oppen at Chartres Cathedral, 1961

Figure 3. The Oppens sailing in Brittany, probably 1961

guests at this party are glimpsed metonymically—'arm waved, shrieks'—and
are likened to the individual waves that go to make up the sea as a whole:

> The shallow surface of the sea, this,
> Numerously——the first drinks——
> The sea is a constant weight
> In its bed.   They pass, however, the sea
> Freely tumultuous.

> (NCP, 15)

In this poem, Oppen had wanted, he said, 'to get again to humanity as a
single thing, as something like the sea which is a constant weight in its bed'
(SL, 111) and this allusion to the unthinkable mass of the ocean throws the
idea of existing 'numerously' into a metaphysical perspective, contrasting it
with a medium which is 'Homogenously automatic', beyond the purview of
the human. As he had put it in the letter to Zimet, 'since we're not self-
contained . . . we want to be contained——against empty space', and 'Time
of the Missile' seems to take 'sight's limit', the absolute horizon, as the dividing
line between, on the one hand, a space we inhabit and in which we reproduce
(it is 'viviparous'—'bringing forth live young'—a designedly 'technical' word
to chafe against the poem's lyric register), and, on the other, Sartre's 'void' in
which all human meanings expire. To Zimet, Oppen also observed that 'The
universe is stone, but we are not. The universe's time is some kind of elapsed
time, whatever that may be, but our time is historical time, and the difference
between one generation and a next, and we *make* that time' (SL, 29). Poetry,
too, is a making time, a 'taking place', as he puts it in 'Eclogue' (NCP, 39),
and it is also, perhaps, one form that may 'contain' us in face of 'empty space',
the 'closed door of nothingness', and the war-torn landscape of mud and
stone—Oppen's 'ur-scene' again—which in this context seems to represent
some final death of the universe as it threatens to return to a state of inert
materiality. Here once more Oppen's thinking might recall Sartre's inasmuch
as the frightening spectre of 'empty space' or nothingness is also what saves us
from that 'fullness' of Being which threatens to extinguish consciousness. As
Sartre observes, 'The necessary condition for our saying not is that non-being
be a perpetual presence in and outside of us, that nothingness *haunt* being.'[44]

Something similar seems to be the issue in Oppen's poem 'Solution', where
the jigsaw is completed 'but there is no gap, | No actual edged hole | Nowhere
the wooden texture of the table top | Glares out of scale in the picture' (NCP,
45). In a much later letter, Oppen explains that the poem 'describes the refusal
to think outside a field, a set of rules, of definitions'; this kind of thinking, he

---

[44] Sartre, *Being and Nothingness*, 35 (his emphasis).

says, amounts to 'the refusal to talk of metaphysics, the refusal to think the idea of Nothingness (this from Henri Bergson), the absence of a field' (SL, 281, 280). 'Metaphysics' may here denote 'a language that talks *about* physical fact' (SL, 84), but in acknowledging the Nothingness that also 'haunts' being it opens a space in which we might discover not just inert and irreducible 'facts' but a world in which they and we have meaning (hence, perhaps, his stress on 'about' in that quotation). Oppen's own 'metaphysical agony', as he calls it in the letter to Zimet, is 'contained' by the poem's 'lyric praise for vision', for it is 'the human vision which creates the human universe' and in the poem 'The eye *sees!*' (SL, 29, 30). We have come full circle, perhaps, because this act of jubilant seeing now gives us the truth of Oppen's proposition quoted earlier that 'WHAT THE EYES SEE CONTAINS US'. The act of poetic seeing—of *poesis*, of making rather than knowing, in Maritain's terms—allows a 'human universe' to be apprehended in face of an intransigently 'mineral' one. Whether Oppen's talk of a 'human universe' deliberately echoes Charles Olson's earlier essay of that name is unclear;[45] either way, Olson's argument for particularism against 'generalisation' and 'discourse' is close to what Oppen has in mind by his emphasis here on 'seeing'. For each poet, what 'contains' us is not the 'universe of discourse', as Olson puts it, but a 'phenomenal' one which is disclosed through 'direct perception and the contraries which dispose of argument'.[46] 'The eye *sees!*': in moving close to tautology, Oppen's exclamation makes seeing the very condition of subjective life and leaves no room for 'argument'. This 'human vision' discloses what a later poem calls simply 'something for us to stand on' ('World, World————', NCP, 159), the muteness of that 'something' reminding us once again that a 'human universe' is not one which has been 'humanised', but rather one with whose irreducibility we might make a tentative and fragile peace.

The Materials is, as a collection, shot through with that sense of fragility as measured against the 'violence' of the Sequoia seed in 'Return', with its closing image of the 'great weight of brick' (NCP, 49), the 'stone dead dam' which is 'Mother Nature' in 'Blood from the Stone' (NCP, 54), the 'lone universe that suffers time | Like stones in sun' in 'Birthplace: New Rochelle' (NCP, 55), the invocation of 'the living, that other | Marvel among the mineral' in 'Tourist Eye' (NCP, 65), and the contrasting 'terrible ground' of Alsace in 'Survival: Infantry' (NCP, 81). Yet the dark perspectives of some of these poems lead not to fatalism but to an affirmation of the life somehow sprung from a 'dead dam', and the 'Sidereal time' ('Blood from the Stone', NCP,

---

[45] First published in *Origin* (Winter 1951–2).
[46] Charles Olson, *Human Universe and Other Essays*, ed. Donald Allen (New York: Grove Press, 1967), 4.

53) whose empty reaches dwarf human history. The recognition that 'This is not our time' ('Return', NCP, 47) actually compels a counter-recognition: 'So we lived | And chose to live || These were our times' ('Blood from the Stone', NCP, 54). 'Our times', then, in the sense that Oppen and his generation lived them, but hardly 'our times' in any sense that the events recalled here were 'for us'. Indeed, 'Blood from the Stone' salvages small evidences of human authenticity from a history which has conspired to reduce individuals first to the 'inexplicable crowds' of Depression America and then, with the War, 'To a body [to which] anything can happen, | Like a brick' (NCP, 52, 53). It's perhaps not surprising that this is the poem with which Oppen made his return to poetry since its continuing political conviction, tentatively expressed as it now is—'That we can somehow add each to each other?' (NCP, 52)—is buoyed by minutely remembered images whose significance eludes the narrative of 'The planet's | Time' (NCP, 53).[47] *The Materials* may give us little detail of the Oppens' experiences in Mexico, but it does powerfully convey the sense of confinement, exclusion, and loneliness which characterized their time there. Hope has to be drawn from the most fundamental of all facts, that life might be generated from a 'stone universe', and many of the most affecting images are, as a result, associated with childhood and its fragility in face of an impenetrable universe: 'The sparrow's feet, | Feet of the sparrow's child touch | Naked rock' ('Stranger's Child', NCP, 58).

What is most striking about the articulation of these themes in *The Materials* is the omnipresent sense of anxiety—anxiety in the face of a mute material world and anxiety in the concern over the child's vulnerability to the forces contained in the atom ('What will she make of a world . . . of which she is made' ('Sara in Her Father's Arms', NCP, 51)). The poems intermittently celebrate the family ('we turn to the children' ('Return', NCP, 48)), not in a sentimental or purely personal way, but as a counter to the alienating reaches of cosmic time. For the world that emerges here is preponderantly 'A world of things', as Oppen puts it in 'Birthplace: New Rochelle' (NCP, 55). It is a world in which the absolutely reified 'stone universe' finds a counterpart in the false allure of 'The streets of stores' with their 'worn and squalid toys in the trash' ('Image of the Engine', NCP, 42). This is, says Oppen, 'a grimy death of love' in which no transformation, no alternative image of the world seems possible. Yet the idea of the generations *does* suggest a future in which things might be different—the 'Sunnyside Child', for example, is 'Preoccupied || To find his generation, his contemporaries | Of the neighbourhood whose atmosphere, whose sound | In his life's time no front door, no | Hardware ever again can

---

[47] Cf. SL, 31: 'the philosophy they acted on is still the only philosophy it is possible to live by ———that one man adds something to the life of another'.

close on' (NCP, 84). 'Birthplace: New Rochelle', one of the first of Oppen's new poems, is in this respect a pivotal work, since in revisiting his first home, the poet seeks to mend the rift in his own childhood and in that way to secure a sense of continuity and human time. Here he rediscovers 'the rounded rocks of childhood—They have lasted well' (NCP, 55). These particular stones are not seen as 'dead' but are reanimated by the affection with which they are perceived,[48] and Oppen, now aware of himself as 'An aging man', can finally grasp his father's life as 'A generation's mark' which 'intervenes'. In that hard-won recognition of continuity lies the promise of a future:

> My child,
> Not now a child, our child
> Not altogether lone in a lone universe that suffers time
> Like stones in sun. For we do not.
>
> (NCP, 55)

* * * * *

In poems such as 'Birthplace: New Rochelle', it is tempting, but not quite precise, to think of Oppen's way of 'get[ting] thru a back log of things I've wanted to say' (SL, 18) as a version of Freud's 'working through'. The difference is instructive, for where the Freudian process overcomes psychic resistances through interpretation, Oppen's way with his 'materials' tends to emphasize their intractability to any discursive or narrative scheme. So he writes, for example, that ' "in everything that is real there is an irreducible element"   of an hallucination, the irreducible element is that you experienced it' (UCSD 16, 18, 1), and in his later interview with L. S. Dembo he remarks rather similarly that 'that which is absolutely single really does exist—the atom, for example. That particle of matter, when you get to it, is absolutely impenetrable, absolutely inexplicable.'[49] Comments such as these indicate the extent to which Oppen's sense of an 'impenetrable' material universe is set over against a conception of the 'human universe' as one in which existence registers its singularity in the non-discursive language of the poem. As we saw in the case of *Discrete Series*, the moment of existence or 'isness' is at once simple and complex, constituting an instance of apparently powerful immediacy but one that is actually mediated through an often difficult and indeterminate syntax. In 'Time of the Missile', for example, when 'The eye *sees!* It floods in on us from here to Jersey tangled | in the grey bright

---

[48] Cf. 'From a Photograph' (NCP, 68) where the poet's daughter hugs him 'as if I were a loved and native rock'.

[49] Dembo, ' "Objectivist" Poet', 63.

air' (NCP, 70), the 'It' remains somehow unspecifiable—it is, again, what 'contains' us—and the relation of its 'flooding' to the condition of being 'tangled' seems deliberately to resist visualization. At the very moment of jubilant seeing, then, there is a certain resistance or opacity in the expression that prevents its reduction to discursive process; once again, 'the figures of perception' stand over against 'the figures of elocution, or even of mere assertion, which I profoundly distrusted' (SL, 82).

I want to suggest that it is by means of such opacities that Oppen stages the irruption of the existential in the political, for it is quite misleading to argue that 'When Oppen put pen to paper again, it was . . . as an existentialist, not as a socialist.'[50] For Oppen, as for Sartre, the insights of Marxism and existentialism came to be regarded not as incompatible but as complementary, not least because, as Fredric Jameson notes in his account of Sartre, each called in question the priority of thought over being ('existentialism with the principle that existence precedes essence, Marxism with the determination of consciousness by social reality'[51]); in this sense, as Sartre would argue in *Search for a Method* (1960; English translation 1963), existentialism was a necessary supplement to a post-war Marxism which had grown mechanical and economistic. In Oppen's case, his involvement with the left since the thirties had made him similarly aware of a tendency in Marxist practice to privilege ideology over experience, and we have already seen that during the period in Mexico the Oppens suffered a growing disenchantment with the communist world, both in terms of Party practice and the policies of the Soviet Union. Burton Hatlen is correct in his view that Oppen never repudiated his communist past,[52] but Oppen was nonetheless often critical of the Party's opportunism, particularly in the wake of the Nazi-Soviet Pact of 1939: 'Communism and our communism——the 15 years or more: many lies, absurdities, cruelties, self deception———and yet were we wrong even for ourselves?' (UCSD 16, 17, 9).[53]

Maritain's claim that 'poetry has its source in the pre-conceptual life of the intellect' (3) offered what must have seemed a highly attractive alternative to the degraded knowledge that was now 'politics', but most importantly for Oppen it opened a way back to politics grasped as experience rather than

---

[50] L. S. Dembo, *The Monological Jew: A Literary Study* (Madison: University of Wisconsin Press, 1988), 137.

[51] Fredric Jameson, *Marxism and Form: Twentieth-Century Dialectical Theories of Literature* (Princeton: Princeton University Press, 1971), 206.

[52] Hatlen, ' "Not Altogether Lone in a Lone Universe" ', 331.

[53] This note seems to have been written in the early seventies. See also UCSD 16, 18, 3, on 'the limited truths of Communism and its unlimited lies'. Oppen also declares (UCSD 16, 18, 1) that 'We gave twenty-five years of our lives to that agony, to that obsession, and now we want to do something else.'

as 'ideas'. This would also be the main point of Sartre's *Search for a Method* which aims

to engender within the framework of Marxism a veritable *comprehensive knowing* which will rediscover man in the social world and which will follow him in his *praxis*—or, if you prefer, in the project which throws him toward the social possibles in terms of a defined situation. Existentialism will appear therefore as a fragment of the system, which has fallen outside of Knowledge.[54]

In their different ways, Sartre and Oppen were each looking for a means of articulating together forms of interiority and exteriority so as to avoid the 'idealist' dichotomy of subject and object and to recover instead 'the *unsurpassable opaqueness* of the lived experience'.[55] Sartre, for example, would name as the 'crucial discovery' of dialectics that 'man is "mediated" by things to the same extent as things are "mediated" by man';[56] Oppen, as we have seen, hit on Maritain's similar if more poetic formulation that 'creative subjectivity awakens to itself only by simultaneously awakening to Things'. In each case, this way of *situating* the subject emphasized the irreducibility of experience to knowledge and, for Oppen, made poetry as its privileged embodiment the source of a kind of generative opacity within political thinking. In that sense, Oppen seems to have associated poetry with the acknowledgement of a certain indeterminacy and resistance that might save politics from ideology and mere 'argument'. It is in this context that we should understand his earlier refusal, as he put it in 1959, 'to write communist verse. That is, to any statement already determined before the verse. Poetry has to be protean; the meaning must begin there. With the perception' (SL, 22). This is a poetry in which, says Oppen, 'the thinking occurs at the moment of the poem, within the poem' (UCSD 16, 14, 12).

These issues would be more systematically reviewed in Oppen's only published essay, 'The Mind's Own Place', which appeared in 1963.[57] It is an uneven performance, perhaps with too many targets in its sights. Oppen finds the poet caught between 'the grim grey lines of the Philistines and the ramshackle emplacements of Bohemia' (173), attempting to rise above 'the

[54] Sartre, *Search for a Method*, trans. Hazel Barnes (1963; New York: Vintage Books, 1968), 181 (his emphases). Cf. Sartre, *Critique of Dialectical Reason*, trans. Alan Sheridan-Smith, ed. Jonathan Rée (London: NLB, 1976), 40: 'Our extremely slight dissociation of ourselves from the letter of Marxist doctrine (which I indicated in *The Problem of Method*) enables us to see the meaning of this question as the disquiet of the genuine experience which refuses to collapse into non-truth.'
[55] Sartre, *Search for a Method*, 9 n. 6 (his emphases).   [56] *Critique of Dialectical Reason*, 79.
[57] 'The Mind's Own Place' (Summer 1963), repr. in *Selected Poems of George Oppen*, ed. Robert Creeley (New York: New Directions, 2003), 173–82. Further references will be given in the text.

terrible thin scratching of the art world' (175). The lessons of early modernism remain as urgent as ever:

It is possible to find a metaphor for anything, an analogue: but the image is encountered, not found; it is an account of the poet's perception, of the act of perception; it is a test of sincerity, a test of conviction, the rare poetic quality of truthfulness. (175)

With Oppen's emphasis on the 'act of perception' and 'the data of experience' we are on familiar Objectivist ground (an earlier draft of the essay quotes from Zukofsky's introduction to the *Anthology* at this point[58]) but the argument quickly moves forward to weigh the political implications of this poetics:

It is part of the function of poetry to serve as a test of truth. It is possible to say anything in abstract prose, but a great many things one believes or would like to believe or thinks he believes will not substantiate themselves in the concrete materials of the poem. It is not to say that the poet is immune to the 'real' world to say that he is not likely to find the moment, the image, in which a political generalization or any other generalization will prove its truth. (176)

It is a puzzling passage. On the face of it, Oppen seems to be urging the incompatibility of poetry and politics on the grounds that poetry deals with acts of perception not with generalizations. At the same time, his account of belief is curiously vague ('things one believes or would like to believe or thinks he believes'), vague to the point of trivializing the very notion of belief. Over against generalization we have 'the moment, the image', or what we might call the spatio-temporal 'thereness' of the poem, the singular occasion which exemplifies a concreteness that cannot be assimilated to any generic category or event. Oppen quotes some lines from a poem by Denise Levertov, 'Matins', to demonstrate how a poet might 'construct a form out of no desire for the trick of gracefulness, but in order to make it possible to grasp, to hold the insight which is the content of the poem' (176).

It is ironic that Levertov should provide the exemplary text here since 'The Mind's Own Place', as Oppen put it in a letter to June, 'is almost written *at* her, and at her latest poems, some of which are very bad' (SL, 57). Oppen objected especially to a poem in Levertov's *The Jacob's Ladder* (1961) called 'During the Eichmann Trial' which ended with these lines:

> A cage, where we may view
> Ourselves, an apparition
>
> Telling us something he
> Does not know: we are members
>
> One of another.[59]

58 Linda Oppen Papers, UCSD 33, 17, 5.
59 Denise Levertov, *Poems 1960–1967* (New York: New Directions, 1968), 65.

Oppen observes: 'I think too that we are members of each other:—I believe that;... or would like to... but what a poem it would be in which one saw and tasted that!' (SL, 81). The criticism hinges in part on Oppen's feeling that Levertov's assertion is not 'substantiated' in the poem, not given a realized palpability that allows the thought to be 'grasped'; hence his declaration in the essay that 'the poet's business is not to use verse as an advanced form of rhetoric, nor to give to political statements the aura of eternal truth' (182). Levertov had also written a review of Paul Goodman's *The Lordly Hudson: Collected Poems* which provoked Oppen's criticism.[60] In an exchange of letters, he intimated not only that Goodman's political verse failed to 'substantiate' its ideas but also that Levertov had been drawn to praise second-rate work because she approved of its politics. One can sympathize with Levertov's annoyance at Oppen's rather high-handed criticism (she responded with an indignant eight-page letter (UCSD 16, 6, 21)) but he was adamant that the poet must at all cost avoid 'edifying conclusions. or comforting conclusions' (SL, 58). If the poem provides 'a test of truth. A test, at least, of conviction' (SL, 79) it is because propositions are somehow exposed there and lack a pre-formed discursive context to support and naturalize them. The poem therefore 'rejects' them as foreign matter; as Oppen puts it in his notes, 'Everything which is not earned is corrupt' (UCSD 16, 14, 5).

The asperity of comments such as this, self-directed as they often are, suggests that more was at stake in the exchange with Levertov than just a critical attitude toward a friend's poems. Oppen was, in short, wrestling here with a problem that was also very much his own. 'The Mind's Own Place' was written several months before the publication of *The Materials* and it plays an important part in Oppen's assessment of where his work was heading. The new volume was, as we have seen, evidence of his 'starting now as if from scratch' (SL, 26), but in his own assessment of it *The Materials* could hardly be thought of without reference to *Discrete Series*. Inevitably, perhaps, those poems provided a standard against which to measure his new work, and while Oppen was sometimes highly critical of his youthful writings, he also found that their 'bareness, the lack of defense' (SL, 152) demonstrate an early

---

[60] Originally published in *The Nation*, 13 Apr. 1963, the review is collected in Levertov, *The Poet in the World* (New York: New Directions, 1973), 231–5. For the exchange, see also Burton Hatlen, 'Feminine Technologies: George Oppen talks at Denise Levertov', *American Poetry Review*, 22/3 (1993), 9–14. Reporting the disagreement to Robert Duncan, Levertov described Oppen as 'an honest man of strong feeling, contentious mind, and a sort of nervous subtlety that makes me aware of what's blunt & almost simple-minded in myself'. *The Letters of Robert Duncan and Denise Levertov*, ed. Robert J. Bertholf and Albert Gelpi (Stanford, Calif.: Stanford University Press, 2004), 397.

commitment to the values of 'perception' as opposed to 'elocution'.[61] From this point of view, Oppen's breaking of his long silence necessarily involved a return to *Discrete Series*, reluctant though it may have been in the first instance, and his unpublished notes are littered with reflections on the relation of the early volume to his work of the sixties and seventies. The poems of *The Materials* were the product of wider and more intense experience; Oppen worried whether 'I haven't just a habit of form, rather than a conviction. The form of the old poems that I wrote. And it chokes on this sort of content' (SL, 19). Yet while his new content, drawn from experience of the Depression and the War, seemed to require a new form, Oppen was concerned about the temptation to rhetoric or 'elocution' which the new materials seemed to invite. In theory at any rate, the function of the poem is not to impose meaning but to allow the world, as it were, to 'shine' through it. Oppen writes accordingly in one of his notebooks, 'The poem replaces the thing, the poem destroys its meaning——I would like the poem to be nothing, to be transparent, to be inaudible, not to be——I felt that most strongly writing Discrete Series' (UCSD 16, 14, 5). 'Transparency', a certain 'silence' or reserve, these are qualities Oppen frequently pits against 'noise': 'not to make noise: to keep one's attention outward toward silence' (UCSD 16, 15, 3), and again: 'when space is not silence, the matrix of silence, it is chatter, noise' (UCSD 16, 18, 5).

The fixing of the attention 'outward' should turn the poem away from egoism and its rhetoric; for this reason, Oppen would subsequently claim that his later poems 'were written in violation of my own speech'.[62] Given the political dimension of his materials, however, this 'silence' was not always easy to achieve and a poem like 'Blood from the Stone' exhibits a tension between the deliberate stylization of perception in its opening lines and the more clearly rhetorical shape of the second stanza:

> . . . Belief?
> What do we believe
> To live with? Answer.
> Not invent—just answer—all
> That verse attempts.
>
> (NCP, 52)

---

[61] For Oppen's negative view, see SL, 379 n. 4: 'not more than three or four of the poems should have been printed'. For the view that *The Materials* simply duplicates the style and concerns of *Discrete Series*, see Oren Izenberg, 'Oppen's Silence, Crusoe's Silence, and the Silence of Other Minds', *Modernism/Modernity*, 13/1 (2006), 789: 'Oppen's next poems . . . are—to put it perhaps too bluntly—not much different in kind than his first ones.'

[62] 'A Conversation with George Oppen', conducted by Charles Amirkhanian and David Gitin, *Ironwood*, 5 (1971), 24. Cf. UCSD 16, 17, 3: 'the consciousness of the senses alone lacks center, lacks self. It also lacks exterior, proof of exterior. The hypothesis of the exterior is the primary work of the mind.'

This may explain the 'shades of Auden' remark quoted earlier (p. 37) and the touch of dissatisfaction lurking behind a comment in Oppen's notes, that since *Discrete Series* 'I have resigned myself to coming on stage, to *talking* for silence is impossible' (UCSD 16, 14, 5). The distinction here is clarified by another unpublished note, where he observes: ' "Discrete": I had tried NOT to speak not to talk' (UCSD 16, 13, 13), a comment that suggests that, much as Oppen wants to begin again 'from scratch', it is the distant, partly forgotten *Discrete Series*, with its *refusal* of 'talking' and 'coming on stage' that seems intermittently to present itself to him as a more effective and fuller realization of the ideas he had so recently absorbed from Maritain and which would direct much of the work to come.[63]

If *Discrete Series* was to remain another kind of 'ur-scene' or founding moment for Oppen, then, it was one whose full effect was felt belatedly, with the poet consciously and unconsciously reconfiguring it in the light of his beginning again. I am tempted to think about his rereading of *Discrete Series* in terms of Freud's notion of *Nachträglichkeit* or 'deferred action' which he developed in his case history of the Wolf Man to describe the way in which a traumatic experience takes on its full meaning only at a later stage.[64] This is not, of course, to suggest that the production of *Discrete Series* was in any sense traumatic for Oppen, but only that, when we are creating a narrative of his career, the structure of belatedness might speak first to his deliberate 'forgetting' of the early book and then to his subsequent return to it as a kind of prefiguring of what he was about to embark upon. John Forrester neatly defines the movement of *Nachträglichkeit* as 'the articulation of two *moments* with a time of delay',[65] and this 'articulation' is not simply a matter of recovering a lost memory, but rather of a restructuring which forms the past in retrospect as the original experience is reworked. As Freud observed in his study of the Wolf Man, 'these scenes from infancy are not reproduced during the treatment as recollection, they are the products of construction'.[66]

As we trace Oppen's career on into the early sixties, we shall encounter precisely what Forrester terms this 'articulation of two *moments* with a time of delay' as we try to bring *Discrete Series* into relation with Oppen's later

---

[63] And compare this rather defensive reflection on *The Materials* made in 1963: 'Shall we live without discourse? The poems are discursive, discursive thought. [B]ut they come out of some moment of silence, some time when I sat on a hill and said to myself, they are an attempt to explore THAT' (UCSD 16, 19, 3).

[64] *Pelican Freud Library*, ix. *Case Histories II*, ed. Angela Richards, trans. James Strachey (Harmondsworth: Penguin Books, 1981), 233–366.

[65] John Forrester, *The Seductions of Psychoanalysis: Freud, Lacan, and Derrida* (Cambridge: Cambridge University Press, 1990), 206.

[66] *Pelican Freud Library*, ix. *Case Histories II*, 284.

work. At least we have to undertake a sort of double reading of the poems, placing them at once in the context of thirties Objectivism *and* in that of the poet's philosophical concerns in the early sixties. For in revisiting *Discrete Series* after such a long absence, the early volume did seem to him increasingly to contain the germ of everything that was to follow—of the later long poem 'Of Being Numerous', for example, Oppen notes that 'the seeds of it [are] all in Discrete' (UCSD 16, 19, 12). For him, it seems, the early poems now come into proper focus only when viewed retrospectively, when their loosely theorized Objectivism is articulated with another body of ideas which Oppen now regards as somehow latent within them. In fact, having, as it were, 'forgotten' those early poems, Oppen in now recalling them also began to reread them quite deliberately in the light of his later concerns—concerns which stood in stark contrast to those of Pound and 'high' modernism. So he would talk in 1973 of 'The "Marxism" of Discrete Series' (SL, 254), and in a letter to his friend John Crawford later that year he expressed gratitude 'for the recognition that from Discrete Series to the Marxism was not a "break" —————by any means' (SL, 255; original in capitals). At the same time, though, Oppen is at pains to emphasize his conviction that Marxism is primarily a matter of action rather than intellection: 'Marx's books are Marx's books, but the Marxist political parties are ways to relieve the suffering, and simple ways they are, *or* they are abominations. . . . Discrete put aside for the sake of "active" Marxism———Marxism in action' (SL, 255). 'Marxism', then, is primarily a matter of action, and although Oppen invites Crawford to discover it in *Discrete Series*, his critical view of consumerism and urban life in that early volume is really only retrospectively informed by a thinking we might properly call 'Marxist'.

And just as the 'Marxism' of *Discrete Series* is discovered as latent within the poems, so in other retrospective views of the volume Oppen regards it as a prefiguring of subsequent philosophical themes. Much later, in 1972, he notes, for example, that in his early volumes 'I had thought I could arrive at the concept of Being from an account of experience as it presents itself in its own terms' (SL, 410 n. 29). Here, rather similarly, Oppen reads his later interest in Heidegger back into *Discrete Series*, the emphasis on 'being' dissociating those early poems from the pitfalls of Poundian 'argument', from the closed 'game' of a knowledge known in advance. So, in a letter of 1967, Oppen remarks on what he calls 'a superstition concerning my relation to H[eidegger]':

The poem which happens to be printed as the first poem in Discrete Series—my first book—was written in 1929. That, I've learned, was the year in which H. was giving his Inauguration Speech in which he spoke of the mood of boredom (in the translation

I have) which leads, again in the translation I have, to 'the knowledge of what-is'. (SL, 156)[67]

The poem reads as follows:

> The knowledge not of sorrow, you were
>   saying, but of boredom
> Is————aside from reading speaking
>   smoking————
> Of what, Maude Blessingbourne it was
>   wished to know when, having risen,
> "approached the window as if to see
>   what really was going on";
> And saw rain falling, in the distance
>   more slowly,
> The road clear from her past the window-
>   glass————
> Of the world, weather-swept, with which
>   one shares the century.

> (NCP, 5)

Maud[e] Blessingbourne is a character from a minor work by Henry James, 'The Story in It', where we are told that 'She got up and stood by the fire, into which she looked a minute; then came round and approached the window as if to see what really was going on.'[68] In the context of Oppen's poem the allusion to James expresses a shift of attention away from the domestic interior and toward some larger, more profound ground of experience. In a letter to L. S. Dembo, the first critic to trace the poem's source, Oppen would later remark that 'I wanted James in the book [*Discrete Series*]—secretly, superstitiously, I carved his initials on that sapling book' (SL, 241). The poem thus presents an intriguing conjunction of stylistic difficulty—the exemplary Jamesian parenthesis through which the poem unfurls—and pure contingency. Oppen's allusion to James is not used, we might note, as Pound would have used it, to signal the tradition in which modernism takes its place, but remains instead 'secret', 'superstitious', and designedly oblique. And fittingly so, perhaps, since the sentence which precedes the one from which the poem takes its cue runs thus: 'What their silence was charged with, therefore, was not only a sense of the weather, but a sense, so to speak, of its own nature.' The indeterminacy of '*its* own nature' allows James to elide

---

[67] The speech was translated as 'What is Metaphysics?' and included in the 1949 collection *Existence and Being*.

[68] 'The Story in It', in *The Complete Tales of Henry James*, ed. and introd. Leon Edel, xi (London: Rupert Hart-Davis, 1964), 308.

the silence in the room with the weather outside, thus gesturing toward a condition which somehow exceeds the awareness of those present (hence Maud[e] 'approached the window *as if* to see what really was going on'). That condition is not one of 'sorrow' but of boredom, of a domestic ritual in which time seems to stand still.

It's not surprising, then, that when Oppen read Heidegger's 'What is Metaphysics?' he was struck not only by the temporal coincidence of his poem and Heidegger's speech, but also by the proximity of their respective conceptions of boredom. Heidegger had argued that

Real boredom is still far off when this book or that play, this activity or that stretch of idleness merely bores us. Real boredom comes when 'one is bored.' This profound boredom, drifting hither and thither in the abysses of existence like a mute fog, draws all things, all men and oneself along with them, together in a queer kind of indifference. This boredom reveals what-is in totality.[69]

The coincidence of Heidegger and Oppen thinking along the same lines at almost the same time is certainly striking, but this example also implies a way of reading which is haunted by chance and contingency, by coincidence and tenuous connection to a degree that makes it possible for Oppen to remark that the early poem was actually 'strengthened' by his later reading of Heidegger (UCSD 16, 2, 12). There are, we might conclude, no clear beginnings or points of origin; at least, Oppen's rereading of his early poems testifies at once to the double impossibility of simply going back to *Discrete Series* to find it as it had 'originally' been or of writing again as if 'from scratch'. Oppen's experience of returning to poetry coloured his subsequent practice of writing at the deepest level, marking the 'now' of the poem's present tense as the site of a 'beginning again'. It is fitting that Heidegger should preside over these tentative and 'superstitious' speculations about the origin of a poem since, as we shall see in the next chapter, it was his work above all which seems to have conditioned Oppen's notion of poetic thinking. And in a text that Oppen may already have known, *An Introduction to Metaphysics*, the following passage may have spoken to him with a particular directness:

But we do not repeat a beginning by reducing it to something past and now known, which need merely be imitated; no, the beginning must be begun again, more radically, with all the strangeness, darkness, insecurity that attend a true beginning. Repetition

---

[69] 'What is Metaphysics?', in *Existence and Being*, introd. Werner Brock (Chicago: Henry Regnery Co., 1949), 333–4. This is the paperback edition owned and marked by Oppen, held at the Mandeville Special Collections; the hardback is differently paginated and unless otherwise specified this will be the edition to which reference is made. Cf. UCSD 16, 15, 9: 'Little people huddling together, asking each other how to be happy. . . . The mood of boredom, which has disclosed to them what is; the mood of dread which is the introduction to the awareness of Being they are sure is merely to put themselves in danger, they will not permit it'.

as we understand it is anything but an improved continuation with the old methods of what has been up to now.[70]

The Materials had made it clear that origins are always somehow barred—the moment of our birth is as a 'locked room' to us—but it is precisely this fact of our belatedness that signals the possibility of a real beginning rather than an empty repetition. A truly poetic thinking, a thinking moving beyond the 'known', would necessarily share the 'Strangeness, darkness, insecurity' that attends such beginnings.

[70] Martin Heidegger, *An Introduction to Metaphysics*, trans. Ralph Manheim (New Haven: Yale University Press, 1959), 39.

3

'That it is', or *This in Which*

Having begun his career again, Oppen now took stock: 'The Materials: to restate the themes: solidly' (SL, 122), and he then went on to differentiate that volume from the one which was to follow it, *This in Which* (1965): 'This in Which means what it means in the Psalm. But contains some private amusements in that it means also the achievement of form; that the materials in achieving solidity, form, appear in the light of the miraculous. Or so I mean them to. ——And I don't mean to write the same book again' (SL, 122).[1] In the closing stages of composing *This in Which*, he wrote in his notes that 'I have by now clearly got a step, or a half step, beyond The Materials perhaps beyond the materials' (UCSD 16, 19, 7). The manuscript was delivered to the publisher early in October 1964 and appeared almost exactly a year later.[2]

What did this 'step beyond' amount to? At first we might in fact be struck by thematic continuities between the two volumes: for example, there is impatient criticism of the slums and tract houses ('The Bicycle and the Apex', NCP, 143), and of the hardship of the urban poor on Bergen Street ('Street', NCP, 127). And once again Oppen dramatizes problems of identification with others, striving to come to terms with the anonymous masses who people 'streets | without horizon' ('Technologies', NCP, 93). At times, the political failure of the thirties suggests the impossibility of authentic identification: 'I had hoped to arrive | At an actuality | In the mere number of us | And record now | That I did not' ('Pro Nobis', NCP, 157), while 'The People', regarded in the Depression years as 'Suffering | And beautiful', are now seen to be 'more ambitious | Than we knew | Of wealth | And more ruthless' ('The People, The People', NCP, 130). The 'image | Of a woman' which stands in this poem for that 'mountain | Of human flesh' which is 'The People' seems to have been suggested by the character of Guinevere in Norman Mailer's *Barbary Shore* (1952), a novel which Oppen discovered long after its publication but which

---

[1] Reference is made here to the poem called 'The Psalm' (NCP, 99).
[2] Oppen delivered the manuscript of *This in Which* on 9 Oct. 1964 (SL, 97), but in an unpublished letter of 1964 (UCSD 16, 1, 5) he speaks of 'the year and a half since I finished This In'.

he quickly commended to June as 'the only book of my time ——my time ——that can be considered at all (UCSD 16, 1, 4)'.[3] In Mailer's allegorical novel there was much to resonate with Oppen's own experience. The main character, Mickey Lovett, is a war veteran, wounded in combat but now unable to remember how ('Probably I was in the war').[4] In a kind of frozen dialectic, Lovett interacts with other members of the Brooklyn boarding-house in which he lives: McLeod, a communist with declining revolutionary hopes and Beverly Guinevere, the seductive landlady whose charms are subtly entwined with an ascendant consumerism. Mailer called this 'the first of the existentialist novels in America',[5] and certainly it maps a path from the political hopes of the thirties through to the horizon-less fifties where, in the concluding words of the novel, 'the blind will lead the blind, and the deaf shout warnings to one another until their voices are lost'.[6]

By the mid-sixties, Mailer was moving to a very different conception of 'politics' and so, in his own way, was Oppen, with *This in Which* gauging the possibilities of collective identity from a new point of view. We find again those forms of reification in which the passion of living congeals into a miserable fascination with commodities, but in this volume there is also a promise of transfiguration in 'the light of the miraculous', as Oppen puts it, a fulfilment, perhaps, of the poetics he had drawn from Maritain. These poems ambitiously seek 'the sense of home' ('Five Poems about Poetry', NCP, 102), even amidst 'the noise of wealth' ('Guest Room', NCP, 107) and 'the stylish | Or the opulent' features that characterize the temples of phoney art ('Giovanni's *Rape of the Sabine Women* at Wildenstein's', NCP, 112). The voice is now less anxious, the social criticism drier and more assured, and here it is coupled with a determined effort to 'grasp the world' ('Technologies', NCP, 93) in all its actuality.[7]

Not merely 'realism', then, but an attempt to speak of 'Being'—this aim of Oppen's becomes transparently clear in *This in Which* and is closely bound up with his intensive and often idiosyncratic reading of Heidegger in the

---

[3] In his notes for a reading, Oppen says that Mailer's novel 'contains a character, Guinevere, who is the character described in this poem——the poem actually derives from that novel' (UCSD 16, 30, 4). See also his much fuller account of the book in UCSD 16, 1, 4 where he explicitly associates Guinevere with 'the mountain of flesh'.

[4] Cf. UCSD 16, 14, 10: 'Mailer's protagonist is typical of his generation in this; that he has lost his memory, he does not know where he came from'.

[5] Norman Mailer, *Advertisements for Myself* (1959; Cambridge, Mass.: Harvard University Press, 1992), 106.

[6] Norman Mailer, *Barbary Shore* (1952; St Albans: Panther Books, 1972), 256. Cf. UCSD 16, 21, 24: 'In paint, in black paint, the windows smeared and blocked with paint——. There is no word in the book which is not a word in the allegorical meaning'.

[7] Cf. UCSD 16, 14, 5: 'The gesture of This In Which given in the first of the Five Poems about Poetry: to hold, to grasp the thing.'

early sixties. The importance of Heidegger to Oppen's thinking has often
been acknowledged, though the intensity and breadth of his engagement
with the philosopher's writings has yet to be properly gauged.[8] Oppen had
been reading Heidegger since his return to New York and this is registered
in one of the epigraphs to the new volume which quotes a phrase from
Heidegger's *An Introduction to Metaphysics*, 'the arduous path of appearance',
the choosing of which means 'to take upon oneself being-there as a de-cision
between being, nonbeing, and appearance'.[9] It is likely, too, that his title,
This in Which, also derived from a passage in this work, one of the first of
Heidegger's texts Oppen seems to have encountered and one which contained,
as we have seen, that memorable account of boredom. In the chapter called
'The Limitation of Being', Heidegger wrote that 'The *polis* is the historical
place, the there *in* which, *out* of which, and *for* which history happens.'[10] The
phrasal echo might be fortuitous, but Oppen's use of his title to signal, as
he put it in a letter of the period, a conception of the world 'as something
IN WHICH we exist among other existences'[11] both recalled the epigraph he
had taken from Maritain and Heidegger's own attempt to break with the
emphasis on subjectivity he discerned in Western philosophy since Descartes.
As the editors of the first Heidegger essays in English had noted in their
introduction, 'it is a foremost contention of Heidegger that man must be
envisaged "amidst" what is, human and non-human, "in the whole"'.[12]
That last phrase may have stuck in Oppen's mind as he seems to echo it
in a much later interview: '"This in Which"—means the world, or reality
seen as about it whole'.[13] This association of *This in Which* with Oppen's
reading of Heidegger is further supported by the recent discovery of the poet's
paperback copy of *Introduction to Metaphysics*, the title page of which bears
the annotation '"This in which" all truth is contained—the universe contains
all truth—[*illegible*]'.[14]

---

[8] Oppen's interest in Heidegger has been much noticed but never analysed in the detail it
deserves. The best accounts are Randolph Chilton, 'The Place of Being in the Poetry of George
Oppen', in GOMP, 89–112; Paul Naylor, 'The Pre-Position of Being, Seeing and Knowing in
George Oppen's Poetry', *Contemporary Literature*, 32/1 (1991), 100–15; Susan Thackrey, *George
Oppen: A Radical Practice* (San Francisco, Calif.: O Books, 2001), 33–45.

[9] Heidegger, *An Introduction to Metaphysics*, trans. Ralph Manheim (New Haven: Yale
University Press, 1959), 113.

[10] Ibid. 152, my emphases.

[11] Unpublished letter, quoted in Burt Kimmelman, *The 'Winter Mind': William Bronk and
American Letters* (Madison: Farleigh Dickinson Press, 1998), 144.

[12] Heidegger, *Existence and Being*, 141.

[13] 'A Conversation with George Oppen', conducted by Amirkhanian and Gitin, 24.

[14] Oppen's copy of *An Introduction to Metaphysics*, trans. Ralph Manheim (New York: Anchor
Books, 1961) was amongst books recently found at the house used by the Oppens on Eagle Island,
Maine by Lauren Holden. It will be deposited in the Mandeville Special Collections at UCSD.

Looking back on *This in Which* some ten years after its publication, Oppen would place it in a continuum of three books: 'I knew there would be three books when I started. "The Materials"—I had in mind gathering again to begin, to assert my "noumenalism"; "This In Which"—means the world, or reality seen as about it whole; and then [*Of Being Numerous*] the social, the fact that one does live historically, argued out.'[15] Elsewhere in his notes he expressed more formulaically the difference between the two later volumes, seeing *Of Being Numerous* as an expression of 'What it is rather than that it is', phrases which again have a deliberate Heideggerian inflection (UCSD 16, 4, 5).[16] Oppen's way of linking the two books reminds us again not only that he has *not* forsaken the political for the existential, but also that for him, as for Heidegger, primacy is to be given here to ontological rather than to ontic questions (as Andrew Bowie puts it in a different context, 'Heidegger's "fundamental ontology" makes the prior question the ontological "thatness" of things, the fact of their being at all, not the ontic "whatness" of their determination by a particular science'[17]). This may certainly remind us of poems like 'Psalm', with its fondness for the 'small nouns' (NCP, 99) which seem to register a simple 'faith' in the world's existence rather than a desire to act upon it in any way. Here again Oppen is close to Heidegger who saw it as the essential task of the philosopher to 'preserve the *force of the most elemental words* in which Dasein expresses itself'.[18]

These echoes of Heidegger were not just isolated examples of a temporary enthusiasm. The sixties saw a steady stream of English translations of the philosopher's works and Oppen seems to have monitored them with intense interest.[19] Indeed, in a late interview, Mary Oppen recalled that the couple 'read a great deal of Heidegger' at this time, mainly encouraged by their new son-in-law, Alexander Mourelatos, a philosopher specializing in the texts of the Presocratics. Mourelatos, who married Linda Oppen in 1962, 'began to

[15] 'Conversation with George Oppen', conducted by Amirkhanian and Gitin, 24.

[16] 'An Adequate Vision,' ed. Michael Davidson, 17: 'But Numerous actually takes more space for a simpler undertaking than *This in Which*. The relationship between things—the relationship between people; What it is rather than That it is.' Compare e.g., Heidegger, *Being and Time*, trans. John Macquarrie and Edward Robinson (Oxford: Blackwell, 1962), 174 on 'This characteristic of Dasein's Being—this "that it is"', and Heidegger, *Poetry, Language, Thought*, trans. Albert Hofstadter (New York: Harper & Row, 1971), 65 for the discussion of 'this "that it is" of createdness' where Heidegger concludes that 'In general, of everything present to us, one can note that it is'.

[17] Andrew Bowie, *Aesthetics and Subjectivity: From Kant to Nietzsche* (Manchester: Manchester University Press, 1990), 112–13.

[18] *Being and Time*, 262 (emphases in original).

[19] The most comprehensive listing of English translations of Heidegger's work is in Miles Groth, *Translating Heidegger* (New York: Humanity Books, 2004), 223–303. Oppen noted in 1967 that 'Having no German at all, much less Heideggerian German, I am dependent on translations, therefore my knowledge of H. is sharply limited' (SL, 156). For details of Oppen's reading of Heidegger, see Appendix A, below.

give us whatever new translations were around', recalled Mary.[20] For Oppen, reviving his poetic ambitions in the early sixties, the work of Heidegger must have seemed to offer a complex development and intensification of some of the ideas he had already absorbed from Maritain. Above all, it was Heidegger's elaboration of a philosophical poetics that seemed to him to provide an alternative to the ideological investments of an earlier modernism. Interestingly, although Mary, in the interview just cited, remarked that Heidegger's controversial politics presented 'a real problem', there is little evidence, published or unpublished, that Oppen himself was much concerned on this score.[21] I have found only one passage in his notes where he confronts the issue. Here he seems to refer to a study of Heidegger by Laszlo Versényi who, he says,

feels that H[eidegger] may lead to rather bad things——One is aware of that danger. It is not possible to read H without experiencing some fear. Still, H's awareness of the world is among the most vivid, the most poignant in literature—We almost have to agree to take a chance on that. There is an extreme rawness, like a raw sun. My feeling is that we should risk it. (UCSD 16, 15, 7)[22]

Oppen certainly took the 'risk', assuming perhaps that his own inherent scepticism about mystical ideas of 'folk', 'nation', and the agrarian 'idyll' would insulate him from the dubious charms of Heidegger's 'ontological pastorale'. [23] And the 'rawness'? In some of his late essays, Heidegger offered a response to those terrors of the new atomic age that had haunted *The Materials*, and he did so by making the retrieval of a certain poetic or 'meditative' thinking a pressing necessity. Here in short was a development of that poetics of being that Oppen had already discovered in Maritain and which would now allow him to move on from the dark perspectives of *The Materials* to that sense of the 'miraculous' that is so distinctive a feature of *This in Which*.

---

[20] Dennis Young, 'Conversation with Mary Oppen', *Iowa Review*, 18/3 (1987), 23. See also the discussion of Heidegger in David McAleavey, 'Oppen on Literature and Literary Figures and Issues', *Sagetrieb*, 6 (1987), 117–20. Mary remarks that 'Our son-in-law gets these books for us, every time he sees a Heidegger quote he usually sends it to us' (118). In a communication to me (8 July 2003), however, Mourelatos says that 'I have no such recollection myself, and find no evidence of it in copies of letters I sent them.'

[21] See Young, 'Conversation with Mary Oppen', 23. Young asks: 'Did you ever reconcile Heidegger's politics', and Mary replies 'No. That was a real problem.'

[22] Oppen probably refers to Laszlo Versényi, *Heidegger, Being and Truth* (New Haven: Yale University Press, 1965). According to Mourelatos (personal communication), Oppen owned a copy of this work. In the passage concerned, Versényi is referred to simply as 'V'. Versényi remarks on various negative implications of Heidegger's philosophy: 'Man is no longer in possession, in control, of himself, let alone of beings and Being. He is possessed by Being for its disclosure' (127).

[23] The phrase 'ontological pastorale' is taken from Philippe Lacoue-Labarthe and Jean-Luc Nancy, *Retreating the Political*, trans. Simon Sparks (London: Routledge, 1997), 62.

Heidegger offers a powerful distinction between what he calls 'calculative' and 'meditative' thinking—the former is rooted in the will and sees the world as nothing more than a resource to be exploited. Nature, he says in a famous passage, 'becomes a gigantic gasoline station, an energy source for modern technology and industry'.[24] Against which, 'meditative thinking' offers a radically different way of being which Heidegger calls, after the early German mystic Meister Eckhart, 'releasement', 'letting go' (*Gelassenheit*).[25] In the essay 'On the Essence of Truth', Heidegger proposes that 'The freedom to reveal something overt lets whatever "is" at the moment *be* what it is. Freedom reveals itself as the "letting-be" of what-is.'[26] Heidegger defines this 'overtness' as the Greek *aletheia*, 'unconcealment', thus contrasting 'our ordinary idea of truth in the sense of propositional correctitude' with 'that still uncomprehended quality: the revealedness [*Entborgenheit*] and revelation [*Entbergung*] of what-is'.[27] In a marginal comment on the essay, Oppen observed similarly that '*Truth* is not a statement, not a thing',[28] and in his notes he transcribed the following passage:

The initial revelation of what-is-in-totality, the quest for what-is-as-such, and the beginning of the history of the West, are one and the same thing and are contemporaneous in a 'time' which, itself immeasurable, alone opens the Manifest to every kind of measurement.[29]

That temporal perspective is further elaborated in Heidegger's discussion of Parmenides in *Introduction to Metaphysics*. There he argues that with the Sophists and Plato a cleavage opened up between thinking and being, with the latter term assimilated to the 'suprasensory realm' of the idea. 'Truth' then became not disclosure of being, but 'the correctness of the logos. With this the logos has departed from its original inclusion in the happening of unconcealment.'[30] 'This differentiation', argues Heidegger, 'is a name for the fundamental attitude of the Western spirit. In accordance with this attitude, being is defined from the standpoint of thinking and reason'[31]—or 'argument', to use the word Oppen applied critically to Pound. As one commentator notes, the 'enframing' of the modern world by technology 'drives out our ability

---

[24] Heidegger, *Discourse on Thinking*, trans. John M. Anderson and E. Hans Freund (New York: Harper & Row, 1966), 50.
[25] Ibid. 54. This work was probably the source of Oppen's interest in Meister Eckhart.
[26] Heidegger, *Existence and Being*, 333.   [27] Ibid. 334.
[28] Oppen's copy of *Existence and Being*, 302. He is commenting on the following passage: 'But if rightness (truth) of statement is only made possible by the overt character of behaviour, then it follows that the thing that makes rightness possible in the first place must have a more original claim to be regarded as the essence of truth.'
[29] Ibid. 336. The passage is quoted in UCSD 16, 13, 2.
[30] Heidegger, *Introduction to Metaphysics*, 106, 186.   [31] Ibid. 145.

even to *see* the whatness, objectness, the in-itselfness of beings'.[32] Instead, we are enmeshed in the representational thinking of logic which, says Heidegger, entails 'letting something take up a position opposite to us, as an object'.[33] The subject–object relation which has dominated Western thinking thus entails a fundamental violence to the world: 'To re-present here means to bring what is present before one as something confronting oneself, to relate it to oneself, the person representing it, and to force it back into this relation to oneself as the normative area.'[34] For Heidegger, then, experience is not to be considered as something distinct from thinking (its content or raw material); rather, as Krzysztof Ziarek explains, 'experience, refigured as event, is a form of thinking which acts upon reality and effects it, "lets it be" through the act of transposing it into language. . . . For Heidegger being means participating in the linguistic event [*Ereignis*] which opens a world and history.'[35] This opening of a world situates man not as a distanced observer, but as one being amidst others ('being' thus denoting a 'being-with'[36]). 'Letting be' means allowing other beings to disclose or present themselves rather than conforming them to external judgement and interpretation: 'The *Being-true* (*truth*) of the assertion must be understood as *Being-uncovering*', as Heidegger puts it in *Being and Time*.[37]

Here we can begin to see how Oppen found in Heidegger an authoritative development of the 'ontological simplicity' celebrated by Maritain and expressed in poems such as 'Psalm'. For Heidegger, Greek philosophy originated in 'astonishment' before the question of Being and the relation of the one (Being) to the all (being).[38] This wonder in face of existence leads to a view of the world to which Oppen was instinctively responsive. In Julian Young's words, with Heidegger, 'one understands the world as something contingent, fragile, precious, something which far from being *of course* there, *might not have existed at all*'.[39] This fragility and sense of possibility are reflected in the play of disclosure and concealment that, for Heidegger, characterizes our

---

[32] Julian Young, *Heidegger's Later Philosophy* (Cambridge: Cambridge University Press, 2002), 53.

[33] Heidegger, *Existence and Being*, 328 (original in italics).

[34] Heidegger, 'The Age of the World View', trans. Marjorie Green, in William V. Spanos (ed.), *Martin Heidegger and the Question of Literature: Toward a Postmodern Literary Hermeneutics* (Bloomington: Indiana University Press, 1976), 11.

[35] See Krzysztof Ziarek, *The Historicity of Experience: Modernity, the Avant-Garde, and the Event* (Evanston, Il.: Northwestern University Press, 2001), 52.

[36] Heidegger, *Being and Time*, 161: 'because Dasein's Being is Being-with, its understanding of Being already implies the understanding of Others'.

[37] Ibid. 261.

[38] See e.g. *What is Philosophy?*, 81 ff. Cf. Dembo, ' "Objectivist" Poet', 172–3 where Oppen says, 'The sense of awe, I suppose, is all I manage to talk about'.

[39] Young, *Heidegger's Later Philosophy*, 60 (his emphases).

grasp of Being. For Being as the condition for entities to be is not some thing about which we can speak: 'Being lies in the fact that something is, and in its Being as it is; in Reality; in presence-at-hand; in subsistence; in validity; in Dasein; in the "there is".'[40] Since '[n]o thing corresponds to the word and the meaning "being" ',[41] Being is 'neither a subject of predication nor a predicate'.[42] As soon as we refer in language to the being of an entity, Being withdraws into this particular being, so while naming or 'saying' discloses beings it simultaneously registers the absence of Being from language.[43] How then are we to talk about 'the marvel of all marvels: that what-is *is*'?[44] 'The little word "is" ', as Heidegger calls it,[45] quickly lost its primal force: 'In the form of statement logos itself became something already-there. It became something handy that one handles in order to gain and secure the truth as correctness.'[46] This 'already-there' measures knowledge by its conformity with fact, whereas 'the unconcealedness of beings—this is never a merely existent state, but a happening'.[47] Oppen follows Heidegger closely in his conviction that 'if we still possessed the word "is", there would be no need to write poems' (SL, 249).

But of course we do not possess the word 'is' in the full plenitude of presence, and we are in that sense forever plagued by a lingering sense of anteriority, of perceiving what-is not in the splendour of its disclosure but in a degraded state of already-having-been. Yet while this recognition might seem to promise nothing but a thoroughgoing pessimism, Oppen shares Heidegger's view that poetry is the privileged means by which we might recover our sense of being. The following passage, from 'Hölderlin and the Essence of Poetry', is duly transcribed in Oppen's notes:

poetry is the inaugural naming of being and of the essence of all things—not just any speech, but that particular kind which for the first time brings into the open all that

[40] Heidegger, *Being and Time*, 26. See also the discussion in Paul Naylor, 'The Pre-Position of Being, Seeing, and Knowing in George Oppen's Poetry', 100–15.

[41] Heidegger, *Introduction to Metaphysics*, 88.

[42] Stephen Mulhall, *Heidegger and Being and Time* (London: Routledge, 1996), 9.

[43] See e.g. David A. White, *Heidegger and the Language of Poetry* (Lincoln, Nebr.: University of Nebraska Press, 1978), 86. Cf. Kryzstzof Ziarek, 'The Reception of Heidegger's Thought in American Literary Criticism', *diacritics*, 19/3–4 (1989), 119: 'It would seem that Heidegger does not advocate the unity of Being and word, since the word points to Being as already withdrawn, concealed, other. The word is not a meaning added to a thing; it lets the thing be, in the sense that it relates it to the self-withdrawing clearing of Being.' Magda King, *A Guide to Heidegger's Being and Time* (Albany, NY: SUNY, 2001), 137 observes that 'Heidegger thinks that meaningful tautology is the only way in which we can express that being is not something, but the sheer "other" to all beings.'

[44] Heidegger, *Existence and Being*, 386.   [45] Heidegger, *Identity and Difference*, 66.

[46] Heidegger, *Introduction to Metaphysics*, 188.

[47] Heidegger, *Poetry, Language, Thought*, 54.

which we then discuss and deal with in everyday language. Hence poetry never takes language as a raw material ready to hand, rather it is poetry which first makes language possible. Poetry is the primitive language of a historical people.[48]

The primacy assigned to poetry is closely connected, for Oppen, with, as he puts it in another of his notes, 'The idea, in Heidegger, that man may have to discard humanity in order to live' (UCSD 16, 19, 7).[49] Oppen gives no source for this idea, but it is likely that he is alluding again to Heidegger's essay 'What is Metaphysics?'. There we find an elaboration of what is called 'essential thinking'. Whereas calculative thinking 'uses everything that "is" as units of computation', essential thinking 'expends itself in Being for the truth of Being': 'The need is: to preserve the truth of Being no matter what may happen to man and everything that "is".'[50] Heidegger thus argues that 'this sacrifice is the *expense of our human being* for the preservation of the truth of Being in respect of what-is'.[51]

Heidegger's distinction sheds some light on Oppen's dismissal of 'simple realism' as an adequate description of what he sought in his early books; rather, 'I had thought I could arrive at the concept of Being from an account of experience as it presents itself in its own terms' (SL, 410 n. 29). Such comments point up the inadequacy of any view of Oppen's work which simply situates it in a smooth line of development from Imagism. For whereas Imagism was absolutely founded on a subject–object dualism, what Oppen now saw himself as attempting entailed a much more fundamental reaction to customary modes of thinking, and it was here that his earlier poems seemed to him to resonate with Heidegger's systematic critique of modern subjectivity and the technology which 'enframes' it. Against the idea of a 'distanced' subject, aloof from the world in its objectivity and intent on manipulating and judging what is before it, Heidegger—and Oppen with him—seeks a fundamental elision of thinking with being.[52] We are dealing, then, not with 'representation', with 'letting something take up a position opposite to us, as an object',[53] but with an event—the emergence of a 'world'—in which things

---

[48] The passage, from *Existence and Being*, 307, is quoted in UCSD 16, 22, 58.

[49] Cf. SL, 395 n. 8: 'Heidegger I think does not assume the permanence of man, and indeed, how can we? This is the difficult thing to confront: we begin to confront it in that word.' Cf. UCSD 16, 19, 7 where Oppen quotes the following from *Introduction to Metaphysics*, 140: 'The question of what man is must always be taken in its essential bond with how it stands with being.'

[50] Heidegger, *Existence and Being*, 388, 389.

[51] Ibid. 389 (my emphases). Cf. *Identity and Difference*, 30–1: 'Hence facing the present squarely, it [thought] gets a glimpse—beyond the human situation—of the pattern of Being and Man in what is befitting both, that is, con-cern.'

[52] For an extended discussion of 'distancing' as a recurrent feature of Western thought, see David Kolb, *The Critique of Pure Modernity: Hegel, Heidegger, and After* (Chicago: University of Chicago Press, 1986).

[53] Heidegger, *Existence and Being*, 328.

come into their own as beings rather than simply presenting themselves as available for human ends. In the wake of Objectivism, Oppen does, of course, speak of 'objects', but he does so with a particular Heideggerian inflection. Heidegger, for example, writes:

It is through the work of art as *essent being* that everything else that appears and is to be found is first confirmed and made accessible, explicable, and understandable as being or not being.[54]

In his copy, Oppen rings the words I have italicized and writes 'i.e. as an object', thus linking objectness to the disclosive force of being rather than making it a condition of subservience to subjectivity. Several pages later, in another passage marked by Oppen, Heidegger speaks of 'the preponderant power of being [which] bursts in its appearing',[55] a phrase which may have suggested the idea in the poem 'Leviathan' that 'What is inexplicable | Is the "preponderance of objects"'' (NCP, 89).

Here, perhaps, we might also understand Oppen's departure from the emphasis placed on the verb as transfer of energy by Pound and Ernest Fenollosa, for that syntax can only endlessly reaffirm the subject–object dualism which, in Oppen's view, it is poetry's function to overcome. So he notes to himself:

The fact that things and people BE. This is the major subject of thought and feeling. It is almost impossible to say to most readers. They regard the verb as all but meaningless, perhaps because it is intransitive: it is not an action of one thing on another. (UCSD 16, 16, 8)[56]

What Oppen seeks is, as he puts it, 'The fusion of subject and object where all is acted upon' (UCSD 16, 17, 1), a formulation that suggests that the poem will constitute not so much an expressive act as the medium of confluence and receptivity. Once Oppen had begun to read Heidegger, his idea of 'the objectification of the poem' increasingly entailed not just the displacement of the subject, but a definition of thinking as a process inevitably *missing* its object as it sought disclosure rather than knowledge. Hence the limitations of propositional discourse, for 'The "is" in a proposition has nothing to do with real existence . . ., but with "being valid for", "holding good for"'.[57] As Heidegger put it in 'What is Metaphysics?', 'Being is not a product of thinking. It is more likely that essential thinking is an occurrence of Being.'[58]

---

[54] Heidegger, *Introduction to Metaphysics*, 134 (my emphases).   [55] Ibid. 137.

[56] For a fuller discussion of Oppen's divergence from Pound and Fenollosa's theories of grammar, see Ch. 5, below.

[57] John D. Caputo, *The Mystical Element in Heidegger's Thought* (Athens, Ohio: Ohio University Press, 1978), 146.

[58] Heidegger, *Existence and Being*, 387.

By not operating within the constraints of logic or representation, poetry has the capacity to release its objects from instrumentality, instigating instead what Oppen calls a 'cadence of disclosure' (SL, 97). That 'cadence' carries, for him, an explicitly Heideggerian charge: 'Prosody: the pulse of thought, of consciousness, therefore, in Heidegger's word, of human *Dasein*, human "being there" ' (UCSD 16, 14, 3).

Poetic thinking thus conceived is not a matter of articulating a thought already had, but rather of deploying the resources of writing to disclose the texture of thinking as it takes shape. 'I write in order to know,' says Oppen, 'As action and process' (UCSD 16, 16, 4). The aim, however, is not some kind of spontaneous production or automatic writing; rather, it is to reveal thought as embodied in the irreducible spatio-temporal 'thereness' of the poem, with its phonic echoes and silences, its syntactical shape and typographical layout.[59] Hence, as we shall see, Oppen's fascination with those 'little words' which show 'that this in which the thing takes place, this thing is here, and that these things do take place'.[60] That 'taking place' is itself, of course, the event (or advent) of the poem: 'I do not mean to prescribe an opinion or an idea, but to record the experience of thinking it', writes Oppen (UCSD 16, 19, 4). This, finally, is the objectification of the poem, as thought becomes present to itself as 'being'. Yet it is, by its nature, an avowedly strange sort of thinking, one conditioned by the possibilities of poetic form and open to the 'accidents' of emerging rhythmic contour and lineation. 'I am concerned', Oppen writes in his *Daybook*, 'with "thinking" (involuntary thoughts) that requires the poem, the verse.'[61] And just as such thinking is not settled in advance and can even seem to the thinker 'involuntary', so the world it creates is one of openness and possibility, of truly beginning again.

* * * * *

[59] For some suggestive remarks on poetic 'thereness', see Eynel Wardi, *Once below a Time: Dylan Thomas, Julian Kristeva, and Other Speaking Subjects* (Albany, NY: SUNY, 2000), 4. Oppen brings these elements together in his comment (SL, 97) that 'A new syntax is a new cadence of disclosure, a new cadence of logic, a new musical cadence. A new "structure of space" '.

[60] Dembo, ' "Objectivist" Poet', 163. The phrasing here takes us, of course, to the title of Oppen's *This in Which*. The studied repetition of 'this' also points up that word's status as the 'canonical deictic'—see Geoffrey Bennington, *Legislations: The Politics of Deconstruction* (London: Verso, 1994), 290: ' "This" can refer to itself as word or utterance or token or event, whereas "I", "here" and "now" can only refer to the agent of the saying, and the place or time in which what is said is said.' The best account of the importance of deictic markers to Oppen is Naylor, 'Pre-Position of Being, Seeing and Knowing in George Oppen's Poetry'. For a poetic statement of 'taking place', see Oppen's 'Eclogue' (NCP, 39).

[61] 'Selections from George Oppen's *Daybook*', ed. Dennis Young, 2. Cf. SL, 123: 'the poem is not built out of words . . . it is the poem which makes the words and contains their meaning'.

Not surprisingly, perhaps, the poems that most successfully enact this event of incipience are those in which a jubilant seeing once again comes to the fore, as in the poem cited by Oppen to characterize the new collection, 'Psalm':

> In the small beauty of the forest
> The wild deer bedding down————
> That they are there!

> (NCP, 99)

The poem's epigraph, 'Veritas sequitur . . .', 'Truth follows from the being of things', is taken from Aquinas; Oppen probably came upon it in his copy of Maritain's *Existence and the Existent*, where it provides the epigraph to chapter 1, 'Being'.[62] Maritain's introduction to that chapter perfectly describes the overall focus of *This in Which*: 'It is that existent universe, set firmly upon primary facts, which we are required to discover, not deduce'.[63] So in 'Psalm' the wild deer are discovered 'bedding down', and the crux of the poem lies in the absolutely simple recognition of the 'primary fact' 'That they are there!'

The deer may recall those of Williams's *Spring and All* ('the imagination strains | after deer | going by fields of goldenrod') or of Stevens's 'Sunday Morning' ('Deer walk upon our mountains'),[64] but more suggestive is the possible allusion to Rilke's 'Eighth Elegy':

> With all its eyes the creature-world beholds
> the open. But our eyes, as though reversed,
> encircle it on every side, like traps
> set round its unobstructed path to freedom.
> What *is* outside, we know from the brute's face
> alone; . . .[65]

Discussing the poem in a letter, Rilke observed that 'the animal is *in* the world' whereas 'we stand *before it* by virtue of that peculiar turn and intensification which our consciousness has taken'.[66] Oppen's deer are similarly figures for a

[62] Jacques Maritain, *Existence and the Existent: An Essay on Christian Existentialism*, trans. Lewis Galantiere and Gerald B. Phelan (1948; Garden City, NY: Image Books, 1956), 20. Oppen's copy of this edition was amongst the books found on Eagle Island, Maine by Lauren Holden. It will be deposited in the Mandeville Special Collections at UCSD. In 'Interview with George Oppen', *Sagetrieb*, 3/3 (Winter 1984), 20, Reinhold Schiffer asked Oppen, 'Do you think you got to Aquinas through Maritain?'; Oppen replied, 'Yes, very definitely, very definitely.'

[63] Maritain, *Existence and the Existent*, 20.

[64] William Carlos Williams, *The Collected Poems 1909–1939*, ed. A. Walton Litz and Christopher MacGowan (Manchester: Carcanet Press, 1986), 218; Wallace Stevens, *Collected Poetry and Prose* (New York: The Library of America, 1997), 56.

[65] Rainer Maria Rilke, *Selected Works, ii. Poetry*, trans. J. B. Leishman (London: Hogarth Press, 1960), 242. Oppen owned this volume. See also 'Quotations', NCP, 140: 'The infants and the animals | And the insects | "stare at the open" . . .' and the uncollected poem '[Sympathy]', NCP, 301: '. . . Rilke's "the animals and the insects | stare at the open" . . .'.

[66] Quoted in Heidegger; *Poetry, Language, Thought*, 108.

non-symbolizing, non-appropriative approach to the world. As he puts it in 'The Building of the Skyscraper', this is to discover 'Not a declaration which is truth | but a thing | Which is' (NCP, 149), and this emphasis upon being produces a language which not only intimates a certain irreducibility—'The small nouns | Crying faith | In this in which the wild deer | Startle, and stare out' ('Psalm', NCP, 99)—but which does so through an insistent use of what in linguistics are termed shifters or deictics, those 'little words' that derive their meaning purely from the occasion in which they are uttered: 'They who are there', 'this in which', and so on. As Oppen put it in a late interview, 'what I'm doing is making that Heideggerian gesture of "pointing" ',[67] an allusion, perhaps, to the account of 'saying' given in *On the Way to Language*: 'we understand saying in terms of showing, pointing out, signalling. . . . *The essential being of language is Saying as Showing.*'[68] This 'pointing' is not even primarily to objects designated by words but to the event of language itself.[69] As Giorgio Agamben puts it, 'The opening of the *ontological* dimension (being, the world) corresponds to the pure taking place of language as an originary event, while the *ontic* dimension (entities, things) corresponds to that which, in this opening, is said and signified.'[70] Oppen's 'pointing', his way of shifting emphasis from the content of his words to the pure fact of their utterance, implies a poetics of being that does not now require the impacted syntax of *Discrete Series* and can thus produce more fluent and expanded structures.[71]

A passionate revelation of 'place' (again, the world that 'contains us') now points to a more certain recognition that 'This is our home, the planets | Move in it | Or seem to, | It is our home' ('A Narrative', NCP, 152).[72] Oppen is reclaiming 'the childish | Here' ('Philai Te Kou Philai', NCP, 97) and the poems seek to make their own spatio-temporal occasion equivalent to the

---

[67] 'Interview with George and Mary Oppen', conducted by Kevin Power, *Montemora*, 4 (1978), 195. Cf. SL, 300: 'I point'.

[68] Martin Heidegger, *On the Way to Language*, trans. Peter D. Hertz (New York: Harper & Row, 1971), 123 (emphases in original).

[69] See Giorgio Agamben, *Language and Death: The Place of Negativity*, trans. Karen E. Pinkus with Michael Hardt (Minneapolis: University of Minnesota Press, 1991), 25: 'The sphere of the utterance thus includes that which, in every speech act, refers exclusively to its taking place, to its instance, independently and prior to what is said and meant in it. Pronouns and other indicators of the utterance, before they designate real objects, indicate precisely *that language takes place*. In this way, still prior to the world of meanings, they permit the reference to the very *event of language*, the only context in which something can be signified' (emphases in original).

[70] Ibid. 26.

[71] See also Giorgio Agamben, *Remnants of Auschwitz: The Witness and the Archive*, trans. Daniel Heller-Roazen (New York: Zone Books, 1999), 137 on the implications of Emile Benveniste's proposed 'semantics of enunciation'.

[72] See Wlad Godzich and Jeffrey Kittany, *The Emergence of Prose: An Essay in Poetics* (Minneapolis: University of Minnesota Press, 1987), 19: 'deixis indicates, in a fashion that is in some sense wordless (that is, it assigns no labels), that which surrounds it and contains it'.

disclosure of this world of being, presenting themselves as singular moments of what is called in 'The Occurrences' 'the creating | *Now*' (NCP, 144). Even the 'stone universe' is somehow redeemed, with Oppen able to celebrate 'the pure joy | Of the mineral fact || tho it is impenetrable | As the world, if it is matter || Is impenetrable' ('A Language of New York', NCP, 114). Here Maritain's awakening 'to ourselves and to things' produces forms of ecstatic perception expressive of a love powerful enough to overcome 'a ruined ethic || Bursting with ourselves' ('Philai Te Kou Philai', NCP, 98) and to realize the sense of 'home' in 'The act of being, the act of being | More than oneself' ('World, World————', NCP, 159). In 'A Narrative', for example:

> River of our substance
> Flowing
> With the rest. River of the substance
> Of the earth's curve, river of the substance
> Of the sunrise, river of silt, of erosion, flowing
> To no imaginable sea. But the mind rises
>
> Into happiness, rising
>
> Into what is there. I know of no other happiness
> Nor have I ever witnessed it. . . .

                    (NCP, 155; ellipses in original)

The 'act of being' reveals itself as a 'being | More than oneself', with the mind 'rising' with the sun, its momentary perception caught up in the all-bounding 'earth's curve'.

As the last lines of the poem put it, this is 'the open | Miracle || Of place':

> . . . I thought that even if there were nothing
>
> The possibility of being would exist;
> I thought I had encountered
>
> Permanence; thought leaped on us in that sea
> For in that sea we breathe the open
> Miracle
>
> Of place, and speak
> If we would rescue
> Love to the ice-lit
>
> Upper World a substantial language
> Of clarity, and of respect.

                    (NCP, 156)

Oppen's 'ice-lit || Upper World' may recall the allegory of the cave in Book VII of Plato's *Republic* where the prisoners ascending to the upper world are suddenly able to 'gaze upon the light of the moon and the stars and the spangled heaven' and to find a new 'clarity' after the 'false notions' and the darkness of the cave.[73] The odd phrase 'thought leaped on us in that sea', which is picked up again as a quotation in 'World, World————', ' "Thought leaps on us" because we are here' (NCP, 159), may echo a passage in Heidegger's essay 'What is Metaphysics?'. There we are told that 'Philosophy is only set in motion by leaping with all its being, as only it can, into the ground-possibilities of being as a whole.'[74] The first lines of the passage quoted from 'A Narrative'—'I thought that even if there were nothing || The possibility of being would exist'—also seem to find a context in Heidegger's essay as an answer to the famous question posed on the same page: 'Why is there any Being at all—why not far rather Nothing?' And Oppen's 'I thought I had encountered || Permanence' becomes clearer in the light of that much later comment: 'I begin to understand that the earlier books have been taken to be a simple realism——I was in these books speaking of Being: I had thought I could arrive at the concept of Being from an account of experience as it presents itself in its own terms' (SL, 410 n. 29).

* * * * *

These various echoes of Heidegger in Oppen's texts may tell us something further about a certain idea of 'poetic thinking'. For while we have remarked the larger patterns of congruence in their thinking—the critique of subjectivism and 'calculative' thinking, the concern about power and technology, the idea of the poem as inaugural event, and so on—Oppen's attention often seemed to focus more on particular words and phrases than on the larger outlines of philosophical or political argument. Indeed, the notoriously difficult texture of Heidegger's thinking probably appealed to him precisely because it seemed to resist facile appropriation and in that way to instigate a suitably complex and at times quite opposite thinking on the part of the reader. Rather like Heidegger himself, Oppen was often fascinated by a single phrase or sentence which seemed to promise illumination, and possibly access to another world of thought. Michael Heller catches precisely the right emphasis here when he observes that the poet

read not for omnivorous knowledge of a subject but to find a passage or even a phrase which would show him an opening or way out of intellectual, emotional or even philosophical impasses. It would seem, from the evidence, that such a passage, or the writer it represented, was an intense transformative nexus from which something enormous or significant might begin.[75]

[73] Plato, *The Republic*, trans. Benjamin Jowett (Oxford: Clarendon Press, 1888), 216.

[74] Heidegger, *Existence and Being*, 380.

[75] Michael Heller, ' "Knowledge is Loneliness Turning": Oppen's Going Down Middle-Voice', *Ironwood*, 26 (Fall 1985), 53. Cf. David Halliburton, *Poetic Thinking: An Approach to Heidegger*,

Much of Oppen's thinking thus entailed intensive consideration of what he called the 'seed phrases' (SL, 102) that he culled from favourite texts; like Heidegger's *Grundworte*, such phrases were to be prized above the propositional structures of a more conventional thinking.[76] Just as Heidegger himself claimed that 'Philosophizing ultimately means nothing other than being a beginner',[77] so Oppen would take Heidegger's texts as a source of beginnings rather than of settled propositions, 'with all the strangeness, darkness, insecurity that attend a true beginning'.[78] In fact, he absorbed Heidegger's critique of calculative thought to such a degree that his own reading of the philosopher entailed a kind of 'letting go' (at once voluntary and involuntary) which opened the original texts to rereadings and even misreadings governed by chance and coincidence. To pursue this aspect of the encounter with Heidegger is to see how much of Oppen's thinking was driven by a need to test and evaluate verbal formulations which seemed to him to embody what Maritain had called 'basic *presences* or existential certainties'.[79] This habit of fixing the attention on particular phrases ran parallel to the tendency toward syntactical fragmentation in Oppen's later work, and it is particularly pronounced in his various encounters with what he took to be cruxes in Heidegger's texts.

To understand Oppen's traffic with the philosophical materials which fascinated him, it's necessary, then, to grasp the way in which these became inextricably enmeshed with the patterns of his own thought. To track Heidegger's influence on Oppen thus entails more than noting ideas held in common; more importantly, it is to acknowledge the strange weave of chance and coincidence, of voluntary and involuntary memory, that, for Oppen, constitutes the measure of true poetic thinking. We have already noted his 'superstition concerning my relation to H[eidegger]' and its effect on his rereading of 'The knowledge not of sorrow'. His thinking there seems to him to bear an uncanny relation to Heidegger's, a relation which is complicated by another experience which he recounts in the same letter to Frederic Will:

And boredom was an odd word to use. I am touched by a superstition remembering my hesitation over that word, the attempt to remove it, and the sense of having been

---

137 on Heidegger's 'habit of construing the text as a nexus of leading words or themes adding up to a kind of statement that he can play off against his own thinking'.

[76] See Groth, *Translating Heidegger*, 165 on Heidegger's practice of translation as 'a procedure that works paratactically, word by word, rather than syntactically, by way of an analysis of propositions.'

[77] Quoted in Rudiger Safranski, *Martin Heidegger: Between Good and Evil* (Cambridge, Mass.: Harvard University Press, 1998), 1.

[78] Heidegger, *Introduction to Metaphysics*, 39.

[79] Maritain, *Creative Intuition*, 382 (emphasis in original).

given it. Followed by a much later event, involving dream and all the trappings, in which I had dreamed quite literally of being given a phrase over a telephone and, the following morning wrote into a poem a quotation from a short essay of Heidegger's which I had been reading the night before. When I checked the quotation—Not there![80]

This dream, which Oppen thought sufficiently important to record also in an extended and carefully dated note to himself (SL, 134–7), exemplifies a kind of poetic thinking which is quite different from what he elsewhere criticized as 'argument'. For Heidegger's phrase delivers itself as a kind of dreamlike (and deceptive) dictation from 'outside', as it were.[81] Oppen quotes the passage as follows: 'Substance itself which has been the subject of all our planning | And by this we are carried into the incalculable' (SL, 156). These two phrases have a quite disproportionate effect on Oppen: he was, he says, 'convinced that a part of the statement was of crucial importance to me, of such importance as to alter the subjective conditions of my life, the conditions of my thinking, from that point in time' (SL, 135). Yet the phrase belongs to Heidegger and while Oppen feels he has been 'given it', he guiltily tries to 'remove' it, to overwrite it with words of his own so as to avoid, he says, the charge of 'plagiarism'.

Here we seem to be moving once again within the realm of something akin to Freud's *Nachträglichkeit* or 'deferred action', with the later rewriting of the passage having an effect quite in excess of the original and triggering a complex of contradictory feelings. Having made his changes, Oppen is still unsatisfied and decides to 'look up the original phrase and use it in quotation marks' (SL, 136). This he does, but even after reading the short essay 'ten or more times in dizzy incredulity' he still can't locate it. Every reader has had this experience at one time or another, but for Oppen it seems to signal some deep connection between the loss of an original text and the writing that is generated from that loss. On the one hand, the withdrawal of text and meaning produces anxiety and disorientation. Oppen would later describe this sensation in relation to another dream:

my dream every night for some time has been a dream of reading from a rather flimsy paper or perhaps a sort of gauze,———I look, and I read words to myself, but I question as I read whether I have actually seen these words. I start again at the beginning and test whether or not I will read the same words, but I am not able to

---

[80] I quote here from a draft of the letter to Frederic Will in SL, 156–7. The draft (UCSD 16, 11, 44) varies slightly from the published text from which Oppen's attempt to 'remove' the word has disappeared. Oppen's dream is also discussed in Thackrey, *George Oppen*, 39–43.

[81] Cf. UCSD 16, 16, 6: 'The nature of the image is the nature of the dream: not thinking, but a thought placed into the mind.'

remember what I had read, I am not sure that I am repeating them as I read them before ———this has been night after night[82]

As in the Heidegger dream, there is an experience of going back to something only to discover that it is different from what it had been, that it is constituted anew in every attempt to stabilize rereading as a repetition. At the same time, though, while such an experience may certainly produce anxiety, as it does in this dream, it is also the source of something *new* and in that sense we might see it as a sort of model for Oppen's notion of poetic thinking. As he puts it in a passage quoted earlier, 'the thinking occurs at the moment of the poem, within the poem—As the image forms in the mind, forms in the present and surrounds me tho it may speak of the past' (UCSD 16, 14, 12). The poet may recall a past experience, then, but that experience is fundamentally recast, perhaps so as to be almost unrecognizable, when caught up in the force-field of present perception. We are dealing not with a situation in which a given subject appropriates something other as an object of knowledge, but rather one in which (as for Heidegger) thinking and being are somehow elided. In this sense, the poetic imagination intuits rather than knows, and referentiality is thus constantly undermined by the slipping away, the evanescence, of a prior term which would make 'accurate' reference possible.

This seems to be the lesson of Oppen's Heidegger dream. Here again are those troublesome phrases, this time as they are incorporated into the long poem called 'Route' in the later *Of Being Numerous*: ' "Substance itself which is the subject of all our planning" || And by this we are carried into the incalculable' (NCP, 201). For Oppen, these words are at once familiar and unfamiliar, and their tenuous existence, absorbed into the poem as a modified quotation with apparently no findable source, renders them genuinely uncanny. Yet if we go to Heidegger's essay, 'The Principle of Identity' in a short book called *Identity and Difference*, the 'lost' sentence is actually located with surprisingly little difficulty:

To the extent that Being is challenged, Man is likewise challenged, that is to say, Man is 'framed' so he will safeguard the Existence which concerns him as the very substance of his planning and calculating, and thus pursue this task into the immeasurable.[83]

As Oppen recalls the passage, he finds himself deliberately changing the word 'incalculable' to 'infinite' and then to 'unthinkable' (SL, 135–6). The final

---

[82] ' "Disasters": Versions and Notes', *Ironwood*, 26 (Fall 1985), 150–1.

[83] Heidegger, *Essays in Metaphysics: Identity and Difference*, trans. Kurt F. Leidecker (New York: Philosophical Library Inc., 1960), 26. A later translation makes Heidegger's meaning rather clearer: 'To the same degree that Being is challenged, man, too, is challenged, that is, forced to secure all beings that are his concern as the substance for his planning and calculating; and to carry this manipulation on past all bounds' (*Identity and Difference*, trans. Joan Stambaugh (New York: Harper & Row, 1969), 35.

version of the poem restores 'incalculable', though in fact Heidegger's word as translated here isn't 'incalculable' in the first place, but 'immeasurable'. Oppen's account of his dream carefully situates it as a remembered event, but his citation of its key terms triggers a series of erasures and reinscriptions which bar access to Heidegger's original text. Yet while the dream thus dissolves into a tissue of misrememberings, these are still not so extreme as to have prevented Oppen from finding the passage after his dogged rereadings of the text. Nonetheless there *is* a genuine failure of recognition here which testifies, I think, to the extent to which 'recollection' made it possible for Oppen to find in Heidegger's essay a content which wasn't actually there. It's something Adorno has described in his own rereading of a text by Ernst Bloch:

when I reread it after more than forty years I could not find in it what I read out of it. It has mystically disappeared in the text. *The substance of the text unfolded only in memory*. It contains much more than it contains, and not only in the vague sense of potential associations. It unambiguously communicates what it unequivocally refuses to communicate.[84]

'The substance of the text unfolded only in memory': once again we are close to Freud's notion of *Nachträglichkeit*, with meaning remembered but unlocatable as a property of the actual text itself.

If we go back now to the essay in question, we find that Heidegger is considering the way in which 'Our whole existence is challenged everywhere; now as if set upon, now as if pushed—to plan and calculate every-thing.'[85] Man, he says in the passage singled out by Oppen, is 'framed [*gestellt*]', enclosed by the total world of technology so that his existence, and even what is 'immeasurable', threatens to be completely dominated by the imperatives of 'planning and calculating'. As this text echoes in Oppen's memory, however, there is a curious displacement of emphasis, so that it is the notion of 'substance' that now becomes central. Oppen's misremembered version of the passage turns it into a statement that 'substance', the realm of 'things' which humanity has sought to order and plan, might somehow assert its autonomy, thus presenting some absolute limit to human 'calculation' (in an unpublished note Oppen observes that 'the existence of matter cannot be explained. We do not explain it, but find it. "and by this we are carried into the incalculable"' (UCSD 16, 16, 13)). Oppen's thinking here may recall his reading of 'What is Metaphysics?' and his claim that Heidegger is there proposing that 'man may have to discard humanity in order to live' (above, p. 70). Indeed, the (mis)reading of 'The Principle of Identity' suggests even more extremely

---

[84] T. W. Adorno, *Notes to Literature*, 2 vols., trans. Shierry Weber Nicholsen (New York: Columbia University Press, 1992), ii. 219 (my emphases).
[85] Heidegger, *Essays in Metaphysics: Identity and Difference*, 25.

to Oppen that Heidegger is gesturing toward 'simply the acceptance of the inevitable final death of mankind' (SL, 136).[86] Not surprisingly, perhaps, Oppen's construal of the text then makes it echo the argument of his own earlier poem 'Time of the Missile' (NCP, 70), with its vision of a non-human world 'Which can destroy us, | Re-arrange itself, assert | Its own stone chain reaction'.

It's clear, then, that Oppen's reading effects a radical departure from the sense of the original passage in Heidegger's essay, though curiously enough the coincidence of loss of origin with a sense of some absolute limit does resonate with Heidegger's talk elsewhere of the 'earth' as 'that which is by nature undisclosable, that which shrinks from every disclosure and constantly keeps itself closed up'. The earth 'shatters every attempt to penetrate into it', and while it may seem to yield in the face of 'the technical-scientific objectivation of nature, . . . this mastery nevertheless remains an impotence of will'.[87] At the time of *This in Which*, Oppen could not have known the essay from which these passages come ('The Origin of the Work of Art', translated in 1971) but he was acquainted with Heidegger's idea of the earth from Frederic Will's essay 'Heidegger and the Gods of Poetry'. In his 1967 letter to Will he remarks that 'tho the sentence [from *Identity and Difference*] is not in Heidegger, [it] is close to your emphasis: "the earth steps forth in all its massiveness" ' (SL, 157). Will is glossing Heidegger's account of the Greek temple which focuses 'the strife of world and earth which is for Heidegger the structure of Being in art'.[88] 'The work', says Will, 'lets the earth step forth in all its massiveness. . . . The world in the artwork is continually drawing the medium forth, while the medium pulls the world back into it.'

Oppen had already crystallized his own version of Heidegger's 'earth' in what would become a favourite word, 'impenetrable'. In 'A Language of New York', as we have seen, he speaks of 'the pure joy | Of the mineral fact || Tho it is impenetrable || As the world, if it is matter || Is impenetrable' (NCP, 114), and this idea of an aspect of the world which is resistant to thought plays an important part in his subsequent work. Such resistance can be the source of 'joy' in the sheer facticity of the world, or it can be associated with

[86] Oppen's misreading is even clearer in another letter to Frederic Will (UCSD 16, 11, 44): 'we have constructed even an ethic which has no purpose but the benefit of technology, and we are convinced that we have gained control of a great part of the world and that we are concerned with nothing but human comfort. But it is substance itself which is the subject of our planning, and by this we are carried into the incalculable————On everyone's mind nearly all the time is————substance; so much more profound a concern than heroes and gods, leprechauns and ghosts————'.

[87] Heidegger, *Poetry, Language, Thought*, 47.

[88] Frederick Will, *Literature Inside Out: Ten Speculative Essays* (Cleveland, Ohio Press of Western Reserve University, 1966), 29.

the dull inertness of an objective world which mutely exceeds humanity (as in the earlier evocations of the 'stone' universe). Either way, this resistance registers something essentially immune to thought: 'that which is, and is not a concept but is here of its own right is impenetrable, unintelligible' (UCSD 16, 16, 3). At the same time, it is a condition of authentic thinking which, in contrast to 'calculative' thought, discloses what Heidegger calls the 'rift' between language and reality.[89] The 'impenetrability' which attaches to the other is not, however, equivalent to absolute unintelligibility: as the poems show, it is available to reflection, but its resistance to reduction establishes it as powerfully different, as non-identical. Indeed, Oppen remarks in a note to himself: 'my "impenetrable". It is the point from which thought begins. There is no thought or possibility of thought the other side of it' (UCSD 16, 14, 8). That idea of 'beginning' seems an appropriately rich crystallization of the importance of Heidegger's thought to Oppen, signalling their shared sense of a world in the act of disclosing itself and at the same time acknowledging that thought itself is always a projective act, a risky beginning rather than a reassuring end. Thought has its limits, then, something modernism had often ignored to its cost; in acknowledging such limits a new poetic thinking might take its distance from avant-gardism and learn that 'The self is no mystery, the mystery is | That there is something for us to stand on' ('World, World————', NCP, 159). The simple fact, Oppen announced at the end of that poem, is that 'We want to be here', but how might a poetics of being incorporate a related proposition, that 'The act of being' amounts to 'the act of being | More than oneself'? Oppen, as we have noted, was not about to succumb to Heideggerian mystifications of 'nation' and 'folk', but he would later observe of *This in Which* that 'in the writing of the book I became more and more distant from the people I was writing of' (UCSD 16, 15, 10). As if deliberately to correct that tendency, in Oppen's next book the matter of urban proximities would come centre stage.

---

[89] See below, Ch. 7, for Oppen's later gloss on the idea of the 'rift'.

4

'What it is': *Of Being Numerous*

In proposing now to explore, as he later put it, the condition of 'What it is rather than That it is' (UCSD 16, 14, 5), Oppen's new serial poem, 'Of Being Numerous', from which his 1968 volume took its title, might be expected to move from a concern with 'the world, or reality seen as about it whole' to 'the social, the fact that one does live historically'.[1] Here Oppen would attempt to show 'Man embedded in the sensory and the historic' (UCSD 16, 16, 2).[2] In line with this shift of focus, the volume is strongly marked by the political pressures of the time. Indeed, the assassination of President Kennedy in November 1963 had opened what for Oppen was to be 'a period of crisis':

There is at least in 'everyone's' mind——I suppose I mean the intellectual——that something very violent is going on, and that perhaps they are fools. We begin to remember again how much we really do care, how much we have at stake, how very endangered we are, how far we are from the belt-buckled semi-fascist population, and how close we are to each other. (SL, 96)

It was a time of conspiracy and strongly alleged police corruption. 'If Oswald was not the assassin, he must have been elaborately framed. And by the Dallas police,' surmised Oppen (UCSD 16, 1, 4). The country seemed locked in an agony of self-destruction, and he observed that 'what we could have, if we tried very hard, is perhaps a civil war. Because "they" know very well who did it, and are surely not repentant' (UCSD 16, 1, 4).[3] That sense of conflict and division would be played out in 'Of Being Numerous'. By 1965, America's growing involvement in Vietnam confirmed Oppen's sense of 'the

---

[1] UCSD 16, 14, 5: 'The relationship between things—the relationship between people; What it is rather than That it is'. The other quoted passages here are from 'A Conversation with George Oppen', conducted by Amirkhanian and Gitin, 24.

[2] In parenthesis, he labelled this 'Auerbach's phrase', perhaps thinking of the account in Erich Auerbach, *Mimesis: The Representation of Reality in Western Literature*, trans. Willard R. Trask (Princeton: Princeton University Press, 1953), 433 of 'a vision of the course of history . . . as being profoundly embedded in the historical data of his existence'.

[3] The letter is dated 2 Dec. 1963. See also the draft of a statement to be sent to *Kulchur* magazine, UCSD 16, 1, 4. This two-page piece concerning the assassination contains the passage about the 'belt-buckled semi-fascist population' already quoted.

violence and disorder of our lives' (UCSD 16, 1, 4); between July 1965 and December 1967 America would drop more bombs on Vietnam than the Allies had delivered to Europe in the whole of the Second World War.[4] Oppen remarked to his niece that he had not so far 'written a Wasteland' or 'a decisive expression of a period', but that he 'mean[t] to try in the next [book, *Of Being Numerous*]' (SL, 108).[5] In doing so, he returned to the eight-part poem 'A Language of New York' which had appeared in *This in Which*. Revised and expanded, this poem was renamed 'Another Language of New York'. Oppen arrived at a final version early in 1966, though, as Burton Hatlen has noted, he did not retitle the poem until close to its publication in 1968.[6] The revised title was carefully weighted: Hatlen has pointed up the importance of 'Language' in the transitional version, but the changing of 'A' to 'Another' seems also to signal, as Oppen noted to himself, something 'other than Williams's [language] of Paterson' (UCSD 16, 19, 12).[7] Perhaps, too, the historical perspectives of Williams's poem no longer seemed accessible to Oppen. Certainly, the urban landscape of 'Of Being Numerous' often registers a disturbing loss of historical and linguistic depth; three years after publishing the volume, Oppen would write of 'the increasing meaninglessness or uselessness of New York City. It no longer seems to possess even the historical meaning that it had'.[8]

Against the backdrop of national violence and a 'rootless speech' (NCP, 173), Oppen's long poem would seek to gauge 'how close we are to each other', though its open form and intermittent opacities would emphasize that its situation was, to use one of Oppen's loaded words, 'precarious' in the extreme.[9] 'Of Being Numerous' was to test what 'existential certainties' might exist at a time when social and political structures seemed blatantly to deny human 'closeness'—'the poem was written', Oppen noted to himself, 'in despair of the historical, the sense of continuation' (UCSD 16, 22, 2). The problem of grasping history as 'continuation' and of locating the conditions in which an authentic future might be possible lies at the heart of 'Of Being Numerous'. For this is

---

[4] Michael Heale, *The Sixties in America: History, Politics and Protest* (Edinburgh: Edinburgh University Press, 2001), 81.

[5] In an unpublished comment (in capitals in the original) he writes that 'There cannot, apparently there cannot, be a Whitman of the factories | have tried and I cannot' (UCSD 16, 13, 6).

[6] For dating, see SL, 126. Oppen dates one draft of 'Another Language of New York' as 'Aug 1964–Aug 1965' (UCSD 16, 22, 38). For the title, see Burton Hatlen, 'Opening Up the Text: George Oppen's "Of Being Numerous"', *Ironwood*, 26 (Fall 1985), 292.

[7] In a cancelled draft, Oppen also wrote of 'the city from Jersey' (UCSD 16, 22, 3).

[8] 'A Conversation', conducted by Amirkhanian and Gitin, 21. And cf. UCSD 16, 16, 2: 'NY in the twenties—It had a strange, antique, substantial gloom—very exciting—which it no longer possesses.'

[9] See Oppen, 'Letters to Andy Meyer', *Ironwood*, 26 (Fall 1985), 111: 'Precariousness || *prex precis* | Webster says:—prayer || like a new fire | will burn out the roots'.

a work informed by a very real sense of crisis, as Oppen tries to understand the generational conflict which threatens to destroy historical continuity. At a more immediately personal level, too, the war in Vietnam—a war with no foreseeable end—almost took Oppen back to his decision to abandon writing in the thirties, when poetry had somehow been overtaken or exceeded by events. At the same time that he was completing the poem that, finally, would be titled 'Of Being Numerous', Oppen remarked in a note dated January 1966 that 'If we launch that "general war in Asia", I think I will have to give this up again', and 'I perhaps cannot write poetry in war time. I couldn't before, and perhaps cannot now. I become ashamed, I become sick with shame' (UCSD 16, 19, 12). Oppen's 'sickness' is produced in part by a sense of deadly repetition, of the traumatic experience of Alsace occurring again, bringing back the 'guilt of that foxhole'.[10] Yet this personal 'shame' is a limit the poem must overcome, as Oppen's final title acknowledges, and the ethical dilemmas that concern him here are grounded in much larger questions that relate ultimately to the very nature of human finitude. Death, in fact, is a constant presence in the poem, as Oppen seeks to arrive at a sufficiently complex sense of mortality to avoid the false consolations of both optimism and pessimism.[11]

The change of title corresponded to the poem's expanding frame of reference. Oppen was no longer concerned only with the experience of living in New York, but with larger ethical and political questions about life in mass society. 'Of Being Numerous' was written while he was reading Heidegger and pondering the philosopher's account of anxiety and 'Being-toward-death'. Existentialism was by this time a powerful presence in American culture and for many its account of estranged individualism offered a persuasive alternative to the now widely unpopular Marxist ideas of social collectivism that had briefly flourished in the thirties.[12] As we have seen, while Oppen was certainly drawn to various aspects of existentialism, he was not inclined to use it as a stick with which to beat the Marxist thinking that had always been so important to him. Indeed, he was fascinated by and in many ways drawn to the New Left which seemed to offer the only credible opposition to the escalating conflict in Vietnam.[13] What would make 'Of Being Numerous' a complex and difficult poem was Oppen's attempt to articulate these different tendencies together. So, for example, where the protagonist of Sartre's *Nausea* (newly translated

[10] Oppen, 'Non-Resistance, etc. Or: Of the Guiltless', *West End*, 3/1 (1974), 5. See David McAleavey, 'The Oppens: Remarks towards Biography', *Ironwood*, 26 (Fall 1985), 309–18.

[11] See e.g. UCSD 16, 1, 4: 'it is my ability to make some kind of peace with death, my conviction not of immortality perhaps, but of what is immortal'.

[12] See e.g. George Cotkin, *Existential America* (Baltimore: Johns Hopkins, 2003).

[13] See e.g. UCSD 16, 1, 7: 'It does seem to me that the New Left, the young left, has created the finest public conversation which has ever taken place in the nation, has created the only intelligent public conversation this country has known'.

in 1965) famously explains that 'I for my part live alone, entirely alone. I never speak to anybody, I receive nothing, I give nothing', this 'shipwreck of the singular', as Oppen would call it in his poem, has to be weighed against the ambiguities of a *collective* singular, the 'people' or 'humanity'.[14] Several poems in *This in Which* had already spoken of the false promise of identification with 'humanity' and this intermittent disillusionment with the new incarnations of 'the People' echoes complaints about social conformity and passive consumerism that had already become commonplace in the fifties.

For Oppen, American culture is mired in 'rootless speech' (NCP, 173), a language which has no relation to being (it is 'Anti-ontology' (NCP, 172)) and which betrays any sense of historical 'continuation':

> And in the sudden vacuum
> Of time . . .
>
> . . . is it not
> In fear the roots grip
>
> Downward
> And beget
>
> The baffling hierarchies
> Of father and child
>
> As of leaves on their high
> Thin twigs to shield us
>
> From time, from open
> Time
>
> (NCP, 181–2; ellipses in
> original)

As a 'shield' against this 'open | Time', Oppen seeks a sense of historical 'continuation' in the 'baffling hierarchies' of the family for which birth and death register the possibility of, as he had put it in the earlier 'World, World————', 'being more than oneself' (NCP, 159). The lines suggest that a sense of authentic 'rootedness' is indissociable from our fear of death. As we shall see, the poem brings us back repeatedly to the uncomfortable recognition that any workable sense of 'numerousness' we may now find will be inextricably bound up with the full acceptance of our own mortality. As Oppen put it in a later interview:

---

[14] Jean-Paul Sartre, *Nausea*, trans. Robert Baldick (Harmondsworth: Penguin Books, 1965), 16. See also 'An Interview with George and Mary Oppen', conducted by Kevin Power, *Montemora*, 4 (1978), 196: 'My difference with Sartre is that I don't in the least dislike the world. There isn't the horror of the roots, the horror of it being there, not at all, and I think it's very definite in the poems.'

'This In Which'—means the world, or reality seen as about it whole; and then the social, the fact that one does live historically argued out, that we speak of Crusoe as rescued, and it's argued out, the matter of age, people do feel some metaphysical connection. The old men knew their own lives not the end of the world, . . . returning on a different level to the political issue.[15]

This 'metaphysical connection', as Oppen calls it, underpins the politics of the long poem. Without it and without the sense of finitude which governs it, 'We stand on || That denial of death that paved the cities' and that 'pavement || Is filthy as the corridors | Of the police' (NCP, 178). Against this denial, Oppen declares elsewhere in true Heideggerian fashion that 'death does not "occur" but is always approaching, occurs as a locomotive on a track "arrives"' (UCSD 16, 18, 1).[16]

It is curious that Oppen's emphatic concern with death in 'Of Being Numerous' has never been fully acknowledged in accounts of the poem, especially since the opening section brings it powerfully to the fore. We begin with a quotation (from Robert Brumbaugh's *Plato for the Modern Age*) that echoes Oppen's earlier epigraph from Maritain, stressing that an understanding of others is the crucial condition of any self-knowledge:[17]

> There are things
> We live among 'and to see them
> Is to know ourselves'.
>
> Occurrence, a part
> Of an infinite series,
>
> The sad marvels; . . .

> (NCP, 163)

Any sense we may have of our own existence as a special or singular 'occurrence' must be tempered by the fact that we are also 'a part | Of an infinite series'. But:

> Of this was told
> A tale of our wickedness.
> It is not our wickedness.

With the idea of a 'series' comes, inevitably, a fascination with origin and inaugural event. Oppen's lines allude to and dismiss the Bible's 'tale' of man's

---

[15] 'Conversation', conducted by Amirkhanian and Gitin, 24.

[16] Cf. James M. Demske, *Being, Man, and Death: A Key to Heidegger* (Lexington: Kentucky University Press, 1970), 7: '[Death] is not something occurring just at the end of a man's life, but something always present, from the very beginning of life, as a constitutive element of existence.'

[17] See Robert S. Brumbaugh, *Plato for the Modern Age* (New York: Crowell-Collier, 1962), 85: 'There are objective forms which attract us, and when we see them clearly, we know our real natures and in some sense actually achieve, through this knowledge, a transcendence of time.' As is often the case, Oppen's 'quotation' significantly modifies his original.

fall into mortality and 'the expulsion from Eden', as he put it in his notes.[18]
Yet while the narrative of Original Sin is rejected here, Oppen's opening lines
still seem to allude to some loss of presence and immediacy—the individual as
merely one term in an 'infinite series', perhaps, or the very condition of 'being
numerous' as somehow random or indeterminate, lacking a convincing 'tale'
to give it historical substance. The syntax here is characteristically difficult:
'The sad marvels' seem to be in apposition to the 'infinite series', but the next
line then leaves us groping for a referent for 'this'. Readers are forced to make
the sense for themselves here (a situation which is highly characteristic of the
poem as a whole). My own suggestion is that we understand the 'sad marvels'
(of human history) as belonging to an 'infinite series' of births and deaths, the
'sadness' of which cannot be blamed on some original 'wickedness' but which
has to be grasped instead as the very condition of human finitude.

The prose section that follows then carries special weight since it seems to
propose some insight into that condition:

'You remember that old town we went to, and we sat in the ruined window, and we
tried to imagine that we belonged to those times—It is dead and it is not dead, and
you cannot imagine either its life or its death; the earth speaks and the salamander
speaks, the Spring comes and only obscures it—'

In a letter to his young friend Steven Schneider, Oppen disclosed that 'The
long quotes in the first section are Mary, verbatim, telling me about Bonnefoy;
the next words, beyond what I've quoted, were "that's what Douve is about"'
(SL, 129).[19] Schneider, then living in Paris, had sent Oppen his translation of
Yves Bonnefoy's *Du mouvement et de l'immobilité de Douve* in late March 1965
(SL, 388 n. 5). The long serial poem seems to have fascinated the Oppens:
'It's been a joy to have the Bonnefoy', Oppen wrote (UCSD 16, 10, 16), and
another letter suggests that he had begun to read the poem in French before
Schneider's translation arrived.[20] Schneider reacted to Oppen's interest by
sending Bonnefoy a copy of *The Materials*, though unfortunately we don't
know how the French poet responded to it (UCSD 16, 10, 15). Schneider
was also translating another of Bonnefoy's volumes, *Hier régnant désert*, and
offered to send Oppen his version (UCSD 16, 10, 16). A copy of the French text,
incorporating Mary's autograph translations of many of the poems, is among

---

[18] 'An Adequate Vision: A George Oppen Daybook', ed. Michael Davidson, *Ironwood*, 26
(Fall 1985), 21. The repeated 'of's in the title and the opening section hint at the poem's concern
with belonging, at the same time as they may echo the first line of *Paradise Lost*, 'Of man's first
disobedience'.

[19] For Mary's interest in Bonnefoy, see also David McAleavey, 'Oppen on Literature and
Literary Figures and Issues', *Sagetrieb*, 6 (1987), 114.

[20] UCSD 16, 10, 14: 'we are very glad to have the English of Bonnefoy——and will
re-approach him'. The letter is misfiled with the 1963 correspondence with Schneider.

the Oppens' books at the Mandeville Special Collections.[21] Schneider also sent Oppen a marked up copy of W. D. Snodgrass's translation of one of the poems from the book, 'A San Francesco, Le Soir', a version containing various infelicities and errors. Mary Oppen was sufficiently intrigued to attempt her own version of the short poem.[22]

At first sight, the sombre tone of Bonnefoy's work with its often lofty, classical vocabulary might seem far removed indeed from the concerns of Oppen, whose own poem is, after all, intent on capturing the demotic energies of the contemporary city. Yet Bonnefoy's preoccupation with time and change in *Douve* generates a poetic vision which is in some ways surprisingly close to Oppen's. For both men, poetry must recognize what is called in *Douve* 'the vast unutterable [*indicible*] matter' of the world (stone is its privileged embodiment there too) and in 'Of Being Numerous' 'the pure joy | Of the mineral fact'.[23] While Bonnefoy speaks of 'the thickness [*l'épaisseur*] of the world' (D, 64), Oppen describes it as 'impenetrable'. This sense of the 'metaphysical *thereness*' of things and 'their stubborn atomicity, and their opaque silence'[24] underlies the central concern with 'presence' in Bonnefoy's work. For, as Maurice Blanchot observes, where Hegel had famously dismissed out of hand any notion of immediacy, Bonnefoy grounds his poetics in a desire to 'recapture the act of presence, the true place, that site where there gathers in an undivided unity what "is" '.[25] Yet this irreducible sense of 'being' depends too upon its opposite—as one critic observes, '[Bonnefoy] has often stressed that it is in absence, and because of death, that "presence" comes to full realization.' 'Presence' thus entails not a romantic transcendence of time, but, on the contrary, 'an epiphany of finitude'.[26] To put it another way, the emphasis, shared by both poets, on what Bonnefoy terms 'the *here and now*' is not at all some pure present but rather 'our limitation', the finite limits which define

[21] Yves Bonnefoy, *Hier régnant désert* (Paris: Mercure de France, 1958). Schneider's translation was never published and Oppen's copy seems to have disappeared.

[22] Schneider enclosed the 'snodweed' translation, as he called it, in a letter of 8 Apr. 1965 (UCSD 16, 10, 16). The page, with Mary Oppen's version added to it, is in UCSD 16, 19, 12. The translation is not included in those written into the Oppens' copy of Bonnefoy's volume.

[23] Yves Bonnefoy, *On the Motion and Immobility of Douve*, trans. Galway Kinnell (1968; Newcastle upon Tyne: Bloodaxe Books, 1992), 101. Further references to D will be given in the text.

[24] Yves Bonnefoy, 'Shakespeare and the French Poet', in *The Act and the Place of Poetry: Selected Essays*, trans. John T. Naughton (Chicago: University of Chicago Press, 1989), 19. An English translation was published anonymously in *Encounter*, 18/6 (June 1962), 38–47. Compare Oppen's 'the great mineral silence | Vibrates, hums, a process | Completing itself' (NCP, 179).

[25] Maurice Blanchot, *The Infinite Conversation*, trans. Susan Hanson (Minneapolis: University of Minnesota Press, 1993), 34. In *Act and Place of Poetry*, Bonnefoy notes that 'as Hegel has shown, seemingly with relief, speech can retain nothing that is immediate' (107).

[26] John T. Naughton, *The Poetics of Yves Bonnefoy* (Chicago: University of Chicago Press, 1984), 19.

existence. [27] Hence the paradox of Douve's existence in Bonnefoy's long poem, as the dead woman still somehow alive, both in 'movement' and 'immobile': 'each instant I see you being born, Douve, || Each instant dying' (D, 49) and 'even dead | She will again be light, being nothing' (D, 67). Douve's death and her assimilation into the 'earth' become a force capable of 'Illuminating | Vast unutterable matter': 'Let the cold by my death arise and take on meaning', she says (D, 101).

The quotation from Mary Oppen at the beginning of 'Of Being Numerous' thus brings together a number of key elements from Bonnefoy's poem, though its central contention—that 'It is dead and it is not dead'—remains designedly enigmatic. In some notes to this section Oppen glosses the phrase 'That which "is dead and it is not dead"—the permanent',[28] though the designation of the latter word also remains unclear.[29] Does the floating 'it' refer, perhaps, to the past, to the 'infinite series' of births and deaths already mentioned? At least we can see why the arrival of Spring, with its traditional associations with renewal, might 'obscure' the past and its connotations of closure and finitude. Like Douve, the past is 'dead and it is not dead' and while we cannot return to it or reanimate it, it continues to live within us. At the same time, though, this contradiction also infects our future: for Oppen and for Bonnefoy, any sense of the future as open possibility is also bound up with a knowledge of inevitable closure.[30] Yet just as Bonnefoy urges the recognition that 'You will have to go through death to live, | The purest presence is blood which is shed' (D, 79), so Oppen's use of Mary's comments on *Douve* seems to hint at an alternative to the 'sad marvels' recalled in the 'tale of our wickedness' by glimpsing our position as being at the *beginning* of an 'infinite series' as well as at its end; history might thus perhaps carry again that 'sense of continuation' that Oppen finds wanting in contemporary American culture, opening a future which exceeds the horizon of the individual life.

Bonnefoy's poem provides a useful clue to Oppen's thinking here, for while the biblical 'tale' tells us of the ways in which we have had to endure the consequences of an original act, *Douve* seeks to evoke a presence whose absoluteness releases us momentarily from the entailments of an already completed narrative. Mary tells of the earth speaking (perhaps recalling Douve's

---

[27] Bonnefoy, *Act and the Place of Poetry*, 106–7.

[28] Oppen, 'Adequate Vision', ed. Davidson, 21.

[29] See also Hatlen, 'Opening Up the Text', 270–1 on the syntactical problems raised by these lines.

[30] And compare e.g. Heidegger, *Being and Time*, 374: 'This phenomenon has the unity of a future which makes present in the process of having been; we designate it as "*temporality*".' Cf. ibid. 446: 'historiology will disclose the quiet force of the possible with greater penetration the more simply and the more concretely having-been-in-the-world is understood in terms of its possibility, and "only" presented as such'.

account of herself as 'nothing but yearning earth' (D, 97)) and of the salaman-
der which can pass unscathed through fire. In the poem in *Douve* called 'Place
of the Salamander', the creature 'freezes and feigns death', attaching itself to
the wall with a stony gaze, but at the same time the poet sees 'its heart beat
eternal'. In an essay which refers to this passage, Bonnefoy remarks that the
salamander 'here present as the softly beating heart of the world, becomes the
origin of what is'.[31] This sense of being depends upon the sudden perception
of the salamander not as one thing among many (as just one term in an
'infinite series', perhaps) but as a presence which somehow brings everything
to, in Bonnefoy's phrase, 'the transparence of *unity*'.[32] Again, the fortuitous
'rhyme' with 'Of Being Numerous' is striking:

> Clarity
>
> In the sense of *transparence*,
> I don't mean that much can be explained.
>
> Clarity in the sense of silence.

> (NCP, 175)

Oppen's 'clarity' sets itself off from any kind of conceptual thought—it is
'silent' rather than explanatory—and what is seen in its light is allowed to
'be' for itself rather than exemplifying merely membership of a larger class.
This sudden emergence into authentic being has a decidedly Heideggerian
inflection, echoing a passage in *Being and Time* in which it is said that
'When one has an understanding Being-towards-death—towards death as
one's *ownmost* possibility—one's potentiality-for-Being becomes authentic
and wholly transparent.'[33] In Douve, that sudden 'transparence' is enacted in a
grammar of perception for which '*a* salamander' becomes, for poet and reader,
'*the* salamander', the creature having 'freed itself from the world of objects
created by an analytic reason that runs the risk of remaining on the periphery
of things'.[34] I am not suggesting that Oppen knew Bonnefoy's essay,[35] but
his own sense of 'disclosure' could produce very similar effects. In 'Of Being
Numerous', for example:

> There can be a brick
> In a brick wall
> The eye picks
>
> So quiet of a Sunday

---

[31] 'French Poetry and the Principle of Identity', *Act and Place of Poetry*, 120.
[32] Ibid. 121 (emphasis in original).
[33] Heidegger, *Being and Time*, 354 (emphasis in original).
[34] Bonnefoy, *Act and Place of Poetry*, 121.
[35] It was first published in *Revue d'Ésthétique*, 3–4 (July–Dec. 1965).

> Here is the brick, it was waiting
> Here when you were born
>
> Mary-Anne.[36]

Oppen's poem is, of course, less exotic than Bonnefoy's, but like *Douve* its shift from '*a* brick' to '*the* brick' also signals some kind of 'presence'.[37]

Such moments of 'disclosure' allegedly show the potential of language to escape the order of the concept, and Bonnefoy even suggests that 'some words—home, fire, bread, wine—are not entirely concepts, can never be taken quite as "pure notions", for they are bound to potential presences'.[38] Again, we may note the proximity of this view to Oppen's account of his 'faith in the little words' as deriving from their being 'in immediate touch with reality, with unthought or directly perceived reality' (SL, 62).[39] As he acknowledges, such a conception is open to criticism, but it is for him an article of 'faith' whose simplicity registers an acceptance of the world and the existential limits it imposes.[40] Bonnefoy proposes a rather similar view:

> The key to our being, the only path toward wholeness, thus seems to me the acceptance of chance. One might call such acceptance a *sacrifice*, since it implies that the individual should renounce infinite possibilities and choose to venture toward his absolute. One might call it consent to death, since it fixes our eyes on finitude. And one may call it love, for only love with its imperious decisive choices enables us to consent to what has been given us.[41]

Bonnefoy's emphasis on 'consent' and 'acceptance' does seem to resonate with the celebration in 'Of Being Numerous' of '*Amor fati* | The love of fate' which 'if I have given it validity, is I think the major achievement of the poem'

---

[36] This section is indebted to a much earlier poem called 'The Town' which is dated in typescript 'January 1959' and which opens with the lines 'There can be a brick in a brick wall | The eye picks' (USCD, 16, 1, 1).

[37] See SL, 105: 'I believe we can't be astonished by any hallucination whatever. Whereas we are totally astonished by daylight, by any brick in a brick wall we focus on.' Quite fortuitously, Bonnefoy observes (*Act and Place of Poetry*, 125) that 'the word *brick* speaks less clearly to the spirit of poetry than *stone*, because the calling to mind of the manufacturing process prevails, in the reality of this word, over its own being as "brick"—and all the more so because it is the opposite of *stone* in verbal structure'.

[38] *Act and Place of Poetry*, 62.

[39] Cf. Oppen in Dembo, ' "Objectivist" Poet', 167: 'I, too, have a sense . . . of the greater reality of certain kinds of objects than of others.' Compare, too, Rilke in 'The Ninth Elegy', *Selected Works*, ii. *Poetry*, trans. J. B. Leishman (London: Hogarth Press, 1960), 244: 'Are we, perhaps, *here* just for saying: House, | Bridge, Fountain, Gate, Jug, Fruit tree, Window,- | possibly: Pillar, Tower?'.

[40] See Oppen in Dembo, ' "Objectivist" Poet', 162: 'I realize the possibility of attacking many of the things I'm saying and I say them as a sort of act of faith.'

[41] *Act and Place of Poetry*, 62 (emphasis in original).

(SL, 121).[42] An unpublished note gives a fuller idea of what this Stoic notion might imply:

The reconciliation, finally, even to death in amor fati, the love of fate. It is—even—an impatient love, like all love. Like all love expressed in events; it requires occurrences. (UCSD 16, 19, 10)[43]

We have already received intimations of this 'amor fati' in Oppen's earlier poem 'World, World————', where the declaration that 'We want to be here' (NCP, 159) echoes Nietzsche's injunction to 'not merely bear what is necessary, still less conceal it . . . but *love* it',[44] thus suggesting that a sense of collective identity must be rooted in this desire to 'be here'.[45]

* * * * *

The passage beyond the self is toward something we might call 'humanity' or 'numerousness' which not only includes the self but which also offers an horizon exceeding that of the individual life. The limits which define our existence would not be bearable, Oppen suggests, if we did not have some inherent 'ethical motivation' which makes us 'care about the idea of what's going to happen to humanity, including after one's death'.[46] Yet to 'care' for 'humanity' in something more than a merely sentimental way we shall need to weigh its meanings very carefully since, as we saw in the case of 'The People', such collective singularities have a tendency to evaporate into empty rhetoric. Oppen had worried away at this problem even in the poems of *Discrete Series* and notably, as we saw in Chapter 2, in 'Party on Shipboard' where, as he puts it in an unpublished note, 'like the waves, the people appearing as individual, are accidents of the single mass, a single body' (UCSD 16, 19, 13). While working on 'Of Being Numerous', he recalls this poem in which, he says, 'I try to get again to humanity as a single thing, as something like a sea which is a constant weight in its bed' (SL, 111).[47] In the work following

---

[42] Oppen may have taken this from Nietzsche's *Ecce Homo*, as Davidson suggests (NCP, 381), or from Simone Weil, *Waiting on God*, trans. Emma Craufurd (London: Routledge and Kegan Paul, 1951), 18.

[43] Denise Riley, *The Words of Selves: Identification, Solidarity, Irony* (Stanford, Calif.: Stanford University Press, 2000), 128 observes that '*Amor fati*, though literally and simply the love of one's fate, may be poised anywhere between a desperate and a nobly Stoic resolve to accept what I cannot avoid anyway, "by taking on deliberately what I am fortuitously" (Merleau-Ponty).'

[44] Friedrich Nietzsche, *On the Genealogy of Morals, Ecce Homo*, trans. Walter Kaufmann (New York: Vintage Books, 1969), 258.

[45] See UCSD 16, 19, 12: 'And the basic position—which is that we are in love with fate and . . . we are absolutely committed to the necessity of being numerous.'

[46] Oppen in Dembo, ' "Objectivist" Poet', 166.

[47] The connection between 'Of Being Numerous' and 'Party on Shipboard' is drawn in another unpublished note (UCSD 16, 19, 12) where Oppen observes that after writing the former

Discrete Series, this attempt to see humanity as 'single' begins to acquire a specifically Heideggerian pathos, for like Being, 'humanity' as a collective entity seems constantly to elude articulation and to 'withdraw' into individual beings.

'Of Being Numerous', he says in one interview, 'asks the question whether or not we can deal with humanity as something which actually does exist.'[48] Tellingly, the poem does not speak of 'humanity', preferring instead 'populace' and 'people(s)', words which with their root connection to an idea of 'commonness' seem to offer an alternative to what Oppen calls elsewhere 'the metaphysical concept of humanity', 'a single figure, A monster' (UCSD 16, 5, 9).[49] Yet against this particular 'singleness' which offers a false ideal of a social unity without division or difference there is the equally problematic notion of 'singularity'. While numerousness leaves us, as he puts it in the poem, 'pressed, pressed on each other' (NCP, 165), it is also a condition we seem to have chosen for ourselves:

> Obsessed, bewildered
>
> By the shipwreck
> Of the singular
>
> We have chosen the meaning
> Of being numerous
>
> (NCP, 166)

The motif of shipwreck, linked here to the tale of Robinson Crusoe, runs through the poem. Oppen may have been alluding to Marx's polemic against 'Robinsonades', as Henry Weinfeld has suggested (GOMP, 376), but his interest in Defoe's novel may also have been rekindled by stories of Buñuel's filming *Robinson Crusoe* (1954) in Mexico (the film, as already noted, was scripted by Oppen's friend, Hugo Butler).[50] The theme of shipwreck had many literary antecedents, of course. Section 26, for example, seems to allude to *Moby Dick* with its talk of 'Behemoth, white whale' (NCP, 179), and an early draft of section 12 (UCSD 16, 19, 8) incorporates a quotation from Owen Chase's *The Shipwreck of the Whaleship Essex*, Melville's principal source for his

---

'I think I'll be a long time starting again. I've come to the end of what was attempted in Discrete Series. . . . But the seeds of all of it in Discrete.' He then refers to 'Party on Shipboard'.

[48] Oppen in Dembo, ' "Objectivist" Poet', 8.

[49] Cf. UCSD 16, 22, 58: 'The word | Populace, not humanity | Which cannot be given meaning. But the sense | Of populace | Necessary'.

[50] See Rouverol, *Refugees from Hollywood*, 47–62. Rouverol (personal communication) observes that Oppen 'must have been to one of the projection-room showings of *Robinson Crusoe*, not just because of Hugo but because the dialogue director was a friend too'.

novel.[51] For other memorable literary shipwrecks one may recall Mallarmé's 'A la nue accablante tu' and, of course, of *Un coup de dés*, poems which seem to inform an intermittent motif of storm and shipwreck in Bonnefoy's *Douve*.[52]

Whatever the literary echoes, though, Oppen's meaning seems clear enough: as he says in section 6, the fact that we speak of Crusoe as having been 'Rescued' shows that 'We have chosen the meaning | Of being numerous' (NCP, 166). In his various comments on this part of the poem, Oppen speaks of 'a dead end, the shipwreck of the singular' (SL, 116), and of 'the concepts evolved from the fact of being numerous, without which we are marooned, shipwrecked' (SL, 121).[53] This theme had appeared in some of his earlier poems: in 'From Disaster', for example, the shipwreck was associated with the social 'disaster' of the thirties (NCP, 50), while in 'Myself I Sing' a man marooned sits down near a sand dune and 'finds himself by two' (NCP, 56), meaning, as Oppen noted elsewhere of the poem, that 'we find ourselves, conceive ourselves by reaction to some other existence' (UCSD 16, 17, 12).[54] Only if such singularity is imagined to have 'unearthly bonds', as he puts it in section 9, only if individualism acquires some false metaphysical sanction, can 'the shipwrecked singular and his distance from them, the people' appear in anything but a negative light (UCSD 16, 14, 6). And curiously enough, such 'light' gives more than merely metaphorical illumination, for Oppen now speaks of 'the bright light of shipwreck' (NCP, 167, 173) and toward the end of the sequence of 'The narrow, frightening light || Before a sunrise' (NCP, 181). It may be that 'Of Being Numerous' is coloured by the deathly light that pervades Bonnefoy's *Douve* and particularly by the sun which is seen there 'in its bright agony | Lighting the place where all was revealed' (D, 139). Either way, the illumination in Oppen's poem is highly ambiguous, at once 'frightening' and apocalyptic, while also promising a certain enlightenment.

That positive sense of the image comes across strongly in an unpublished poem which begins 'beautiful as the sea | and the islands' clear light || of shipwreck', a light that here 'prove(s) us part | of the world not fallen || from it' and that embodies what Oppen calls 'conviction   forceful | as light' (NCP,

---

[51] At the end of section 12, Oppen quotes the following passage from *The Shipwreck of the Whaleship Essex*: 'This day his reason was attacked, and he became about 9 o'clock in the morning a most miserable spectacle of madness, calling loudly for a napkin and water.'

[52] See D, 77 ('this land which the storm lights'), 95 ('the road of lightning'), 103 ('Shipwrecked in your night').

[53] Cf. UCSD 16, 14, 10: 'It [the poem] requires only the reader's consent to the proposition that "the shipwreck of the singular" is a physical and unalterable fact, and that "the meaning of being numerous" is not easily stated or found. This is really the whole poem.'

[54] Cf. the reference in 'The Speech at Soli' to 'Friday's footprint' (NCP, 239).

301).[55] The implication is that shipwreck, as in the tale of Crusoe, must prove to us that value resides ultimately in numerousness. At the same time, though, this seascape with its clarity and 'the pebbles | shifting || on the beach', an image worked through in section 26 of 'Of Being Numerous' ('Or see thru water . . .' (NCP, 179)), has an emotional tranquillity that sits oddly with the disaster of shipwreck. Two earlier passages raise the same problem. In section 8:

> Slowly over islands, destinies
> Moving steadily pass
> And change
>
> In the thin sky
> Over islands
> Among days

In a draft of a letter to Rachel Blau DuPlessis, Oppen comments as follows on these lines:

I am sure we really must 'choose'——or find——the 'meaning of being numerous'. Shipwreck is by definition to be 'singular'——tho the poem wavers again to the possibility of watching fate simply in the change and movement of the clouds. (UCSD 16, 19, 12)

The poem does indeed seem to 'waver' again in the next section:

> To dream of that beach
> For the sake of an instant in the eyes,
>
> The absolute singular
>
> The unearthly bonds
> Of the singular
>
> Which is the bright light of shipwreck
>
>   (NCP, 167)

The moral ambiguities of 'watching' and 'seeing' are encapsulated in the quotation from a letter from Rachel Blau DuPlessis which opens section 9: ' "Whether, as the intensity of seeing increases, one's distance from Them, the people, does not also increase" '. 'Distance' would seem to negate an authentic sense of 'numerousness', yet at the same time, as Oppen wrote in two lines subsequently cancelled from the poem, 'To be unable to watch | Is to be destroyed' (UCSD 16, 22, 8). If we avert our eyes (in this case from the horrors of Vietnam) we are lost, even though this act of watching might set us apart from others. The condition of singularity may be equated with 'shipwreck',

---

[55] Cf. 'Two Romance Poems' (NCP, 261): 'bright light of shipwreck beautiful as the sea'.

then, but as the story of Robinson Crusoe reminds us, the wreckage is seen from afar and from the point of view of the survivor. In this sense, Oppen seems to have recognized the inherent ambiguity of the shipwreck motif which, as Hans Blumenberg puts it, poses endlessly 'the insoluble dilemma of theoretical distance versus living engagement'.[56] The passages quoted above from sections 8 and 9 thus complicate the poem's presentation of numerousness by suggesting a partial acceptance of singularity in the spirit of 'amor fati', the lure of the beach and the clouds proving that no more than Crusoe can we simply transcend the condition of singularity in 'numerousness'. At the same time, though, the 'singular' and the 'numerous' are not susceptible of any easy dialectical resolution, and the poem's reflections on contemporary American culture certainly permit no acceptance of ideological variations on 'e pluribus unum'.

Instead, it is the horizon of the individual's death which returns once more to complicate the logic of the poem, as a letter of 1973 confirms:

'The shipwreck of the singular' I wrote. We *cannot* live without the concept of humanity, the end of one's own life is by no means equivalent to the end of the world, we would not bother to live out our own lives if it were———

and yet we cannot escape this: that we *are* single. And face, therefore, shipwreck.

And yet this, this tragic fact, is the brilliance of one's life, it is 'the bright light of shipwreck' which discloses——————'all'. (SL, 263)

There is a painful hesitancy in Oppen's phrasing ('and yet . . . And yet'), with ellipses dramatizing this fundamental paradox, that the 'tragic fact' of singularity is actually 'the brilliance of one's life'.[57] 'Humanity' is apparently rehabilitated here, but less as an existential reality than as a 'concept' or horizon which we need to live out our individual lives. Any utopian sense of 'humanity' or 'numerousness' is bound by the limit which is our own death because it is only from the perspective of that impending end that we can entertain an authentic idea of human 'continuation'. In a curious way, then, the 'shipwreck of the singular' and the 'meaning of being numerous' are not antithetical options, as might first be thought, but are rather mutually

---

[56] Hans Blumenberg, *Shipwreck with Spectator: Paradigm of a Metaphor for Existence* (Cambridge, Mass.: MIT Press, 1997), 67.

[57] Oppen, we might say, has to find this a 'difficult' thought lest it be too easily grasped. Compare, for example, the rather lame expression of a similar idea in William E. Connolly, *Identity/Difference: Democratic Negotiations of Political Paradox* (Minneapolis: University of Minnesota Press, 2002), 19: 'connectedness to a future that stretches beyond my life and our lives provides me with pride in the present and consoles me somehow about the end that awaits me'. Oppen may also be thinking of Whitman's 'Crossing Brooklyn Ferry' with its address to 'The others that are to follow me, the ties between me and them; | The certainty of others—the life, love, sight, hearing of others' (*The Portable Walt Whitman*, introd. Mark Van Doren (New York: Viking Press, 1969), 193).

implicated possibilities. In fact, *both*, it turns out, are sustained by notions of oneness and separation. Hence we may speak of what Oppen called with reference to one of William Bronk's poems, 'Not My Loneliness But Ours', 'The loneliness not of the individual, but of the group' (SL, 77). Part of Bronk's poem reads: 'The human loneliness | is the endless oneness of man. Man is one; | man is alone in his world. We are the one . . .'.[58]

The ironies attaching to social 'oneness' were, of course, writ large at the time Bronk and Oppen were writing their poems. In the period during which 'Of Being Numerous' took shape, it was not only the Vietnam War that presented a spectre of national violence. With the faltering of the Civil Rights movement after the gains of 1964 and 1965, American cities were poised on a wave of rioting, while other oppositional groups—the women's movement, the anti-war movement, student activists—would become increasingly disenchanted with reformism. The consensus politics of the opening years of the decade now swiftly began to unravel; in the year that Oppen received the Pulitzer for *Of Being Numerous*, Richard Nixon became President on a neo-conservative mandate of law and order. So Oppen's poem pressed its questioning of numerousness with a prescient grasp of social fragmentation and of 'Insanity in high places' (NCP, 173). There were no obvious panaceas, and when it came now to mass action Oppen set his sights low, observing in his poem that 'The shuffling of a crowd is nothing— | well, nothing, but the many that we are, but nothing' (NCP, 168). In other words, we must resist any ersatz feeling of oneness while at the same time eschewing a compensatory fetishism of the other oneness that is our singularity. And that, perhaps, is the meaning of the passage in Oppen's letter where he speaks of ' "the bright light of shipwreck" which discloses————— ——"all" ', for it is only in the harsh light of our mortality that we may grasp the concept of 'humanity' in its authentic form, as the sum of those who live on after us. This is, indeed, to arrive at 'the *meaning* of being numerous' and it perhaps explains why the strongest affirmation of numerousness in the poem stresses proximity to others rather than immediate identification with them:

> For us
> Also each
> Man or woman
> Near is knowledge
> Tho it may be of the noon's
> Own vacuity
>
> (NCP, 185–6)

---

[58] William Bronk, *Life Supports: New and Collected Poems* (Jersey City, NJ: Talisman House, 1997), 44.

These lines may echo section 4 of Whitman's 'Crossing Brooklyn Ferry'—'The men and women I saw were all near to me; | Others the same—others who look back on me, because I look'd forward to them'[59]—but Oppen's end in equivocation and the syntax deliberately eschews Whitman's easy assurance. Indeed, the 'us' here reminds us that much of the poem's drama occurs at the level of the pronoun and that it is ultimately to these 'little words', these aptly named linguistic 'shifters', that so much importance here attaches. In the poems that make up 'Of Being Numerous', Oppen is constantly 'testing' pronouns, exploring what he calls the 'distances' (NCP, 178) that open up between 'I', 'we', 'one', and 'they'.

Section 1 begins with what must be an all-inclusive 'we', but by section 3 there are 'others' whom 'we' encounter, a difference clarified in terms of generations in section 4. With section 6, 'we' may be 'pressed on each other', but far from being all-inclusive this is now a populist 'we' implicitly oppressed by some vaguely defined other ('We will be told at once | Of anything that happens'). With sections 9, 10, and 11, the poet seems to speak as 'I', this singular expressing a sincerity to be clearly distinguished from 'art' (169). Sections 12–14 then complicate matters by introducing a variously inflected 'they': first, a primitive people who were 'patient with the world' but who are gone never to return;[60] then, by way of contrast, a contemporary 'they':

> unable to begin
> At the beginning, the fortunate
> Find everything already here. They are shoppers,
> Choosers, judges; . . . And here the brutal
> Is without issue, a dead end.
>
> They develop
> Argument in order to speak, they become
> unreal, unreal, life loses
> solidity, loses extent, baseball's their game. . . .
>
> (NCP, 170)

The strongly repudiated 'they' of this passage recalls the 'they' of *Being and Time* where Heidegger speaks of 'an impassioned freedom toward death—a freedom which has been released from the Illusions of the "they", and which is factical, certain of itself, and anxious'.[61] Oppen's shoppers, choosers, and judges, however, are still caught up in the unreality of the 'they', where

---

[59] *Portable Whitman*, 196.

[60] The reference is to Thomas Carlyle, 'Goethe'—see Carlyle, *Critical and Miscellaneous Essays*, 7 vols. (London: Chapman & Hall, 1888), i. 206, quoting from *Wilhelm Meister*: 'what a task was it, not only to be patient with the Earth, and let it lie beneath us, we appealing to a higher birthplace'.

[61] Heidegger, *Being and Time*, 311.

everything is 'already here', the social interpellations already in place and the possibilities of power withdrawn. The 'dead end' which this represents leads to the conclusion that 'one may honourably keep | His distance | If he can' (note how the generic 'one' here modulates into the singular 'he').

But there is another 'they'—'those men' Oppen knew in combat—from whom 'I cannot even now | Altogether disengage myself'. Here, to be sure, there is a strong sense of social connection (in contrast to 'talk | . . . of "The People" ') but this too has to be recovered from past experience, 'in a ruined country', and Oppen was adamant in his rejection of any reading of the poem that finds too easy consolation in 'the "comradeship" of war' ('I reject this interpretation of the poem very strongly,' he wrote (SL, 254)). At the same time, the present is characterized by the gloom of the subways (section 17) where 'There is madness in the number | Of the living' and 'A ferocious mumbling, in public | Of rootless speech', and the cracks in the national 'we' (the sequence will end with Whitman's reflections on the capitol building) now begin to open up. Here the 'bright light of shipwreck' refers to the collective singular which is a 'we' sufficiently exclusive as to leave a space in which other people 'burn'. 'If it is true we must do these things | We must cut our throats', the poem concludes, but section 20 shows that it is not in fact 'we' who must commit these atrocities but 'they':

> ———They await
>
> War, and the news
> Is war
>
> As always
>
> That the juices may flow in them
> Tho the juices lie.
>
> (NCP, 174)

In face of this it seems impossible to speak as 'we'—'we do not altogether matter' (NCP, 175)—and the next two sections offer the personal address to Mary-Anne and the poet's claim for clarity as silence ('I don't mean that much can be explained'). Section 23 then returns us to a contemporary 'they', the 'jet set' and the party girls sexually 'filled' while they 'Stare at the ceilings'. Each 'they' signals a degraded numerousness which is somehow contrasted with 'The lump, | Entity | Of substance' which is 'Under the soil'. An early version of these lines suggests that Oppen was thinking once again of the stark reality of his wartime experience in relation to the superficial social rituals of the contemporary world ('the people will change again'):

> Under the sea, under the deep
> Soil hidden

> In the black
> And heavy depths
> Lump, accretion,
> Is one's brother.

>   (UCSD 16, 22, 22)

The removal of the last line makes the final version enigmatic, a gesture toward some mineral 'change' beneath the contemporary surface.[62] It is as if Oppen's revision entails almost literally the burial of a dead comrade, removing mention of his 'brother' and leaving the body as just an unrecognizable 'lump'.

Again, the focus shifts abruptly. If this nation is 'in some sense | Our home', as the next section proposes, and if the American 'covenant' is that 'There shall be peoples', then numerousness should amount to something more than social conformity. Yet that possibility too seems to belong to 'the dark rooms | Of the past', and the immigrant families have been absorbed into the 'middle class' to become ' "The pure products of America———" '. Williams's line which is borrowed here ends, of course, with 'go crazy',[63] and section 26 returns us to a 'they' who 'carry nativeness | To a conclusion | In suicide'. And here we return once more to Oppen's major theme:

> They have lost the metaphysical sense
> Of the future, they feel themselves
> The end of a chain
>
> Of lives, single lives
> And we know that lives
> Are single
>
> And cannot defend
> The metaphysic
> On which rest
>
> The boundaries
> Of our distances.
> We want to say
>
> 'Common sense'
> And cannot. We stand on

---

[62] See UCSD 16, 1, 4 (dated 22 Oct. 1963): 'Yet it is difficult to say that an object exists. Even rocks grow by accretion, and diminish by erosion, so that if I say "This rock" it is already not the same rock. And yet surely this is "is-ness". This constant changing, this constant flowing, ceasing-to-exist, of the object must consist of the mixing and separating of primordial elements which are themselves indestructible, and it is these elements—whatever they may be—whose existence constitutes is-ness . . . a sort of atomic theory by metaphysical necessity.'

[63] William Carlos Williams, *The Collected Poems 1909–1939*, ed. A. Walton Litz and Christopher MacGowan (Manchester: Carcanet, 1986), 217.

> That denial
> Of death that paved the cities. . . .
>
> (NCP, 177–8)

In an earlier draft, Oppen had written 'They carry *liberalism* | To a conclusion | In suicide' and referred to 'The boundaries | Of our *liberalism*' (UCSD, 16, 22, 58), the implication being that the logical end of liberal individualism is suicide as a refusal to accept the condition of finitude and its opening to numerousness (in contrast to 'them', 'We want to defend | limitation'). '[T]hey feel themselves | The end of a chain | Of lives' rather than its beginning and they thus have no sense of a future extending beyond their deaths.[64] It is clear by now that any countervailing sense of 'we' is going to be 'precarious' indeed, and in some of the remaining sections of the poem the pronoun 'one' is used to point up the ambiguous relation of the generic to the particular (see sections 27, 30, 31, 36, and 38).

* * * * *

At this point it is helpful to invoke once more Oppen's distinction between 'That it is' and 'What it is', for the movements of 'Of Being Numerous' do indeed lead us away from the vision of the 'whole' that was sought in *This in Which* and plunge us instead into the currents of what Oppen had called 'the sensory and the historic' (UCSD 16, 2, 48). As 'Route' puts it, 'The context is history | Moving toward the light of the conscious || And beyond' (NCP, 198)—to think 'history' in this sense is to move from past to future and, as Oppen notes elsewhere, 'the concern of a man with the future after his death is a metaphysical construct' (UCSD 16, 14, 4). The whole issue of social identification when weighed in this 'metaphysical' balance might come down, then, to the matter of history as shared time, the time 'we make' (SL, 29). If 'the concept of "humanity"' has proved to be a 'failure' (SL, 63) it is because the 'we' who discover a common world in immediate experience are increasingly fragmented into an 'us' and an anonymous 'they' whose subjectivity we never grasp directly. The emphatic use of shifters to establish '*this* world *here*' makes the poem itself a possible defence against social anonymity, though it can only be a partial one, as the experience of 'nearness' and 'connection' is increasingly threatened by a growing sense of mere contemporaneity. Sociologist Alfred Schutz, whose terms I am borrowing here, proposes a distinction between, on the one hand, the experience of living with 'my fellow man' and, on the other, the awareness of my 'mere contemporary' who is 'one whom I know coexists

---

[64] Cf. UCSD 16, 19, 13: 'Francis Ponge who says: "Every desire to flee weights me with a new link to the chain".'

with me in time but whom I do not experience immediately'.[65] Here, perhaps, we can see how Oppen thinks the relation of 'That it is' to 'What it is', for in each case 'being' is in tension with forms of predication. As Schutz puts it, there is on the one hand 'a pre-predicative experience in which I become aware of a fellow human being *as a person*' while on the other the 'contemporary' is understood in a purely predicative way, 'that is, in terms of his typical characterisation' (Oppen's 'shoppers, | Choosers, judges', for example).[66] The pre-predicative relation to the other is, we might say, a disappearing feature of numerousness, and while Oppen does retrieve an authentic 'we' as the poem approaches its close, it is one rooted in the family rather than in a larger social group. It is ultimately in 'the baffling hierarchies | Of father and child' (section 29) and in marital love (section 32) that we finally discover something 'Which is ours, which is ourselves, | This is our jubilation' (section 33).

Yet it is the achievement of Oppen's poem to see such 'jubilation' against a background which shows up the very fragility of this sense of 'ourselves'. As the starkly moving section 38 reminds us, human finitude must ultimately compel the inclusive pronouns of authentic numerousness toward objectification and division:

> You are the last
> Who will know him
> Nurse.
>
> Not know him,
> He is an old man,
> A patient,
> How could one know him?
>
> You are the last
> Who will see him
> Or touch him,
> Nurse.
>
> (NCP 187)

The reiterated 'him' is the final condition of singularity, the patient no longer a person to be known, but just 'an old man' who can only be seen and touched. But the very 'transparency' of the diction here and the studied impersonality of its pronouns also affirm ' "the bright light of shipwreck" which discloses————— "all" ', a disclosure which, paradoxically, makes this

---

[65] Alfred Schutz, *The Phenomenology of the Social World*, trans. George Walsh and Frederick Lehnert (London: Heinemann, 1972), 142–3, 181. See also Paul Ricoeur, *Time and Narrative*, 3 vols., trans. Kathleen Blamey and David Pellauer (Chicago: University of Chicago Press, 1988), iii. 112–16.

[66] Schutz, *Phenomenology of the Social World*, 164, 194.

absolute singularity the unsentimental ground of what is truly held in common. In the spirit of 'amor fati', though, 'We want to be here', and section 39 attempts to state that paradox:

> Occurring 'neither for self
> Nor for truth'
>
> The sad marvels
> In the least credible circumstance,
> Storm or bombardment
>
> Or the room of a very old man
>
> (NCP, 187–8)

A draft of notes on the poem's sources suggests that the quotation is from one of Meister Eckhart's sermons which has already been used in section 5: 'consciousness || Which has nothing to gain, which awaits nothing, | Which loves itself' (NCP, 165). Eckhart is defining 'happiness':

we say that it consists neither in knowledge nor in love, but in that there is something in the soul, from which both knowledge and love flow and which, like the agents of the soul, neither knows nor loves. To know this is to know what blessedness depends on. This something has no 'before' or 'after' and it waits for nothing that is yet to come, for it has nothing to gain or lose. Thus, when God acts in it, it is deprived of knowing that he has done so. What is more, it is the same kind of thing that, like god, can enjoy itself.[67]

Oppen's 'neither for self | Nor for truth' seems to parallel Eckhart's qualified view of love and knowledge, suggesting perhaps that the poem in its final moments must weigh death (in fox-hole or in hospital) against 'consciousness' as the very principle of 'actuality' (an equation Oppen derives from Hegel[68]).

As in other parts of the poem, Oppen's syntax is deliberately awkward and incomplete, refusing to let this difficult thought degenerate into platitude. A rejected draft of an early version of section 24 shows, though, how these ideas were initially brought together:

> In this nation
> Which is in some sense
> Our home
>
> As those who spoke of a covenant:

---

[67] *Meister Eckhart: A Modern Translation*, trans. Raymond Bernard Blakney (New York: Harper and Brothers, 1941), 229. Oppen's copy of the book is held at UCSD. He gives a version of this passage, substituting 'consciousness' for 'happiness' in UCSD 16, 19, 9. For Oppen's notes on 'Of Being Numerous', see 'An Adequate Vision: A George Oppen Daybook', 21.

[68] As is shown in the next chapter, Oppen's often repeated sentence 'Consciousness in itself and of itself carries the principle of actualness | for it itself is actual' derives from Hegel's 'Preface' to *The Phenomenology of Spirit*.

You shall die
But shall exist as a people

In which they found
Meaning.

Consciousness
'Which has nothing to gain, which awaits nothing,
Which loves itself'

(UCSD 16, 19, 12)

This, then, is finally the 'Meaning' of being numerous, though the disjunction between the 'tragic fact' of one's own death and the continued existence of the 'people' returns us to 'consciousness' or, we might say, to a phenomenology of ordinary life in which the balance must constantly tip toward the burden of singularity. It is this emphasis on singularity that ultimately underlies the ambivalence that colours the whole poem. There is a fundamental recognition that 'The human is dependent on brotherhood, we must love one another or die' (UCSD 16, 17, 7), but while this may be 'the meaning of being numerous', Oppen also adds 'Not that I have much hope of it' (UCSD 16, 17, 7). And again, in its confrontation of 'the problem of the concept of humanity' the poem, says Oppen, 'does not mean to solve such a problem, but to permit the problem to remain a problem while giving MEANING, if I can, to its terms' (UCSD 16, 17, 2).[69]

Comments such as these urge caution when we are trying to fathom Oppen's 'position' in 'Of Being Numerous'. Indeed, where in an earlier essay I had proposed Emmanuel Levinas's concept of 'ethics' as in some ways analogous to Oppen's sense of 'numerousness', that now seems to me to offer the kind of ground that the poem may desire but that it also constantly undercuts.[70] Levinas's ethics defines a relation which presupposes that the self comes into being only by first recognizing its responsibility to others. 'Ethics' in this usage, then, denotes the claims of others rather than a body of moral rules and values; these claims are absolute, amounting to what Jean-François Lyotard has called 'obligation without conditions'.[71] While Oppen believes that 'we are absolutely

---

[69] Cf. UCSD 16, 16, 13: 'Of Being Numerous: whether we are bound each to each other: this question is the content and the meaning of our lives (the poem does not succeed in answering the question——nor did I expect to answer. It remains the question.'

[70] See my 'Of Being Ethical: Reflections on George Oppen', in Rachel Blau DuPlessis and Peter Quartermain (eds.), *The Objectivist Nexus: Essays in Cultural Poetics* (Tuscaloosa: University of Alabama Press, 1999), 240–53. The Levinasian reading has been taken up in Tim Woods, *The Poetics of the Limit: Ethics and Politics in Modern and Contemporary American Poetry* (Basingstoke: Palgrave, 2003) and G. Matthew Jenkins, 'Saying Obligation: George Oppen's Poetry and Levinasian Ethics', *Journal of American Studies*, 37/3 (2003), 407–33.

[71] Jean-François Lyotard, *The Differend: Phrases in Dispute*, trans. Georges Van Den Abbeele (Manchester: Manchester University Press, 1998), 117.

committed to the necessity of being numerous' (UCSD 16, 19, 12), the relation of numerousness to singularity in the poem remains indeterminate. In fact, he suggests in a comment on 'Route', the other long serial poem in *Of Being Numerous*, that the ultimate singularity at which we arrive is not actually that of the other at all: ' "Route" is very closely connected to "Of Being Numerous", the learning that one is, after all, just oneself and in the end is rooted in the singular, whatever one's absolutely necessary connections with human history are.'[72] 'Route' is in many ways a darker poem than 'Of Being Numerous', with the larger perspectives of 'humanity' now coming under even greater pressure.

> Tell the beads of the chromosomes like a rosary,
> Love in the genes, if it fails
>
> We will produce no sane man again
>
> (NCP, 192)

Love is 'in the genes', it is what is 'autonomous in us' (SL, 177), though to say this is to recognize a 'minimum' truth, as Oppen puts it, 'that a morality is possible within a family. It is, as you say, "in the chromosomes" ' (UCSD 16, 10, 15).[73] Such 'truths', though, might always 'fail' and 'Route' is at every point shadowed by the disaster of war, Oppen recalling at length the terrible story of Pierre and the Alsatian men who hid for years in holes to evade the Germans, a memory which echoes contemporary horrors, the politicians 'insane and criminal', the 'madmen' who 'have burned thousands | of men and women alive' (NCP, 201): 'We are at the beginning of a radical depopulation of the earth', Oppen concludes (NCP, 201).

The apportioning of guilt might seem a foregone conclusion given the angry rhetoric of the poem, but characteristically Oppen also finds himself guilty, guilty of leaving his wife and daughter to go to war ('Why | did I play all that, what was I doing there'), guilty of causing that youthful automobile accident ('The wheels of the overturned wreck | Still spinning————'), and guilty, too, of not attempting to rescue his comrade from the fox-hole. This last anxiety is not mentioned directly, though it is not far below the surface in section 6 of the poem:

> We are brothers, we are brothers?————these things are
> composed of a moral substance only if they are untrue. If
> these things are true they are perfectly simple, perfectly

---

[72] Oppen in Dembo, ' "Objectivist" Poet', 172. Cf. UCSD 16, 16, 13 on 'the mass of people breaking up into little groups, trying to get away from each other' and UCSD 16, 26, 4: 'The law and the prophets not that we are united, that we are brothers, but that we are here.'

[73] As 'Route' makes clear, this is to distinguish 'love' from the 'force of clarity' which 'is not autonomous in us' (NCP, 193). As noted in Ch. 2, above, the idea probably derives from Maritain.

impenetrable, those primary elements which can only be
named.

A man will give his life for his friend provided he wants
to.

In all probability a man will give his life for his child
provided his child is an infant.

(NCP, 197)

The austerity of these lines and their unblinking awareness of the limits set
by singularity emphasize that war imposes many intractable burdens of guilt,
as Oppen acknowledged in an unusually personal statement for the magazine
West End some years later:

If I fought, and fought to kill, I would suffer guilt, the guilt of guilt AND the guilt of
fear, the desire to run, the guilt that I've told of, the guilt of that foxhole (and who
does one fight? The deceived, the idiot, the stupid and also those with no choice, those
who must be heroes to refuse the crime).

If I killed, I would suffer guilt. If I did not, I would suffer . . . I don't even know a word,
a name for what I would suffer[.][74]

A culture of false heroism, a culture which 'stands on' a 'denial of death' while
casually meting it out to others, as in section 18 of 'Of Being Numerous' with
its 'plume of smoke, visible at a distance | In which people burn' (NCP, 173),
such a culture is 'without issue, a dead end' (NCP, 170).

In face of such violence, it is perhaps not surprising that, politically engaged
as the poem indubitably is, the dilemma posed by 'Of Being Numerous'
requires us to look to poetry for an expression of the 'metaphysical' that
can finally recognize 'the benevolence of the real' as something 'more than
the "political" '.[75] But even this approach to 'Of Being Numerous' is not
completely satisfactory, for it is surely not the case that Oppen wants the poem
finally to advocate one particular view, or to demonstrate that by some irony or
other its logic has simply come full circle. The letter from 1973 (quoted above,
p. 97) may tempt us to the latter kind of reading—singularity is shipwreck, but
we can't escape the fact 'that we *are* single. And face, therefore, shipwreck' (SL,
263)—but the apparent circularity of this logic is broken by the assertion that
it represents 'the brilliance of one's life' and 'discloses————————all'. The
single or singular is thus marked by a certain undecidability, incorporating
both existential loneliness and a sense of being which exceeds predication—it

[74] 'Non-Resistance, etc. Or: Of the Guiltless', *West End*, 3/1 (Summer 1974), 5.
[75] The phrase 'the benevolence of the real' occurs in section 13 of 'Route'. In a 1972 letter
(SL, 241), Oppen writes: 'the benevolence of the real. Sometimes called salvation | this, more
than the "political" which makes the failure of the concept of "humanity" maybe crucial'.

is, to put it another way, a matter of who we are rather than what we are, though as the pronominal shifts of the poem insist, this 'who' is disclosed as a shifting play of identifications rather than as any one stable identity. Oppen's poem thus proposes a condition of numerousness *and* singularity, the 'and' marking the irreducibility of one term to the other as an aporia which is not the condition of a blocked 'argument', but rather of the experience of *living between* these two possibilities. This seems to be exactly what Oppen has in mind when he concludes that 'Numerous is an attempt to establish the experience of humanity, and the experience of other universal terms' (UCSD 16, 18, 2).[76] This emphasis on 'experience' recalls the 'opacity' that Sartre's existentialism promised to bring to a politics too instrumentally conceived, an 'opacity' that in 'Of Being Numerous' affects local intelligibility and inhibits any large-scale 'resolution' of its themes.

If we can think of something that is 'more than the "political"' here, it is precisely a poetic thinking which allows one to accept that in the final instance one is 'rooted in the singular' while finding in that singularity a promise of a 'metaphysical sense | Of the future' (NCP, 177–8) that exceeds one's own life. Indeed, that final instance is, we might say, that of the poetic itself, which in the singularity of its utterance commits itself to what is there in the words rather than to what should be there in the world, seeing futurity as inseparable from finitude and finding in 'my' death an absolute singularity which is at the same time absolutely exemplary, a possible bond of numerousness.[77] Yet this accentuation of singularity carries, of course, its own pathos and, as Eric Santner has argued in another context:

To 'count' as singular one has to be, as it were, *supernumerary*, to persist beyond the logic of parts and wholes, beyond cultural systems of exchange, distinguished not by this or that trait but rather by *being left over*, by *remaining* once all particularities have been accounted for. It is death that first endows existence with this kind of singular density.[78]

In his work after *Of Being Numerous*, this sense of 'being left over', of remaining as the *survivor* who, unlike Crusoe, can't be rescued, would constitute a major

---

[76] Cf. Oppen in Dembo, ' "Objectivist" Poet', 162 on 'whether or not one will consider the concept of humanity to be valid, something that is, or else have to regard it as being simply a word.'

[77] See Jacques Derrida, *Aporias*, trans. Thomas Dutoit (Stanford, Calif.: Stanford University Press, 1993), 22: 'If death . . . names the very irreplaceability of absolute singularity (no one can die in my place or in the place of the other), then all the *examples* in the world can precisely illustrate this singularity. Everyone's death, the death of all those who can say "my death", is irreplaceable.'

[78] Eric L. Santner, *On the Psychotheology of Everyday Life* (Chicago: University of Chicago Press, 2001), 72 (his emphases).

element in Oppen's thinking, inflecting his sense of relation to contemporary culture and initiating, as we shall see, a series of reflections about his own problematic Jewishness. As he put it in one of his notes, 'somewhere half-way between the fact of being singular and the fact of being numerous is the fact of being Jewish' (UCSD 16, 14, 15).

5

From Avant-Garde to Hegel

Oppen finished 'Of Being Numerous' early in 1966 and in mid-February of the following year the couple moved to San Francisco, a relocation which would have a significant impact on the form and content of the poetry of his later years. The new volume appeared at the end of March 1968 and Oppen was awarded the Pulitzer Prize in Poetry in May of the following year. He was now 60 years old and a poet with a secure reputation, but none of this curbed his desire to reckon with the new youth culture around him. The poems published in 1972 as *Seascape: Needle's Eye* were accordingly strongly shaped not only by Oppen's return to the landscape of his youth but also by the shockwaves of the 'Summer of Love' which instinctively the couple sought to understand but from which, inevitably, their age excluded them. The first of 'Some San Francisco Poems' remembers their visit to the ill-fated Rolling Stones concert at Altamont in December 1969: '*as the tremendous volume of the music takes | over obscured by their long hair they seem | to be mourning*' ('Some San Francisco Poems', NCP, 221). Oppen, he said later, 'didn't know of the murder' that brought the concert to a halt, but he was struck by the way in which 'before the music started, everyone turned very sharply into himself or herself. Kind of a masturbatory atmosphere.'[1] In the drug-induced euphoria of the late sixties he clearly discerned another example of what he had described in 'Of Being Numerous' as the new 'Dithyrambic' arts, 'audience-as-artists' (NCP, 167). Indeed, the visit to Altamont may have consolidated the various anxieties Oppen had begun to feel about new directions taken in the contemporary arts. Particularly problematic were the claims for a new avant-gardism and Oppen's scepticism about these reinforced his own earlier critique of modernism and inflected the work he would produce in his remaining years.[2]

While a distaste for contemporary avant-gardism had made itself felt in 'Of Being Numerous', another event earlier in 1969 had already incited him

---

[1] 'Conversation', conducted by Amirkhanian and Gitin, 22.
[2] On Oppen's response to contemporary avant-gardism, see also Rachel Blau DuPlessis, ' "Uncannily in the open": In light of Oppen', in *Blue Studios: Poetry and its Cultural Work* (Tuscaloosa: University of Albama Press, 2006), 186–205.

to think through the issues involved. On 21 March of that year, The Living Theatre group organized by Julian Beck and Judith Malina held a symposium on 'Theatre or Therapy?' at the Friends Meeting House on Gramercy Square in New York.[3] Advocates of anarchy, drugs, and nudity, The Living Theatre had by this time achieved notoriety for their commitment to a spontaneous, Artaudian aesthetic that sought 'pure theatre' in the violent conflation of art and reality.[4] Some five hundred people attended the event, including Susan Sontag, Pauline Kael, Stephen Spender, Stanley Kunitz, and Norman Mailer. Reactions to The Living Theatre's tactics were mixed, however. Critic Robert Brustein, who had previously praised the group for its ability to, as he put it, 'break down barriers between what was going on onstage and what was going on in life', now spoke critically of their 'anti-intellectual' bias.[5] Brustein's contribution to the panel was followed by one from Paul Goodman who in 'cautious and moderately conservative tone', argued that contemporary America was confronting not a revolutionary moment but one analogous to the Protestant Reformation. Members of The Living Theatre and The Theatre of the Absurd were quick to show their disapproval. Discussion was drowned by chants of 'Stop analysing! Start living!'; a woman's fur coat was seized and handbags upturned in the auditorium. Bent on destroying 'illusory' theatrical space and ensuring that spectators 'confront the real world through conscious decision-making',[6] actors roamed the crowd, screaming obscenities at the audience and the speakers and spitting at everyone they encountered.

Caught up in the mêlée was Harvey Shapiro, poet, editor of the *New York Times Magazine*, and an old friend of Oppen. Two days later, Shapiro wrote him a three-page letter in which he puzzled over his own ambivalence toward the events of the evening. He couldn't help feeling, he said, that for all the chaos something portentous had been expressed, particularly in the theatre group's aggressive response to one young man who had tried to speak about poetry: 'All words,' they'd screamed, 'dead words by dead people' (UCSD 16, 10, 30).

---

[3] My account of this event draws especially on John Tytell, *The Living Theatre: Art, Exile and Outrage* (London: Methuen, 1997), 257–8.

[4] For an overview of the performance aesthetic to which The Living Theatre contributed in this period, see Daniel Belgrad, *The Culture of Spontaneity: Improvisation and the Arts in Postwar America* (Chicago: University of Chicago Press, 1998).

[5] Tytell, *Living Theatre*, 158, 257–8. Brustein's initial enthusiasm for The Living Theatre had waned by 1969. In an essay of 1970, collected in *The Culture Watch: Essays on Theatre and Society, 1969–1974* (New York: Alfred A. Knopf, 1975) he recalls (10–11) that 'Our third year (1968–69) was undoubtedly the low point in the history of the Yale Repertory Theatre, as well as being the most depressing period of my own life.' The visit by The Living Theatre in that year apparently contributed to the sense of having reached this 'low point'.

[6] Arnold Aronson, 'American Theatre in Context: 1945–Present', in Don B. Wilmeth and Christopher Bigsby (eds.), *The Cambridge History of American Theatre, iii.: Post-World War II to the 1990s* (Cambridge: Cambridge University Press, 2000), 120.

The point of the tirade, observed Shapiro, 'as far as I can understand it, was to demonstrate that theatre is happening all the time, that it does not take place in a theatre under authoritarian direction, that it is created by people freed of their blocks, and therefore an evening of discussion (lousy words) such as this is absurd & shd [*sic*] not take place'. The hostility to language and to 'discussion' confirmed a tendency in the new theatre that Brustein would later comment upon: 'actors were refusing to perform unless they could appear in their own characters and speak their own lines; and it was not surprising, considering their questionable command of the language, that much of this work became physical rather than verbal'.[7] For his part, Shapiro observed mordantly that 'one pure theme emerged—hatred of all those who live by language, and of course hatred of the rational'. Even Norman Mailer, author of the recent *Armies of the Night*, was howled down when he tried to restore order and described as a 'Fascist' and 'money-lover'. Mailer, recalled Shapiro, 'stood there bathed in spit and enjoying it'. But not everyone had Mailer's taste for this sort of thing; indeed, Shapiro noticed that 'An old woman behind me was crying, she remembered Thomas Mann being shouted down by the brown shirts, & it was so similar, even some of the phrases.' And what of the intellectuals? 'Paul Goodman disappeared', noted Shapiro, and 'Susan Sontag was silent (I wd. guess she approved).' Perhaps surprisingly, Shapiro found himself also in approval. 'I enjoyed the carnage,' he told Oppen. 'Something of the split in myself was being acted out & it left me exhausted.' Shapiro could 'see the liberal point of view', but at the same time, he admitted, 'I like the release of energy': 'Something was being acted out that maybe has to be acted out. And sides were being formed.'

In his immediate response to Shapiro's letter, Oppen was unenthusiastic about this expression of 'raw energy'. 'I myself', he observed, 'can live only for "dead words" or rather, for their transparency. Not, surely, not for the opaque "blood"' (SL, 189). And his letter ends: 'The opposition and "the Blood" or the young bloods have rather an advantage   Need only shout, and indeed the blood responds———————' (SL, 190).[8] Oppen's rejection of the event seems straightforward enough, but, as it happens, this was not to be his final judgement. Shortly after, he wrote again to Shapiro saying that he was still 'Much preoccupied with your report of the living theatre', and that having thought more about the event 'I reverse myself' (SL, 191), meaning by this that he had subsequently come to acknowledge that a generation facing

---

[7] Brustein, *Culture Watch*, 86.

[8] The issue here is uncannily prefigured in the 'New Arts' section of 'Of Being Numerous': 'But I will listen to a man, I will listen to a man, and when I | speak I will speak, tho he will fail and I will fail. But I will | listen to him speak' (NCP, 167–8).

the draft might have reason to be impatient with orderly discussion and the kind of academic culture it supports.[9]

Oppen's indecision about the Living Theatre event was not, however, a sign of age or conservatism. As we have seen, he was a staunch opponent of the war in Vietnam and enthusiastically followed the emergence of the New Left and the vibrant youth culture that sustained it. Rather, Oppen's 'reversal', as he called it, resonated with that sense of a fundamental incompatibility between the aesthetic and the political he had first formulated in 'The Mind's Own Place'. Oppen's conclusion there that it is not 'the poet's business to use verse as an advanced form of rhetoric, nor to give to political statements the aura of eternal truth', certainly illuminates his response to the avant-garde activities of The Living Theatre.[10] For Oppen's 'reversal' of judgement showed that he could value such avant-gardism only as a pure expression of the political and nothing more. That might seem an unexceptionable view of the historical avant-gardes since we have grown used to celebrating their attempts to eliminate 'the distance between art and life' as proof of their entry into 'the immediately political sphere'.[11] For Oppen, however, it is a false immediacy that is at issue here: the work is exhausted in its performance, being absolutely of its time and leaving no remainder for further development. Oppen's thinking on this matter has much in common with another important essay of the period, Hans Magnus Enzensberger's 'The Aporias of the Avant-Garde' (1962) which argues against the performance aesthetic that

art without a moment of anticipation cannot even be thought of. It is contained in the very process of creation: the work is preceded by the design. The design, the project, does not appear in its realization. Every work of art, and the master-work in particular, has in it something unfinished; indeed, this necessary residue makes up its durability: only when it fades does the work fade with it.[12]

By contrast, the avant-gardist thought consumes itself in action, while the action itself is deliberately thoughtless, an expression of the 'blood', as Oppen put it, rather than of the intelligence. This substitution of emotion for thought

---

[9] See SL, 191: 'A young man in imminent danger of being sent to Vietnam or some other jungle does not, I suppose, consider it absolutely necessary that universities should function, or that industries should function, or that conferences on education——etc———Neither does his girl[.]' Oppen's 'reversal' is clear in the short poem included in the letter which attributes 'an exotic poetry | Between speech and action || Between action and theatre' to 'A pop culture | Of an elite | Engaged in revolt . . . '.

[10] 'Mind's Own Place', 182.

[11] Peter Bürger, *Theory of the Avant-Garde*, trans. Michael Shaw (Minneapolis: University of Minnesota Press, 1984), 50; Andrew Hewitt, *Fascist Modernism: Aesthetics, Politics, and the Avant-Garde* (Stanford, Calif.: Stanford University Press, 1993), 36.

[12] Hans Enzensberger, *The Consciousness Industry*, ed. Michael Roloff (New York: Seabury Press, 1974), 23.

made performance art something Oppen readily associated with Surrealism which, following Maritain, he had always viewed as pre-eminently an attempt 'to produce art not out of the experience of things but out of the subjectivity of the artist'.[13]

In their damaging subjectivism, Surrealism and performance art seemed to Oppen to take no account of art's limitations and of its inadequacy in the face of certain challenges—an inadequacy, of course, which it would have been contradictory for the avant-garde to acknowledge. In 'The Mind's Own Place', for example, he had observed that 'There are situations which cannot honorably be met by art, and surely no one need fiddle precisely at the moment that the house next door is burning'.[14] There are, in short, emergencies which demonstrate the incommensurability of art's resources to the demands of the real. Such conjunctures might be deemed to offer the avant-garde a ready passage into politics, but in Oppen's more astringent view the attempt to elide the political and the aesthetic has the ultimate effect of undermining both.

Anticipating something of the discourse of postmodernism, Oppen concluded that 'The avant garde has become a mass movement, a mass concern' (UCSD 16, 17, 8). With this new 'urban art' the aesthetic is no longer the property of the avant-garde as formerly conceived but has degenerated into what he rejects as the merely 'stylish [and] the chic', offering little more than a noisy and intoxicated reflection of the bourgeois culture it purports to subvert (UCSD 16, 16, 3).[15] As he writes in another unpublished note: 'The Advance guarde [*sic*] goes where the whole army is going. Meanwhile someone steps off into open, undevastated country. . . . This lateral step has behind it a force which shares the nature of the force of poetry' (UCSD 16, 18, 4).[16] In returning to the military origins of the term, Oppen now suggests that the avant-garde never really outstrips its followers and simply advances more quickly on a

---

13 'Selections from George Oppen's *Daybook*', ed. Dennis Young, *Iowa Review*, 18/3 (1988), 5.
14 'Mind's Own Place', 181.
15 Oppen refers here to what he calls the 'NY School SF School (meaning the Ferlinghettis) etc'. Cf. 'Selections from George Oppen's *Daybook*', ed. Young, 2: ' "avant garde": the distinction between the avant garde and anything I could wish to be is the distinction between writing stylishly and the attempt to say with lucidity some part of what has not been said'. In another comment to himself, Oppen remarks 'I am not avant-garde and do not "experiment": I improvise. I am an amateur, I don't know anything else to be' (UCSD, 16, 13, 3).
16 To make a rather similar point, Enzensberger, *Consciousness Industry*, 43–4, quotes a passage from Baudelaire's *Mon cœur mis à nu*: 'This habit of putting one's trust in military metaphors is characteristic not of unyielding minds but of minds that prefer discipline, in other words conformity, of minds in fetters, provincial minds that can only think collectively.' Enzensberger also notes of this idea of 'the forward march of the arts through history' (27) that 'Nobody knows what is up front, least of all he who has reached unknown territory. Against this uncertainty there is no insurance. Only someone willing to suffer the consequences of error can get involved with the future. The *avant* of the avant-garde contains its own contradiction: it can be marked out only a posteriori' (27–8).

shared terrain. In contrast, the 'lateral step' breaks the cycle of innovation and recuperation, expressing the force of an unassimilable newness and effectively leaving the avant-garde behind.

So Oppen would very deliberately take his distance from both contemporary avant-gardism and from any mainstream tendency urging traditionalism. But what exactly is denoted here by the 'new'? It is certainly not what goes under that name in the debate about the avant-garde which Peter Bürger's *Theory of the Avant-Garde* has fuelled. There the 'new' is a kind of second-order category that denotes 'a critique of traditional literary technique' rather than an authentically avant-gardist assault on the institution of art itself. The new, here, signals a merely 'modernist' horizon that is necessarily limited by its dialectical tie to tradition. As it happens, though, the contrasting avant-garde attempt to eliminate the distance between art and life itself lapses into contradiction since, as Bürger himself concedes, 'An art no longer distinct from the praxis of life but wholly absorbed in it will lose the capacity to criticise it, along with its distance'.[17] While this contradiction may ultimately be responsible for the death of the historical avant-gardes, the 'false sublation' of commodity aesthetics in more recent times seems to have left us looking yet again for a critical 'distance between art and the praxis of life'.[18]

The terms of this debate are clearly not ones Oppen would share and this accounts in part for his fundamental hostility to any concept of the avant-garde. For him, the creative 'now' is not the present tense of 'the praxis of life' but, as we have seen, the spatio-temporal 'thereness' of the poem itself. And if there is some kind of aporia at work here it has to do not with an unresolvable conflict between art and life, but rather with the irreducibility of the poem to discourse which in turn parallels the irreducibility of the real to thought. This aporia stands over against the false immediacy which Oppen associates with the political art of the avant-garde, instigating designedly 'opaque' uses of syntax, ellipsis, and line-ending to prevent an experience of the political from resolving itself into the universal claims of what he had called 'political statement'. Instead of what he perceives as the avant-gardist attack on the real, Oppen's poems announce an antithetical move to recover it. In these terms he speaks of 'the loss of the commonplace' (SL, 411 n. 5), thereby invoking the life-world of the everyday as the ground of shared experience and reversing the avant-garde gesture by which an ordinary urinal is shockingly projected into the realm of 'art'.[19] Indeed, in one late poem, he writes of the need 'to *save* the commonplace' (NCP, 270; my emphasis), to 'save' it perhaps from

---

[17] Bürger, *Theory of the Avant-Garde*, 49.   [18] Ibid. 54.
[19] Compare UCSD 16, 18, 2 where Oppen remarks on 'The anti-poetic in Williams's work—or mine. Anti the readymade.'

the dead embrace of an 'art' which, in the wake of the historical avant-gardes, speaks only in the idioms of style and fashion.

* * * * *

If Oppen felt the need to thus dissociate his sense of the aesthetic from that of sixties avant-gardism, the exchange with Shapiro also prompted him to consider once more the relation of his work to an earlier modernism. For it was in June 1969 that he met Ezra Pound again quite unexpectedly in the office of New Directions in New York. It was for both men an emotional encounter (their first meeting since the early thirties) and prompted Oppen to write two poems in which he deliberately reviewed the claims of the earlier avant-garde.[20] In the first of these, 'Of Hours', his 'Old friend' is clearly rebuked for his egotism—'What is it you "loved" | Twisting your voice', Oppen asks in a sharp reminder of Pound's 'What thou lovest well remains'[21]—but perhaps the most telling aspect of the poem is its way of proposing its own elliptical structure as a critique of Poundian self-certainty: 'Holes   pitfalls open | In the cop's accoutrement', Oppen writes, invoking not only the literally fissured landscape of the war in which he almost lost his own life, but also those syntactical 'holes' and hesitancies that against the poet's will work to undermine his attempt to order and police his poem. Indeed, if the 'sap' of his legacy is 'not exhausted' it is because of his poem's resistant musicality ('Movement | of the stone') rather than because of the truths it claims to represent. In the closing lines, Pound pursues his way 'homeward' but remains 'unteachable'. Oppen implies that it was the poet's monopoly on 'truth' that led to the 'twisting' of his voice, and his own poem attempts a directness which equates sincerity with the recognition of limits—of, we might say, the world's resistance to metaphor (hence we have the 'rubble' of Alsace rather than Pound's visionary stone).[22] Oppen's presentation of Pound has a certain pathos, though it is one that is again complicated by a long-standing suspicion of modernist avant-gardism:

> Lonely sister my sister but why did I weep
> Meeting that poet again what was that rage

---

[20] For a brief account of the meeting, see Oppen, 'Pound in the U.S.A., 1969', *Sagetrieb*, 1/1 (1982), 119.

[21] Pound, *Cantos*, 534–45: 'What thou lovest well remains, | the rest is dross . . .'.

[22] See 'Mind's Own Place', 175: 'It is possible to find a metaphor for anything, an analogue: but the image is encountered, not found; it is an account of the poet's perception, of the act of perception; it is a test of sincerity, a test of conviction, the rare poetic quality of truthfulness.' On 'limits', see 'An Adequate Vision: A George Oppen Daybook', ed. Michael Davidson, *Ironwood*, 26 (Fall 1985), 24: '[William] Bronk. An intellectual insight which becomes an emotional force thru the recognition of its limits, the recognition of its failures'.

Before Leger's art poster
In war time Paris. . . .

(NCP, 218)

The lack of punctuation characteristic of these later poems evokes the moving nature of the two poets' encounter but it subtly allows Oppen's emotion to be inhabited also by a kind of rage in face of a refusal by the artist—Pound or Léger—to acknowledge the incommensurability of his work to the demands of the real.[23]

The second poem, 'Speech at Soli', similarly takes Pound to task for his failure of vision: 'war in incoherent | sunlight it will not || cohere it will NOT . . .' (NCP, 239).[24] Only in a self-legitimating 'game of thought' can the 'incoherence' of war be sublated in aesthetic form. Oppen's title, he explained in an interview, derived from his discovery that 'the etymology of "solipsism" was the name of a place, Soli. The Greeks, apparently, thought that town somewhere in Italy to be a very barbarous place'.[25] In contrast, then, to the Poundian 'solipsism', poetic language, in Oppen's view, allows us not to grasp 'truth' as concept, but, quite the opposite, to accept limits to our cognitive ambitions by creating a language which recognizes what is now firmly established as the 'impenetrability' of the world. This sense of encountering the world as something irreducibly other gives poetic language an unresolved, lacunary quality, with syntactical openness and hesitancy constantly proposing shared relationships and experiences without formulating them absolutely. In a very specific sense, the language, with its 'holes' and 'pitfalls', seems to fail in its attempt to grasp the real, and thought becomes a matter of doubting rather than of asserting or believing.[26] But it is this very failure, the 'holes' opening up in the fabric of language, that allows the disclosure of 'the commonplace that pierces or erodes || The mind's structure' (NCP, 212). In an early letter to Cid Corman, Oppen had explained that

I think of form as immediacy, as the possibility of being grasped. I look for the thinnest possible surface. ——at times, no doubt, too thin : a hole, a lapse . . . There is no

---

[23] See MAL, 177 on Oppen's response to the new Léger exhibit in wartime Paris: 'I nearly went beserk; there was no way to express my anger at these Parisians who could care about such mediocrity at such a time.'

[24] The lines allude, of course, to Pound's Canto CXVI, 810, 'I cannot make it cohere . . .'.

[25] 'An Interview with George and Mary Oppen', conducted by Kevin Power *Montemora*, 4 (1978), 200. Oppen's etymology seems rather awry here. Soli was an ancient Anatolian seaport. According to the *Encyclopedia Britannica*, 'The bad Greek spoken there gave origin to the term solecism (Greek *soloikismos*).' The usual derivation of 'solipsism' is from *solus* and *ipse*.

[26] See SL, 118–19: 'Doubt, rather than faith, is the motivation of an ethic of pity. The one ethic left to us—or, or??' Oppen quotes elliptically his friend and fellow poet William Bronk to the effect that 'it is by our most drastic failures that we may perhaps catch glimpses of something real, of something which is' (SL, 167; the passage is given in full at SL, 396 n.21.).

point in defending lapses———but that is, of all risks the one I plan to live with   I am much more afraid of a solid mass of words. (SL 40)[27]

The discursive order of 'a solid mass of words' is 'pierced' by something that resists thematization, by 'The absolutely incomprehensible, which pierces any possible structure of the mind'.[28]

This particular sense of lacunary structure is quite different from Pound's use of ellipsis and juxtaposition in the late Cantos. As I have suggested elsewhere, *Thrones* (1959), the last main sequence of the poem, shows Pound increasingly drawn to formulations of absolute identity, notably through expressions of archaic monetary values such as '8 stycas: one scat', '2 doits to a boodle', and so on.[29] The 'ideogrammic method' he had derived from Ernest Fenollosa originally seemed to offer resistance to an identificatory mode of thinking that would subsume objects to concepts, expressing instead a kind of remainder always in excess of the process of adequation (in defining the word 'red', for example, the ideogram containing 'rose', 'cherry', 'iron rust', and 'flamingo' produces multiple displacements away from any simple identification of subject and predicate). By way of contrast, expressions such as '2 doits to a boodle' leave no remainder and produce a moment of reified identity in which being can express itself only as quantity, the 'is' a matter of mere equivalence. Such definitions aspire to become performative utterance, the imperfectly veiled assertions of an absolute and remote authority.

* * * * *

The Living Theatre and Ezra Pound, then: two examples of avant-gardism which could not be more unlike each other but which when viewed through the lens of Oppen's ongoing poetic concerns had more in common than might at first appear. For in different ways each foreclosed upon the 'is' of being, the one by making it merely a moment of ephemeral presence, the other by making it contingent on the authority of the writer. Oppen's new work might

---

[27] See also the interesting account of 'perforation' in Oppen's later work, in Eleanor Berry, 'Language made Fluid: The Grammetrics of George Oppen's Recent Poetry', *Contemporary Literature*, 25/3 (1984), 305–22.

[28] 'Selections from George Oppen's *Daybook*', ed. Young, 12. This motif of 'piercing' occurs in several poems. See, in addition to 'The Occurrences', NCP, 212, 'Of this all things . . .', NCP, 129 ('everything is pierced | By her presence'), 'Some San Francisco Poems', NCP, 222 ('Pierced and touched'). Oppen may also have recalled the use of the same word in Simone Weil's *Waiting on God*, trans. Emma Crawford (London: Routledge and Kegan Paul, 1951), 78: 'this nail has pierced a hole through all creation, through the thickness of the screen which separates the soul from God'. Oppen quotes part of the passage about the nail at the beginning of 'Of Hours'.

[29] See my ' "2 doits to a boodle": Reckoning with *Thrones*', *Textual Practice*, 18/2 (June 2004), 233–49. The quotations are from Canto XCVII, but examples of circular definition abound in this sequence.

be read as a search for ever more extreme ways of recovering that 'is' of being by freeing language from the closure of predication and from the pitfalls of 'political generalisation'.[30] After the publication of *Of Being Numerous*, in fact, he seems to have become increasingly preoccupied with what we might call the grammatical conditions of poetic singularity. An important intertext in this regard is Fenollosa's *The Chinese Written Character as a Medium for Poetry*, the 'big essay on verbs', as Pound called it.[31] Fenollosa's attack on Western habits of generalization and what we might now call identity-thinking is well known and I shall not rehearse it here.[32] I shall note just his objection to the conventional definition of the sentence as 'uniting a subject and a predicate':

the grammarian falls back on pure subjectivity. *We* do it all; it is a little private juggling between our right and left hands. The subject is that about which *I* am going to talk; the predicate is that which *I* am going to say about it. The sentence according to this definition is not an attribute of nature but an accident of man as a conversational animal.[33]

Fenollosa argues, of course, that the sentence *should* be precisely 'an attribute of nature' and this because 'The verb must be the primary fact of nature, since motion and change are all that we can recognise in her' (19). In Fenollosa's view, the Chinese language is rooted in the transfer of verbal energies, and it thus mirrors nature in its way of disclosing activities in things rather than submitting them to the rule of external description—the tree 'greens itself' rather than being merely described as 'green', an attribute it otherwise shares with an indefinite number of other things (15).[34]

What is particularly interesting in this comparison with Fenollosa's theory is that while Oppen, as we shall see, has similar reservations about the

[30] 'Mind's Own Place', 176.
[31] *The Selected Letters of Ezra Pound 1907–1941*, ed. D. D. Paige (London: Faber and Faber, 1971), 82.
[32] The best accounts are Herbert N. Schneidau, *Ezra Pound: The Image and the Real* (Baton Rouge: Louisiana State University Press, 1969) and D. S. Marriott, 'An Introduction to the Poetry of J. H. Prynne, 1962–1977', D.Phil. diss., University of Sussex (1993). See also Marriott's 'Aspects of *Ousia* and Transitive Verb Form in Fenollosa's *The Chinese Written Character* and Pound's *Cantos*', in Karl Simms (ed.), *Language and the Subject* (Amsterdam and Atlanta, Ga.: Rodopi, 1997), 65–73.
[33] Ernest Fenollosa, *The Chinese Written Character as a Medium for Poetry*, ed. Ezra Pound (San Francisco: City Lights Books, 1969), 11. Further references will be given in the text. Schneidau notes (62) that conventionally 'the predication seems to come from us instead of the thing itself'.
[34] See Marriott, 'Introduction to the Poetry of Prynne', 9: 'Pound . . . agreed with Fenollosa's objections to the separation of ontological particulars from subject-predicate process in copulative sentence forms. The latter were seen as placing the subject as exterior to the process, converting the process into object transfer rather than placing the subject as integral to the process.'

subject-predicate form, he does not share Fenollosa's ideal of a syntax which is somehow reflective of natural process or the related desire for subject and predicate as 'simply aspects of a unitary process'.[35] Oppen's poetics is, from the first, dissociated from that sort of representationalism, and we may recall that, attractive as Fenollosa's attack on conventional grammar might seem, its mimetic emphasis would eventually supply the 'natural' grounding of Pound's ideogrammic or 'totalitarian' ethics. In Oppen's view, Pound's appeal to some sort of absolutely grounded, 'natural' grammar simply concealed a more conventional rhetorical insistence. His divergence from Poundian modernism was thus inevitable and, as comments in his personal notes and 'Daybooks' show, not just for ideological reasons but for technical, poetic ones as well, hence his repeated criticism of Pound's 'argument' as a 'game of thought' in which each 'piece' has its meaning assigned in advance.[36] It may seem odd that Oppen should fault the elliptical and fragmented modes of *The Cantos* for being an 'argument', but his choice of that word points up a significant divergence between his poetics and Pound's. At issue are not merely the *argumentative* habits of the older poet's work and the hectoring tone of the late stages of his poem, but, more importantly, what Oppen sees as a tendency there to closure and solipsism. The two are, for him, closely connected and together characterize a discourse that must always fall short of the genuinely 'poetic'.

In his own quarrel with conventional grammar, however, Oppen drew not on Fenollosa but on Hegel.[37] As with his reading of Heidegger, he was not attempting to 'master' the philosopher's work but approached it in his own idiosyncratic and intensely directed way. As we saw in Oppen's reading of Heidegger's essay in *Identity and Difference*, particular passages or phrases could take on a kind of talismanic significance for Oppen, not just as those 'luminous details' that for Pound seemed to compress vital truth, but rather as clues to the labyrinth of his own thinking. The 'test' of such materials in the quest for truth was not a matter of judgement weighing the value of 'fact', but

---

[35] Marriott, 'Aspects of *Ousia*', 70.

[36] 'Selections from George Oppen's *Daybook*', ed. Young, 6. Cf. UCSD 16, 16, 9: 'the danger is of the chess-board: on which everything has already been named'.

[37] Fenollosa's own intellectual background was in part informed by a reading of Hegel: see the account in Lawrence W. Chisholm, *Fenollosa: The Far East and American Culture* (New Haven: Yale University Press, 1963). Roxana Preda, *Ezra Pound's (Post)Modern Poetics and Politics: Logocentrism, Language, and Truth* (New York: Peter Lang, 2001), 295 n. 16 argues that Fenollosa was certainly familiar with Hegel's negative account of the Chinese character, but notes (31) that 'While Hegel privileged the name, as *signification of things*, valuing its directness and its appeal to the intellect, Fenollosa preferred the verb as acting out "*transferences of force*" in nature.' For the view that Fenollosa's theory derived from his misunderstanding of Hegel, see Joseph Riddel, 'Decentering the Image: The "Project" of "American" Poetics', in Josué Harari (ed.), *Textual Strategies: Perspectives in Post-Structuralist Criticism* (London: Methuen, 1980), 322–58.

of thought's ability to move forward, to progress beyond some blockage or aporia it had gone out of its way to encounter. In that movement lay also the possibility not of some perfectly finished artwork, but of the discovery of one's own reflection embodied in the 'objective' shape of the poem—yet another twist in Oppen's ongoing definition of Objectivism.

His first significant reference to Hegel occurs in a letter to fellow poet William Bronk in 1967. Here Oppen alludes to 'a sentence of Hegel's: "Disagreement indicates where the subject matter ceases, it is what the subject matter is not"' (SL, 169). In his interview the following year with L. S. Dembo, Oppen quotes Hegel's sentence again, adding: 'The important thing is that if we are talking about the nature of reality, then we are not really talking about our *comment about it*; we are talking about the apprehension of some *thing*, whether it *is* or not, whether one can make a thing of it or not.'[38] The quotation appears yet again in a letter of the same year to Jerome Rothenberg where Oppen uses it to affirm what he calls 'the primary concern with postulation': '"Disagreement marks where the subject matter ends; it is what the subject matter is not"—a remark by that primitive, Hegel' (SL, 179).[39]

The sentence to which Oppen keeps alluding is to be found in the 'Preface' to Hegel's *Phenomenology*, and it is clear from the form of citation he used in a 1972 letter to L. S. Dembo that the text from which he quotes is not J. B. Baillie's translation (1910; rev. edn. 1931), but the revisionary one of Walter Kaufmann in his *Hegel: Reinterpretation, Texts, and Commentary* (1965).[40] Kaufmann provides a complete translation of the 'Preface' with a commentary *en face*, and Oppen, it seems, used this critical edition to undertake a close reading of what Kaufmann describes as 'Hegel's most important essay' (113).[41] The sentence that draws Oppen's attention is rendered by Kaufmann

[38] Dembo, '"Objectivist" Poet', 162. Oppen's observation inevitably recalls Pound's view of 'good prose' and 'good verse': 'It presents. It does not comment' (quoted in Schneidau, *Pound*, 25), though, as will be noted below, his idea of 'presentation' is different in its sense of agency from Oppen's talk of 'apprehension'. Compare, too, Pound's rejection of 'this talk about the matter, rather than presentation' (*Literary Essays*, 29).

[39] For discussion of Oppen's reference to Hegel as 'that primitive', see below, pp. 126–7.

[40] Walter Kaufmann, *Hegel: Reinterpretation, Texts, and Commentary* (New York: Doubleday and Company, 1965); hereafter cited as Kaufmann, with further references given in the text. In the letter to Dembo (SL, 241), Oppen cites a passage as 'Preface to the phenomenology 11. 1 (6)', using the system of section numbering devised by Kaufmann. The quotations given in this letter and elsewhere indicate that Oppen is using the Kaufmann version. The translation by A. V. Miller which is now regarded as definitive was not published until 1977. John Peck ('George Oppen and the World in Common: A Descriptive Polemic', in GOMP, 83) locates the sentence in Hegel's 'Preface' but gives an incorrect page reference to Baillie's translation. The Oppens mention 'Kaufmann's translation of Hegel' in McAleavey, 'Oppen on Literature, Literary Figures and Issues', 120–1.

[41] Herbert Marcuse, *Reason and Revolution: Hegel and the Rise of Social Theory*, 2nd edn. (London: Routledge and Kegan Paul, 1968), 97 describes the 'Preface' as 'one of the greatest

as follows: 'In the same way, the difference is really the limit of the subject matter: it indicates where the subject matter ceases, or it is what the subject matter is not' (372).[42] Hegel is here distinguishing between, on the one hand, an approach to philosophy which evaluates systems of interpretation by differentiating between them in terms of their aims and objectives, and, on the other, one which seeks to work through the various stages of a system, immersing the reader in its detail. The first approach, says Hegel, is merely a beginning and one which necessarily adopts an external perspective: 'For instead of dealing with the subject matter, such talk is always outside it; instead of abiding in the subject matter and forgetting itself in it, such knowledge always reaches out for something else and really remains preoccupied with itself instead of sticking to, and devoting itself to, the subject matter' (372).[43] If we recall Oppen's view that the poet should give 'no possible impression of a statement having been *put* into verse' (SL, 104), we can see why Hegel's definition of dialectical thinking as based in the inseparability of thought and content should confirm this underlying principle of Oppen's poetics. Indeed, the sentence he quotes from the 'Preface' is part of an extended discussion of dialectical or speculative thinking in which Hegel argues that philosophy must remain 'inside' the subject matter, this involving, in Fredric Jameson's words, 'the attempt to think about a given object on one level, and at the same time to observe our own thought processes as we do so'.[44]

Oppen's use of the sentence from the 'Preface' to emphasize what he calls 'the primacy of the subject as against predicate' (SL, 180) is closely bound up with Hegel's call for a language that functions outside the grammatical parameters of the propositional form: 'only a philosophical exposition that

philosophical undertakings of all time'. The fact that Kaufmann translates only the 'Preface' may explain why Oppen's allusions do not extend beyond that part of the *Phenomenology*.

    42 Oppen clearly takes 'difference' in Kaufmann's sense of argument or disagreement (373). Cf. *Hegel's Phenomenology of Spirit*, trans. A. V. Miller (Oxford: Oxford University Press, 1977), 3: 'the specific difference of a thing is rather its limit; it is where the thing stops, or it is what the thing is not'. J. N. Findlay in his 'Analysis' appended to Miller's translation explains that 'merely to differentiate a system from others is to remain resolutely on its fringes' (ibid. 495).

    43 Cf. ibid. 434: 'Instead of entering into the immanent content of the matter, it always looks over the whole and stands above the individual existence of which it speaks, i.e., it simply overlooks it. Scientific knowledge, however, demands precisely that we surrender to the life of the object or—and this is the same—that we confront and express its inner necessity.' As Kaufmann remarks (435), 'What matters to Hegel is that the impetus that leads from point to point should not come from the arbitrary disposition of the writer but from the subject matter.' As Adorno observes in *Negative Dialectics*, trans. E. B. Ashton (New York: Continuum, 1973), 144 Hegel 'wanted a philosophy without detachable form, without a method to be employed independently of the matter'.

    44 Fredric Jameson, *Marxism and Form: Twentieth-Century Dialectical Theories of Literature* (Princeton: Princeton University Press, 1971), 340. Jameson (339) uses the passage containing the sentence Oppen quotes to outline Hegel's theory of dialectical thinking.

strictly precluded the usual relation of the parts of a sentence would attain the goal of being really vivid', observes Hegel (448). The dead 'is' of mere equality expressed in the ordinary proposition is only conditionally true; it is, in Kaufmann's words, 'one-sided and therefore untenable as soon as it is embraced consistently' (133).[45] Hegel thus cautions against 'mixing up the speculative style with the argumentative style so that what is said of the subject sometimes has the meaning of its Concept, at other times only the meaning of its predicate or attribute' (446, 448). Hegel's critique of 'argumentative' thinking (which almost certainly reinforced Oppen's own dismissal of 'argument') emphasizes again 'its freedom from the content and the vanity that looks down on it' (440): 'Truth is its own self-movement, while this is the method of knowledge that remains external to it' (426).[46]

At the core of Hegel's opposition of 'argumentative thinking' to 'the thinking that comprehends' (442) lies his critique of the subject-predicate form of ordinary propositions which, as we shall see, speaks to Oppen's own sense of poetry as 'postulation' rather than as 'argument'. 'Disagreement', in his version of Hegel's sentence, carries us outside the 'subject matter' itself and situates us instead in the realm of a thinking subject engaged in predication. As one commentator puts it, 'Where, as in the "formal proposition", the predicates of a subject signify what is "attributed" to the subject by someone thinking, strong language is needed to indicate that in the "speculative proposition" predicates are activities...of the subject *itself*. It is for this reason, too, that knowledge of objects is revelatory of *self* to the knower.'[47] Fredric Jameson provides a further gloss on this important point, proposing a distinction between 'logical' and 'ontological tautology', the latter being characteristic of dialectical thinking: in the former, 'where a proposition had seemed to link two separate, independent entities, they suddenly turn out to

---

[45] Cf. Quentin Lauer, SJ, *A Reading of Hegel's* Phenomenology of Spirit (New York: Fordham University Press, 1976), 288–9: 'When [Hegel] says that the propositions of mathematics are simply expressions of equality and hence "dead", he is emphasizing once more the dynamic character of the "is" in the "speculative" proposition.' Cf. Marcuse, *Reason and Revolution*, 102: 'The locus of truth is not the proposition, but the dynamic system of speculative judgments in which every single judgment must be "sublated" by another, so that only the whole process represents the truth.' Judith Butler, *Subjects of Desire: Hegelian Reflexions in Twentieth-Century France* (New York: Columbia University Press, 1987), 18 observes of Hegel's style that 'When "is" is the verb at the core of any claim, it rarely carries a familiar burden of predication, but becomes transitive in an unfamiliar and foreboding sense, affirming the inherent movement in "being", disrupting the ontological assumptions that ordinary language lulls us into making.'

[46] Kaufmann, 419 notes in the case of Hegel's example of mathematical demonstration that 'according to Hegel, we witness the development of knowledge about something, but not the development of that which is known.' Findlay, in *Hegel's Phenomenology*, trans. Miller, 503 notes that 'Argumentative thinking connects the content it thinks of with its own self as judging subject.'

[47] Lauer, *Reading*, 295–6 (his emphases).

have been the same thing all along, and the very act of thinking dissolves away. Here [in ontological tautology] the identity is not that between two words or two concepts, but rather between subject and object itself, between the process of thinking and the very reality on which it is exercised, which it attempts to apprehend.'[48] Oppen's own dissociation of 'argument' from 'consciousness' is a move in exactly this direction: 'Not argument of thought, nor even the argument of the I, but the argument of consciousness. | Consciousness in itself and of itself carries the principle of actualness | for it itself is actual.'[49]

In a letter to John Taggart, part of this passage reappears, this time as a quotation: 'Whatever may be doubted, the actuality of consciousness cannot be doubted. "Therefore consciousness in itself, of itself carries the principle of actualness." This is indeed the law and the prophets. It can happen in the poem. Perhaps this should have been the meaning of "objectivism"' (SL, 290).[50] Oppen here seems to be giving his own characteristically free and half-remembered version of the following passage from Hegel's 'Preface': 'The spiritual alone is the actual; it is [i] the essence or being-in-itself; [ii] that which relates itself and is determinate, that which is other and for itself; and [iii] that which in this determinateness and being outside itself remains in itself—or, in other words, it is in and for itself' (396). Oppen's reworking of the passage again emphasizes thought as 'process' rather than as inert 'generalization' and thus runs parallel to Hegel's way of contrasting a 'complex movement of thought' with the 'fixity' of ordinary propositions.[51] That 'process' is blocked by the copulative form of the proposition which tends either to conflate or divide subject and predicate terms, thus situating the subject outside the dynamic form of reflection which, for Hegel, allows the self to find itself in the other. In one of his *Daybooks*, Oppen argues in similar vein that 'We do not sit outside of reality, think abstract thoughts of setting ourselves problems about

---

[48] Jameson, *Marxism and Form*, 341–2.

[49] 'Selections from George Oppen's *Daybook*', ed. Young, 6.

[50] The passage is also referred to a number of times in the unpublished manuscript headed 'The Romantic Virtue' (discussed below, pp. 145–55) and plays an important part in two late poems, 'The Book of Job and a Draft of a Poem to Praise the Paths of the Living' (see NCP, 245) and 'Who Shall Doubt' (NCP, 259). The phrase 'the law and the prophets' is from Matthew 22: 40.

[51] See Raymond Geuss, *Morality, Culture, and History: Essays on German Philosophy* (Cambridge: CUP, 1999), 87: 'speculative propositions' are 'momentary expressions of a certain complex movement of thought and not equivalent to ordinary propositions or sets of such propositions'. Cf. ibid. 94: 'for Hegel, philosophy is a continuous, in fact infinite, process of reflective argumentation in which any individual proposition or set of propositions is no more than an idealized position, a geometric point on the itinerary through which reflection moves. Taken out of this process, isolated and fixed, a proposition is a mere *caput mortuum*.' Hegel (Kaufmann, 416) rejects 'dogmatic thinking' as 'nothing else than the opinion that the true consists in a proposition that is a fixed result and that is known immediately'.

reality which is somehow visible to us. On the contrary, life has led us into the subject matter itself (final phrase derived from Hegel)'.[52]

Another letter from Oppen to Dembo makes the same point by elliptical reference to a related passage in the *Preface*:

'. . . the propositions   : God is what is eternal, the moral world order, or love and so forth. . . . In a proposition of this sort one begins with the word God   This by itself is a senseless sound. . . . only the predicate fills the name with content and meaning. . . . it is not clear why they do not begin with the eternal, the moral world order, etc . . . without adding the senseless sound as well'. . . . | 'the individual is the absolute form . . . the immediate certainty of himself. . . . unconditioned being' (SL, 240–1)[53]

Hegel is arguing that in the propositional form the subject—'God' in this case—is merely a 'senseless sound' and acquires meaning only through its predicate. The subject thus becomes merely 'a fixed point to which predicates are affixed as to their support', and it is not 'represented as the movement of that which reflects itself into itself' (394, 392). In Hegel's terms, then, the subject of the ordinary proposition is not really a subject at all, since as a fixed point it has no way of *becoming itself*. As one commentator puts it, 'It will be true only by *becoming* true, in a process of self-determination which is identical with the process of consciousness coming to *know* it; only as the "result" of this process is the absolute truly absolute.'[54] In his notes Oppen remarked similarly, and with Hegel in mind, that rather than deal in generalizations, the poem should function as 'process of thought. . . . The primacy of the nominative, which Hegel spoke of, the primacy of subject. *Revelation of the nominative: there can be no predicate of revelation. It is never which is which*' (UCSD 16, 15, 9; emphasis in original).

---

[52] 'Selections from George Oppen's *Daybook*', ed. Young, 4.

[53] See Kaufmann, 392, 394: 'The need to represent the absolute as subject has employed the propositions: God is what is eternal, or the moral world order, or love, and so forth. In such propositions the true is only posited straightway as the subject, but it is not represented as the movement of that which reflects itself into itself. In a proposition of this kind one begins with the word God. This by itself is a senseless sound, a mere name; only the predicate says what he is and fills the name with content and meaning; the empty beginning becomes actual knowledge only in this end. For this reason, it is not clear why they do not speak merely of the eternal, of the moral world order, and so forth—or as the ancients did, of pure Concepts, such as being, the One, and so forth—in sum, only of that which supplies the meaning, without adding the senseless sound as well.' For the second quotation, see Kaufmann, 398: 'the individual is the absolute form, i.e., he is the immediate certainty of himself and, if this expression should be preferred, he is therefore unconditioned being'.

[54] Lauer, *Reading*, 277. For further commentary on the passage in question, see Richard E. Aquila, 'Predication and Hegel's Metaphysics', *Kant-Studien*, 64 (1973), 241. Kaufmann (391) observes that 'What Hegel means by a subject is that which makes itself what it becomes.'

By the late sixties, Oppen was describing *Discrete Series* to Jerome Rothenberg as precisely 'my own attempt toward the primacy of subject as against predicate'—'I am for further reducing the mechanism of predicate   which "marks where the subject matter ends" ' (SL, 180). One short poem from that early volume will indicate something of what Oppen has in mind.

> This land:
> The hills, round under straw;
> A house
>
> With rigid trees
>
> And flaunts
> A family laundry,
> And the glass of windows
>
> (NCP, 16)

Verbal energy is so muffled here that when we arrive at 'flaunts' we are almost inclined to read it as some archaic noun, while, paradoxically, the adjective 'round' suggests for a moment that the hills 'round themselves' under straw. The oddness of those ambiguities is further compounded by the deliberately broken-backed syntax of the poem: '*And* flaunts'. No judgement is made, though the sequence of appositional phrases sets up dissociations that the reader is invited to weigh: the round hills, under straw, on the one hand, the rigid trees associated with the house that 'flaunts' itself, on the other. But does this simple contrast really sum up 'This land'? If that phrase implies 'America', then the colon—at once expansive and offhand—suggests that it both does and does not. At the same time, the punctilious semicolon of the second line seems to contrast a careful economy with the poem's unpunctuated final line and its interminable windows. The economy, of course, is in one sense that of the poem itself, as its withholding of predication leaves little room for the poet to 'flaunt' *him*self through conventional forms of introspection or 'argumentative thinking'. The poet's thought, in other words, appears not as 'comment' on the subject matter but is immanent to it. The emphatic 'This' with which the poem opens thus affirms the immediacy of its occasion, even as the spatial figuration highlights the pivotal 'With' as if to confirm the poem's attention to relationality as both its syntax and its theme.

We may now be in a position to see why in his response to Rothenberg's path-breaking anthology *Technicians of the Sacred* Oppen couples 'the primary concern with postulation' with his quotation from 'that primitive, Hegel'. Oppen is being ironic, of course, in his description of Hegel, suggesting that this 'primary concern' is hardly a feature of 'primitive' thought alone. In his follow-up letter to Rothenberg, however, Oppen speaks of *Discrete Series* as 'my own attempt toward the primacy of subject as against predicate Which seems to me a path still toward the "primitive" whether or not in the sense of historical repetition' (SL, 180). Oppen finds in Rothenberg's anthology *Technicians of the Sacred* a 'similarity of approach' between his own technique in *Discrete Series* and 'some of the African and Esquimaux' poems. Oppen may be thinking of the Yoruba 'praise-poems' translated in Rothenberg's anthology. 'Yoruba Praises' is one example:

> Shango is the death who kills money with a big stick
> The man who dies will die in his home
> Shango strikes the one who is stupid
> He wrinkles his nose & the liar runs off
> Even when he does not fight, we fear him. . . . [55]

As Rothenberg notes in his comments on the 'praise-poem', 'At its simplest it's the stringing-together of a series of praise-names (usually independent utterances) describing the qualities owned by a particular man, god, animal, plant, place, etc.' It entails a technique comparable, says Rothenberg, to contemporary modes of collage and assemblage, 'in which a series of phrases are [*sic*] made to turn around a single subject-as-pivot'.[56] One can see how Oppen might have read this description of 'subject' in terms of his idea ('derived from Hegel') that 'life has led us into the subject matter itself'. So too, the open syntax of many of these poems, with their accumulative rather than propositional structures and their dependence on substantival and gerundive forms rather than the grammar of 'argument', clearly seemed to Oppen to share something with his own early poems:

> Crushed fire extending
> fire having watched fire extending
> wood for the fire
> bends expands. . . . [57]

Yet the idea of the 'primitive' was always an ambivalent one for Oppen. In his notes, for example, he defines it like this: ' "Primitive" (the name for it is something like the first light || Primitive. First things in that humanity is the light of the world. The *primitive fact: the existence of the world* and that the light of the world is our humanity (our humanity is the light of the world "Primitive" i.e., first things' (UCSD 16, 15, 5; emphases in original). This is arguably the sense in which 'primitive' would be used as the title

---

[55] Jerome Rothenberg (ed.), *Technicians of the Sacred: A Range of Poetries from Africa, America, Asia & Oceania* (1968; New York: Anchor Books, 1969), 39.

[56] Ibid. 418, 419.

[57] Ibid. 75. This poem, 'Snake Chant/Storm Chant', begins: 'Winding throwing forward | writhing throwing forward | skin of snake rising | to heaven rising . . .'.

of his last volume of poems, the word denoting the originary, the 'first things', or what he calls in an earlier letter 'the open world' (SL, 186).[58] On the other hand, as he notes in another passage in his notes, 'primitive men   tribal men were born into terror much greater than ours', and he concludes that 'the wisdom of primitive man——tho it was wisdom——is the wisdom from which I most wish to free myself || a wisdom whose purpose was to establish limits to freedom, limits to the freedom of the mind' (UCSD 16, 15, 3). These 'limits', imposed by fetish and superstition, and inciting terror and guilt, contrast with the forms of poetic thinking that carry us out into the 'open world'.

Yet, like the Imagist texts to which it is distantly related, a poem such as 'This land' has its own limits. Here, we might say, what Oppen terms 'the primacy of the subject' depends a little too literally on the emphatic foregrounding of nouns in a radically reduced syntactical format. This Oppen acknowledges in the letter to Rothenberg, observing that 'In the later books I've struggled to broaden the statement beyond the nouns   Discrete Series is not concerned with predicates' (SL, 179). Rather as Pound's poetics had developed from the static to the 'moving' image,[59] so Oppen's work would move as we saw in earlier chapters, from the noun-based 'statement' to poems in which shifters, conjunctions, and prepositions would be brought to unusual prominence in an attempt to capture the movement and texture of poetic thinking. In that shift, Oppen's reading of Hegel's 'Preface' offered a powerful means of clarifying what 'objectification' might entail. For as we have already noted and as Oppen would say frequently in interview, the term applied not to the presentation of 'objects' but rather to the objectification of poetic form. And with Hegel's 'Preface' now in mind, 'form' might be dialectically conceived as an objectification of thought, as an externalization of thought which could then be grasped as other to itself rather than as mere self-expression. From this point of view 'objectification' thus refers to two different but related aspects of the poem: first, it names an attitude toward the object-world which regards it as given or as 'postulated', taken for granted. Such a world, to use one of Oppen's favourite words, is ultimately 'impenetrable', preserving its non-identicality in the face of the imperious demands of the ego. Things present themselves for reflection, but it is thought which, instead of conforming them to its own demands, now grasps itself in the object. As Hegel puts it, 'To become true knowledge, or to generate the element of science which is her pure Concept itself, it [spirit] has to work its way through a long journey' (400).

---

58 The letter, touching on the Old English and Icelandic sagas, is to George Johnston, translator of *The Saga of Gisli*. Oppen associates the 'open world' with Northern antiquity.

59 See Pound, *ABC of Reading* (London: Faber and Faber, 1961), 52.

That 'journey' entails 'a relating-to-an-other which at the same time relates to itself';[60] as Hegel puts it, consciousness 'must become an object for itself, but just as immediately an object which is sublimated, reflected into itself' (396). I want to suggest that Oppen is interested in undertaking only part of this 'journey', that he seeks out that first moment of objectification but deliberately stops short of what Hegel terms 'the return into oneself'.[61] As a result, this version of the Hegelian trajectory makes no claim to any final or absolute clarity; indeed, as Charles Taylor observes, from the Hegelian point of view, 'lack of definition and reflective unclarity are essential to art because it is a mode of consciousness embodied in an external work, rather than in the inwardness of conceptual description. When we are conceptually clear, the work is superfluous.'[62] Oppen's version of the Hegelian 'journey' will thus not complete the circle by which (as Adorno puts it) Hegel secures 'the identity of identity and nonidentity'.[63] Instead, poetic form registers a sort of resistance to conceptual resolution, leaving a remainder which thought cannot penetrate: 'That which exists of itself can not be explained   it cannot be analyzed, it is the object of contemplative thought, it is known by "indwelling". The Given' (SL, 115). That proposition demonstrates how Oppen's abbreviated version of the Hegelian 'journey' is inextricably bound up with his concurrent reading of Heidegger whose term *In-sein* is invoked here.[64] So too the emphatic appeal to 'The Given' denotes pre-predicative being (Heidegger's way of avoiding 'what the subject matter is not') and reminds us that Oppen seems not to have read on into the *Phenomenology*, thereby missing Hegel's chapter on 'Sense-Certainty', with its conceptual presentation of shifters or singulars as, paradoxically, universal terms.[65] Everything that we have seen so far of Oppen's poetics suggests, however, that he would have not been persuaded by Hegel's attempt to submit singularity to the rule of the concept.

* * * * *

Oppen's use of a third passage from Hegel's 'Preface' might provide an intimation of the kind of poetic thinking that Heidegger deployed against the

---

[60] Werner Marx, *Hegel's* Phenomenology of Spirit: *Its Point and Purpose—A Commentary on the Preface and Introduction* (New York and London: Harper & Row, 1975), 38.

[61] See e.g. Kaufmann, 432.

[62] Charles Taylor, *Hegel* (Cambridge: Cambridge University Press, 1975), 473.

[63] Adorno, *Negative Dialectics*, 7. See also Adorno, *Hegel: Three Studies*, trans. Shierry Weber Nicholsen (Cambridge, Mass.: MIT Press, 1993), p. xv.

[64] See below, App. A., p. 195.

[65] *Hegel's Phenomenology of Spirit*, 66: 'I point it out as a "Here", which is a Here of other Heres, or is in its own self a "simple togetherness of many Heres"; i.e. it is a universal. I take it up then as it is in truth, and instead of knowing something immediate I take the truth of it, or *perceive* it.'

systematic logic of *The Phenomenology*.[66] Oppen's own refusal to complete the Hegelian circle is, as it were, mirrored in his reduction of two sentences to several disconnected words in the late poem called 'From a Phrase of Simone Weil's and Some Words of Hegel's', published in *Seascape: Needle's Eye* (1972). Hegel's words exist here as little more than a resonant trace:

In   back   deep the jewel
The treasure
No   Liquid
Pride of the living life's liquid
Pride in the sandspit wind this ether this other this element all
It is I or I believe
We are the beaks of the ragged birds
Tune of the ragged bird's beaks
In the tune of the winds
Ob via   the obvious
Like a fire of straws
Aflame in the world or else poor people hide
Yourselves together   Place
Place where   desire
Lust of the eyes the pride of life and foremost of the storm's
Multitude moves the wave belly-lovely
Glass of the glass sea shadow of water
On the open water no other way
To come here the outer
Limit of the ego

(NCP, 211)[67]

It is characteristic of the difficulty of Oppen's later poems that the 'phrase' of Weil and the words of Hegel in the title have so far resisted identification.[68] The title in this sense gives with one hand as it takes away with the other, reminding us that when Oppen borrows philosophical concepts their 'substantiation' in the language of the poem can amount to a radical transformation of the insights of their original owners. Indeed, their sensuous embodiment or objectification

[66] See e.g. David Halliburton, *Poetic Thinking: An Approach to Heidegger* (Chicago: University of Chicago Press, 1981; David White, *Heidegger and the Language of Poetry* (Lincoln, Nebr.: University of Nebraska Press, 1978); Marc Froment-Meurice, *That Is To Say: Heidegger's Poetics* (Stanford, Calif.: Stanford University Press, 1998).

[67] My discussion of this poem modifies a preliminary account in my 'Modernising Modernism: From Pound to Oppen', *Critical Quarterly*, 44/2 (Summer 2002), 51–3.

[68] See Michael Davidson, NCP, 389. In 'Interview with George and Mary Oppen', conducted by Power, 199, Oppen might seem to suggest that the passage from Weil is the one used as an epigraph for 'Of Hours'. However, it is not clear from the context that he is definitely referring to 'From a Phrase . . .' here and the passage itself does not connect in any obvious way with the poem in question.

in the poem undermines their original status as connected 'ideas', suspending them in the promise of an immanent meaning rather than subordinating them to the demands of thematic or propositional development. We note first the lack of punctuation which is characteristic of Oppen's poems after *Of Being Numerous*, along with a foregrounding of substantival over verbal items, and the steady use of enjambement to obtain a marked stress on the initial word of most lines (an almost deliberate reversal of the signature end-stopped rhythms of Pound's *Cantos*). The rhythm is not so much hesitant as inchoate, reminding us that where predication completes, the pre-predicative entails a beginning again. In line with this, the phrase of Simone Weil and 'some words of Hegel's' provide not a key to the poem but merely points from which it will depart on a 'journey' of its own, so we should perhaps suspend for a moment the question of 'sources', and follow the lines of association that the poem most clearly offers. There is, first, the sea to figure space and desire—'the wave belly-lovely'—and the familiar celebration of the impenetrability of the real: 'ob via', the Latin meaning literally what is lying in the way, at hand. The poem seems to push toward some 'outer limit' where the homelessness of drifting 'On the open water' allows an apprehension of 'being' (in his *Daybook*, Oppen quotes Plotinus, 'Being, in which intelligence must come to rest. The defining limit of thought' (UCSD 16, 19, 6)).[69] The 'journey' toward that 'limit' seems to demand that we set our faces against 'the jewel | The treasure', relinquishing hidden riches for what is immediately at hand, 'Pride of the living life's liquid'.

If that sketches the poem's larger theme, there remains the matter of those 'words of Hegel's'. In the letter to Dembo in which Oppen quotes Hegel on predication, he also notes: 'self-consciousness is "the absolute"   self-consciousness is "science"   *science* used for the word *philosophy*' (SL, 241). The section in the 'Preface' to which Oppen alludes—II.6, in Kaufman's version—begins with the statement that 'The living substance is, further, that being which is in truth subject'. This phrasing may lie behind Oppen's talk of 'the living life's liquid', and Hegel's point here—that the experience of the world (substance) leads to self-consciousness (subject)[70]—relates directly to Oppen's references in the letter to 'the absolute' and to 'science' as philosophy. Indeed, as we read on into the next section of the 'Preface' (III. 2, in Kaufman's

---

[69] See the discussion below, p. 137. Variations on the phrase include 'this is a work of the intellect in that it seeks | The extreme outer limit of the ego' (UCSD 16, 15, 2).

[70] See e.g. Butler, *Subjects of Desire*, 9: 'The final satisfaction of desire is the discovery of substance as subject, the experience of the world as everywhere confirming that subject's sense of immanent metaphysical place.' It is just possible that Oppen's 'liquidity' echoes Hegel's opposition of the 'fluidity' of 'pure thinking' to 'the fixity of the pure concreteness which characterizes the ego even in its opposition to differentiated content and the fixity of differentiations which, posited in the element of pure thinking, share in the unconditionality of the ego' (Kaufmann, 408, 410).

numbering) we encounter the passage which provides the principal source for 'some words of Hegel's':

Pure self-recognition in absolute *otherness*, this *ether*, as such, is the ground and basis of science or knowledge in general. The beginning of philosophy presupposes or demands that consciousness dwell in this *element* (398; my emphases)

As Werner Marx observes of this passage, 'reflection is defined as the "element" which science as such, the scientific system, possesses as its pure "ether"; reflection consummates itself as the absolute subject, insofar as its "knowledge in universal form" is "*knowledge purely of itself* in absolute otherness to itself" '.[71]

When Hegel's words are incorporated in Oppen's poem, they acquire a new literalness: while 'ether' signifies a purified, originally divine 'element', it may also denote here the upper regions of space beyond the clouds, 'fair weather', and an 'extremely subtle fluid' (*OED*) that is here 'the living life's liquid'. Its Greek root in 'to kindle, burn, shine' also seems to presage the blazing fire that several lines later signals the 'obviousness' of the real.[72] This almost 'Heideggerian' construal of Hegel's text, with its concentration on isolated words and its attention to etymology, reconfigures 'this element' to make it at once the condition of a non-Hegelian poetic thinking, and a kind of Presocratic first principle that is air or water.[73] Oppen's inflection of Hegel's words thus makes the poem register the movement of spirit toward something other than itself, but it does not complete the spirit's return to itself by which the other becomes a pure property of consciousness.[74] Oppen, then, does not follow Hegel to the position for which 'knowing in its strictest sense is not the relationship of a subject to a world outside itself; it is its reflective relationship to a world within itself'.[75] At the same time, though, as we might now expect, neither is Oppen thinking in terms of some naïve subject–object

---

[71] Werner Marx, *Hegel's* Phenomenology of Spirit, 43 (his emphases).

[72] Oppen's 'fire of straws' may echo Pound's memories of Tangier in Canto LXXIV, 432 in the passage that begins 'but in Tangier I saw from dead straw ignition | From a snake bite | fire came to the straw'.

[73] Oppen developed an interest in the Presocratic philosophers in part through correspondence and conversations with his son-in-law the philosopher Alexandros Mourelatos, whose area of expertise this was.

[74] Adorno's emphasis on Hegel's dissolving of non-identity in identity is not shared by all interpreters, and Judith Butler notes that Kojève and Hyppolite in different ways record Hegel's 'progressive and open adventure of Spirit' (14). A more recent example is Jean-Luc Nancy, *Hegel: The Restlessness of the Negative*, trans. Jason Smith and Steven Miller (Minneapolis: University of Minnesota Press, 2002). Butler also observes (pp. ix–x) that Hegel's subject 'wants to know itself, but wants to find within the confines of this self the entirety of the external world; indeed its desire is to discover the entire domain of alterity as a *reflection* of itself, not merely to incorporate the world but to externalise and enhance the borders of the self.'

[75] Lauer, *Reading*, 281.

dualism. Rather, he seems to discover in the passage from Hegel's 'Preface' a moment in which consciousness both grasps an object as fundamentally other *and* in that action finds its own thought as an object for itself. Werner Marx thus characterizes the structure of Hegelian self-consciousness as 'that of a moment in which the *subjectum* "represents" to itself a "given" *objectum* in such a way that it refers equally to this object—as its other—and to itself as the "self" which has become self-certain in and through this reference'.[76] It is just this 'moment', before spirit's 'return to itself', that Oppen's poem tries to articulate, with its idea of reaching 'the outer | Limit of the ego' and finding 'the pride of life' only in its recognition of what is not its self. There seems, too, to be a personal reference behind these ponderings of self and ego, for the allusion to the 'jewel' at the beginning of the poem relates obliquely to Oppen's feelings of guilt in enlisting in the war and leaving his family to fend for themselves. This theme would figure prominently in some of his later poems, but the following passage from his notes shows the possible line of association here: 'you were so afraid for me,' he writes of Mary, 'you kept taking care of me, passionately, tenderly. You took care of me. The jewel you thought I was, the warrior, the infinitely precious, the vulnerable phallus. And you were right, of course. Who but those who stand behind him are in greater danger than the warrior?' (UCSD 16, 16, 8).[77] This is a lesson learned, and the poem gives a resounding 'No' to the lure of this false 'treasure', seeming then to move from the hesitant 'It is I or I believe' to a highly tentative collective identification ('We are the beaks of the ragged birds').

If all this seems oblique and obscure, it is partly because Oppen's commitment to the irreducibility of the real has to be 'substantiated', as he would say, in a language which abandons predication and the judgemental 'I'. The fragmentary presentation of the first three lines thus warns us in advance that this is a language that will not clarify itself through the normal procedures of 'thought', but will leave us instead with words and phrases which stubbornly refuse to be drawn into any kind of 'argument' (in a passage in his notes, Oppen speaks in one breath of 'argument, the empty ego'[78]). There are literary allusions here, perhaps—to Eliot's 'I should have been a pair of ragged claws | Scuttling across the floors of silent seas' and to Stevens's 'The Idea of Order at Key West'—but these echoes are there to indicate that Oppen's poem

---

[76] Werner Marx, *Hegel's* Phenomenology of Spirit, 36.

[77] The passage also appears as a quotation from George at the head of an autobiographical fragment titled 'Declaration of Independence' in Mary Oppen's papers (UCSD 125, 1, 13).

[78] 'Selections from George Oppen's *Daybook*', ed. Young, 5. Cf. SL, 56–7: 'There seems to me no problem for an artist more difficult than that of separating the brute ego, the accidents of the ego, from the self which perceives.'

will not engage in ironic self-presentation or conjure with some paradigm
of aesthetic order. Instead, there is a desire for some pure exteriority which
allows the 'ego' to be defined only at the point at which it runs up against
what is not itself. In part, this is 'the sandspit wind this ether this other', but
it is also, in a more complex sense, the form of the poem itself whose very
estrangement from the modes of ordinary thought dissolves the ontological
subject in a lacunary grammar and situates the thought process somehow
beyond the entailments of subjectivity.[79] This 'ether this other this element'
define the delimited space of the mind's movement, edged as it is with what is
not itself; a space which is at the same time that of 'the living life's liquid', the
moving ocean that provides no secure habitation.[80] This 'exteriorization' of
thought, if we may call it that, echoes the poem's celebration of the 'obvious'
and its contrast between a flaming of fire 'in the world' and the poor people
who 'hide | Yourselves together'. This rather cryptic reference to the poor may
be to the Book of Job, which as we shall see, was becoming an increasingly
important text for Oppen; there we read (24: 4) that 'the poor of the earth
hide themselves together'. Perhaps, too, we might trace here the phrase from
Simone Weil alluded to in the poem's title. For in her book *Waiting on God*,
which Oppen knew well, she writes of 'A popular Spanish song [which] says in
words of marvellous truth: "If anyone wants to make himself invisible, there
is no surer way than to become poor." '[81] If this is the passage Oppen has in
mind it would support a reading that emphasizes some sort of turn from 'I'
to 'we', redeeming a notion of collectivity by embedding it in the 'obvious'
and in a certain impoverishment (here the 'ragged' birds seem to consort
with the poor).[82] Hence too, perhaps, Oppen's comment in a letter written
in 1971 about 'breaking the words, the sentences, the locutions *open* to make
some room for ourselves' (SL, 227), for the stylistic tactic of fragmentation

---

[79] Cf. Lauer, *Reading*, 284 on Hegel's dialectic: 'thoughts cease to be the "subjective" activities
of the thinker and are identified with the "objective" movement of reality—provided, of course,
that reality itself be permitted to be "conceptual".' Jameson, *Marxism and Form*, 340 remarks
that 'This is not the "I" thinking but rather an observation of the thought process as object'.
Of related interest is Oppen's already quoted 1971 comment, 'I don't want to be tied to the
characteristics of voice, conferred upon me, not chosen. So I have carefully broken with that.
These poems [including those of *Seascape: Needle's Eye*] were written in violation of my own
speech' (*Ironwood*, 5 (1975), 24).

[80] Is there perhaps an echo here of the famous lines from Pound's Canto LXXIV. 463: 'This
liquid is certainly a | property of the mind | nec accidens est   but an element | in the mind's
make-up' ? Berry, 'Language made Fluid', 315 notes that in Oppen's poems after *Seascape*, 'An
imagery dominated by hard, unitary objects, typified by rock, has given way to an imagery of
the liquid, of light; a conception of the world as external has been superseded by a vision of
interpenetration.'

[81] Weil, *Waiting on God*, 91.

[82] See the discussion of the formal and political implications of Oppen's idea of 'impoverish-
ment' below, pp. 152–3.

carries a weight of anti-individualism which places the idea of some shared space over against what he had called in 'Philai Te Kou Philai', with a significantly different sense of the plural, 'a ruined ethic || Bursting with ourselves' (NCP, 98).

Interestingly, it was in just this way that Oppen responded to one interviewer who had rather missed the point of this poem. The interviewer asks:

Have you moved more, in these poems, to an inner landscape? I'm saying this a little clumsily but in the first poem you seem to start inside the 'dark jewel', then move out to the actual world of the 'ragged birds' beaks', and finally return back in to the 'limits of the ego'.[83]

One can sympathize with the interviewer's perplexity, but what is interesting is his ready construal of the poem as 'an inner landscape' and his sense of it achieving closure in a movement of *return*. Oppen is tactful but firm in his response:

I did, however, say *no* to the jewel. Unless the jewel *sees*: unless the jewel, like a mirror, gives something *back*. I was speaking again of my own specific response and not searching that interior. I said *no*, and then said it's the lust of the eyes that moves the belly-wave. It acknowledges the spirit and circumstances of where we are, of being far at sea, of being among the elements. It's a little too complex to reduce but it definitely rejects that inner space. It says *no* to it except where the spirit moves out to infinity, or at least to the given which I take to be infinite.[84]

Again, it is seeing—'Lust of the eyes'—which 'moves the wave belly-lovely' and expresses a desire beyond mere egotism and misplaced heroism. The self is now 'far at sea', 'among the elements', and these figurings of exteriority take us into Oppen's 'primitive' or 'open' world, a world in which poetic form itself begins to be seen as something estranged, projected, as it were, beyond mere self-expression. In a 'Statement on Poetics', not published until after his death, Oppen puts it thus: 'The word in one's own mouth becomes as strange as infinity—even as strange as the finite, strange as things.'[85] His late poems would have much to say about these different kinds of 'strangeness' and about the way in which the infinite and the finite might seem to coexist within that pure 'element' that is poetic thinking.

---

[83] 'Interview with George and Mary Oppen', conducted by Power, 199.

[84] Ibid. For the 'lust of the eyes' (from 1 John 2: 16) and the 'pride of life', see Daniel Defoe, *Robinson Crusoe*, ed. and introd. John Richetti (London: Penguin Books, 2001), 102: 'In the first place, I was removed from all the wickedness of the world here: I had neither the *lust of the flesh, the lust of the eye, or the pride of life*'. Oppen, of course, reverses the sense of Crusoe's words which attribute lack of covetousness to the fact of his sole authority on the island ('I might call my self king, or emperor over the whole country which I had possession of').

[85] Oppen, 'Statement on Poetics', *Sagetrieb*, 3/3 (1984), 26.

6

'A metaphysical edge': *Seascape: Needle's Eye*

'From a Phrase of Simone Weil's and Some Words of Hegel's' shows some fundamental shifts in perspective and style that were closely bound up with the Oppens' removal from the New York of *Of Being Numerous*. Settled in San Francisco, Oppen was fascinated anew by the city of his adolescence and especially now by an acute sense of being at the edge of the continent. A few years after settling there he would remark to his daughter on 'This distance, this edge of the country, and the thing beyond or outside the sense of metropolis' (SL, 405).[1] This move beyond the busy life of New York City was also a move toward new preoccupations. The tension he had previously explored between singularity and numerousness, a pre-eminently social tension, was now projected into a new set of relations for which the 'bare edge of the continent and simply space beyond'[2] became a powerful figure for the poem itself ('the poem is the moving edge', he wrote to John Taggart (SL, 289)) and for a new sense of personal isolation: *Seascape* 'comes to the personal: the man individually facing the temporal' (UCSD 16, 16, 4).[3] 'Of Being Numerous' now seemed far behind him: as Oppen noted to himself several years later, 'Couldn't have written it now———we've become alien alien in the streets of Brooklyn where we knew, I think, everyone in every apartment' (UCSD 16, 15, 8).

Instead of a crowded urban scene, then, San Francisco offered intimations of 'a metaphysical edge' which was, literally, the horizon, the bounding line between the sea and 'the sky, the unlimited space, the unlimited' (SL, 407 n. 1). 'From a Phrase of Simone Weil's', the opening poem of *Seascape*, had made this 'outer limit' a key motif of the new collection. In the 1973 interview in which this phrase 'a metaphysical edge' appears, Oppen goes on to elaborate:

What happens there—the symbol of the needle's eye is the horizon, the horizon at sea, in which these dimensions close, coincide. The detail, the objectivism in the sense it

---

[1] An early draft of 'A Morality Play: Preface' (NCP, 397) refers to 'the complacent little center | Of the city'.

[2] 'A Conversation with George Oppen', conducted by Charles Amirkhanian and David Gitin, *Ironwood*, 5 (1975), 22.

[3] Cf. 'Semite', NCP, 253: 'in the open the moving | edge and one | is I'.

was usually understood, and the sky, the unlimited space, the unlimited. At that point almost touch leaving a needle's eye.[4]

In an unpublished note, Oppen also describes this horizon as 'the edge of the human' (UCSD 16, 17, 3), and these various plays on intersections and interfaces—'*the sublime*—which means, at the threshold' (UCSD 16, 17, 3)—add a further dimension to 'From a Phrase of Simon Weil' which ends:

> On the open water no other way
> To come here the outer
> Limit of the ego

> (NCP, 211)

This idea of some 'outer limit' derives in part from Oppen's reading of Plotinus who defines Being as

that in which thought comes to a stop, though thought is a rest which has no beginning, and from which it starts, though thought is a rest which never started: for movement does not begin from or end in movement. Again, the Form at rest is the defining limit of intelligence, and intelligence is the motion of the Form, so that all are one; movement and rest are one, and are all-pervading kinds; and each subsequent thing is a particular being, a particular rest, and a particular motion.[5]

The 'form at rest' may have reminded Oppen of Zukofsky's 'rested totality' but here it is also adapted to define the point at which the individual 'ego' discovers its own limits in a perception of 'being': 'Being, in which intelligence must come to rest. The defining limit of thought,' is his gloss (UCSD 16, 19, 6).[6] That 'outer limit' thus figures at once the intelligence's furthest reach and that inescapable horizon at which the poet's being must itself 'come to a stop'.

Oppen's 'open voyage', as he describes the new volume (UCSD 16, 16, 2) thus turns away from the city itself ('There is a discarded super-market cart in the ditch | that beach is the edge of a nation' ('Some San Francisco Poems', NCP, 224)) and the gesture instead toward 'a metaphysical edge' is closely associated with figures of risk and self-exposure, figures now coupled with a deep sense of loneliness and perhaps of a necessary isolation (in a letter written shortly before the publication of *Seascape*, he spoke of his and Mary's 'Extremes of loneliness, in a way, metaphysical loneliness, there being two of

[4] Transcript of BBC interview with Charles Tomlinson, produced by George Macbeth, UCSD 16, 34, 4. The interview was recorded on 22 May 1973 during the Oppens' visit to London and transmitted on 28 Aug. 1973.

[5] *Plotinus*, trans. A. H. Armstrong (New York: Collier Books, 1962), 81. Oppen's copy of this selection is held at UCSD.

[6] Oppen's modification of Plotinus appears frequently in his notes: e.g., 'a work of the intellect in that it marks the extreme outer limits of the ego but is not separate from the ego' (UCSD 16, 31, 16).

us   And yet it is surely the breath or is it the ether of life to us ———' (SL, 242)).[7] As in 'A Phrase of Simone Weil's', the rarefied Hegelian 'ether' is at once the subtle 'atmosphere' of the Californian seascape and the mental 'space' in which the poem originates.[8] As Oppen puts it in a letter of 1972, 'Poem   the thing in the mind before the words   to be able to hold it even against the language' (SL, 236). Comments such as this, which abound in his notes of this period, seek to situate the poem in 'the wordless sphere of the mind' (SL, 236), thus releasing it from syntactic and grammatical constraints. 'I try to avoid all this grammar,' he writes,[9] and in a letter of 1970 to the poet Shirley Kaufman about her work he says 'I half-hear, in the poems, where the transition could be less smooth, less bound by syntax', and that eschewal of 'smoothness' accords with his view that the poem should be 'not "too perfect"'.[10] In the same vein, he concludes another letter to Kaufman with the remark that 'my only real talent is failure'.[11] This is something more than an excess of modesty on Oppen's part, for the idea of 'failure' is bound up with a particular conception of non-rhetorical literary form. 'Rhetorical', he observes in his notes, 'it means a flowing speech, it means a deluge of speech' (UCSD 16, 16, 12), and in another passage he defines his objective as 'To slow down, that is, to isolate the words. Clatter, chatter is extreme rapidity of the words' (UCSD 16, 16, 11). The aim should rather be, he says, 'To make the words hit bottom, to find words that will lie in bed rock, not suspended in a mesh of syntax. The image. The impress' (UCSD 16, 14, 9). Smoothness, rhetoric, these are routes to an illusory success in fluency and certainty. Oppen's late poems certainly employ strong rhythmic forms, making emphatic use of the caesura, for example, but this strength paradoxically produces hesitation and disjunction, and tends to be coupled with an emphasis on typographical spacing and on the word in syntactic isolation ('isolated words making possible the audibility of minds and parts of minds which have been inaudible in print' (UCSD 16, 17, 10)).

Oppen's allusions to 'silence' and to something 'inaudible' are bound up with his long-standing rejection of 'voice' and his search for a language whose referentiality is severely curtailed: 'I would like the poem to be transparent,

---

[7] The comments in the letter refer to the couple's 1972 sailing holiday off Maine ('We play with loneliness', Oppen writes). Several years after the publication of *Seascape*, Oppen would define 'the metaphysical dimension' as 'the thought of being alone' (SL, 279). The letter is also drawn on for part of 'The Book of Job', NCP, 243.

[8] See SL, 210: 'The N.Y. poem (meaning of course *Numerous*) is intellectual and philosophic. The San Francisco poems are atmospheric.'

[9] '*Primitive*: An Archaeology of the Omega Point', ed. Cynthia Anderson, *Ironwood*, 31–2 (Spring and Fall, 1988), 313.

[10] Oppen, 'Letters to Shirley Kaufman', *http:/writing.upenn.edu/epc/authors/oppen/oppen_ letter_to_kaufman_1.html.*

[11] Oppen, 'Letters to Shirley Kaufman', *http:/writing.upenn.edu/epc/authors/oppen/oppen_ letter_to_kaufman_4.html.*

inaudible', he writes (UCSD 16, 22, 58) and 'I am forced to express myself in the simplest language I can find precisely because I do not use a colloquial language: there is no social tone which I am able to accept' (UCSD 16, 15, 6). This is a significant move away from the varied registers of *Of Being Numerous* and it coincides with the idea that the poem must represent the point at which 'the intelligence comes to rest'. This idea of thought 'coming to a stop' and resting, somehow mutely, in a perception of being defines a negative theology for which discourse is exceeded by thought of the unspeakable or the unrepresentable. This is once again a rejection of the poem as 'argument' (a rejection Oppen will now repeatedly refer to Hegel's 'Preface') and gestures toward a new kind of absoluteness which is described as 'metaphysical'. It is curious that in his notes Oppen seems originally to have thought of the needle's eye as a symbol equivalent to the Jungian mandala. He had been briefly interested in some of Jung's texts in 1963 and the concept resurfaces unexpectedly in his notes of the *Seascape* period.[12] He had originally repudiated the idea of the mandala, describing it as 'Fool object, | Dingy medallion' in 'A Narrative' (NCP, 153),[13] but in his later notes he speaks of 'needle's eye center center of the mandala shadowless   water, shadow of water ————Void   But is perhaps also the center (tho it is a void) of individuation' (UCSD 16, 19, 13). For Jung, mandala symbols are 'circular or quaternary figures which express wholeness',[14] and Oppen associates this wholeness with the concept of 'ANIMA MUNDI—the spirit of the world, which is the life-spirit' (UCSD 16, 19, 13). Borrowing Jung's concept, Oppen also finds that his figure of the needle's eye is implicated with a concept of the feminine: 'I had even asked myself: What does a needle symbolize? Phallus, I asked? But obviously a needle is a symbol of femininity!!' (UCSD 16, 19, 13). The anima is, for Jung, an 'inner feminine figure [which] plays a typical, or archetypal, role in the unconscious of a man',[15] and Oppen remarks similarly that 'the way to the unconscious is thru the feminine' (UCSD 16, 19, 13), though this 'way' is apparently not the same as the 'open journey' of a properly 'metaphysical' quest (Oppen remarks characteristically on 'the war between the women and

[12] Rachel Blau DuPlessis refers (SL, 384 n. 22) to a three-letter 'Jung series' of 1963 (see SL, 91–3 and *Ironwood*, 26 (Fall 1985), 220–4; there is a fourth letter in UCSD 16, 19, 10). At this time Oppen seems to have read Jung's *Memories, Dreams, Reflections* and the commentary to Richard Wilhelm's translation *The Secret of the Golden Flower*. Oppen's lightly annotated copy of Jung's *Psychological Reflections* is held in the Mandeville Special Collections.

[13] See Oppen, 'Letters to June Oppen Degnan', *Ironwood*, 26 (Fall 1985), 223 where he comments on this passage and reads the mandala as representing 'the closed universe, the closed self'.

[14] Carl Jung, *Memories, Dreams, Reflections*, trans. Richard and Clara Winston (London: Collins and Routledge and Kegan Paul, 1963), 299.

[15] Ibid. 179.

the metaphysical ———women the home-makers' (UCSD 16, 15, 5)).[16] The eye of the needle seems in fact to represent access to something quite remote from the domestic intimacies of 'home'; indeed, quoting from section 6 of 'Some San Francisco Poems' (NCP, 228), Oppen observes: ' "Silver as | The needle's eye" || i.e., it is not the needle's eye[.] Because I am familiar neither with God nor the approach to God but with the place where God might be' (UCSD 16, 15, 12).

The needle's eye thus has a complex symbolic resonance for Oppen, at once acknowledging the power of the feminine and seeking to transcend it, a double movement which encapsulates his sense of himself and Mary as a couple bound together in some shared and exquisite 'metaphysical loneliness'. As long, that is, as 'we' are together, for in *Seascape* and the poems that follow Oppen is dogged by the fear of losing Mary, by the fear that she will predecease him. The figure of the 'open voyage' is thus shadowed by another kind of 'outer limit', the new beginning ineluctably bound up with an end to come:

> Time and depth before us, paradise of the real, we
>   know what it is
>
> To find now depth, not time, since we cannot, but depth
>
> To come out safe,   to end well
>
> We have begun to say good bye
> To each other
> And cannot say it
>   ('Some San Francisco Poems', NCP, 227)

As these lines indicate, the emotional registers of the late poems are complex: elegiac in their sense of a life richly lived ('How shall we say how this happened, these stories, our stories' ('Some San Francisco Poems', NCP, 226)), but fearful in their horror of absolute separation (Hadrian's 'little pleasant soul wandering | Frightened' ('Animula', NCP, 213)). 'One writes in the presence of something | Moving close to fear', Oppen records in one of the 'San Francisco' poems (NCP, 229), those lines reminding us again that while the 'open voyage' is an exhilarating one it is at the same time blighted by the pathos of knowing that the 'outer limit' is also an end. The 'magic infants' ('Populist', NCP, 276) who appear intermittently in Oppen's late texts are witness to a future that the poet will not see: 'Transparent as the childhood of the world | Growing old   the seagulls sound like the voices of children' ('West', NCP, 216). From *Seascape* on, the poems are haunted by the misery of ageing and by Oppen's intermittent sense of losing the people and things

---

16 Cf. UCSD 16, 17, 8 on 'The feminine mind——Locked against the metaphysical'.

he loves. In unpublished notes, Mary Oppen wrote that 'He is not willing to face age. He is anxious. Fear of the Void, unable as yet, to face his remaining years with courage, with grace and with meaning. [A]nd these years are also my remaining years' (UCSD 16, 2, 45).

The tone of Mary's words acknowledges a tension between them that would finally be accounted for by George's painful descent into Alzheimer's, an illness that seems to have troubled him increasingly after the autumn of 1977, though it was not accurately diagnosed until 1982. Confusion, forgetfulness, disorientation, these were constant features of Oppen's world after the illness took hold; combined with feelings of guilt and of artistic failure, they could not but affect the construction of the late poems. Certainly, the anxiety of which Mary writes is much in evidence—'this sad and hungry || wolf walks in my footprints fear fear || birds, stones, and the sun-lit || earth turning, that great || loneliness' ('A Political Poem', NCP, 265). The speaker of these lines is there only in the trace of his footprints and these are already inhabited by the wolf that pursues him—a dissolution of self that is intensified as the earth turns in its great indifference. And yet loneliness is also, for Oppen, increasingly the condition of writing itself—in an unpublished note, for example, he reminds himself of 'The need to feel absolute solitude, to being absolutely alone, while the poem is being written—But I am too timid, too dishonest' (UCSD 16, 14, 2). This solitude is, we might say, a chosen exile, which carries at once the pathos of separation and a sense of privilege.

Much of the emotional complexity of these late poems and their moments of self-criticism derive from that sense of himself as a survivor that Oppen had gestured towards in the shipwreck motif of 'Of Being Numerous'. In the later poems, the motif acquired more autobiographical substance. Oppen had, we remember, 'survived' his family, and, more literally, had when young survived a car wreck in which another died. He was, too, he wrote at the end of the sixties, 'the only surviving male' in his family, recalling thus the suicide of his mother and the probable suicide of his sister, Libby (SL, 207). And most dramatically, of course, Oppen had survived the conflict in Alsace and the tragic fate of Europe's Jews. But survival carries with it a double burden, recalling us to events already outlived while at the same time projecting a sense of loss into the future. In the lines just quoted, Oppen seems to intimate something close to Derrida's remark, that 'When we are with someone, we know *without delay* that one of us will survive the other.'[17] And Derrida also notes here that 'it is always me who says "we" ', an 'asymmetrical' utterance which seems to imply the absence of the other person even as the speaker

---

[17] Jacques Derrida, *Resistances of Psychoanalysis*, trans. Peggy Kamuf et al. (Stanford, Calif.: Stanford University Press, 1998), 43 (his emphases).

identifies with them. This may shed some light on the difficult second poem
of *Seascape*, 'The Occurrences' which begins with these lines:

> Limited air   drafts
> In the treasure house moving and the movements of the living
> Things fall   something balanced   Move
> With all one's force
> Into the commonplace that pierces or erodes
>
> The mind's structure but nothing
> Incredible happens
> It will have happened to that other
> The survivor   The survivor
> To him it happened

(NCP, 212)

The reference to 'the treasure house' remains obscure, though the imperative
to 'Move . . . Into the commonplace' is partly derived from an exchange of
letters with Michael Heller who had written that 'the commonplace is at the
moment lost' (SL, 252).[18] In a prose note, Oppen puts it like this: 'to move
with all one's force, all his strength, toward the commonplace which holds all
meaning' (UCSD 16, 17, 9).[19]

What, though, are the 'occurrences' of the title? Oppen glosses the
word in a letter as follows: 'Occurrences——events   the heavy events
————and down or somewhere to the toys of everyday, small self-interest,
the wings of the wasp' (SL, 419 n. 52). Again, these 'events' seem to be
the catastrophic forces of history as weighed against the trivial concerns of
self-interest. The reference to 'the middle Kingdom' is to Mencius, according
to Oppen (SL, 264), and perhaps specifically to the survivors of the great floods
during the reign of the legendary Emperor Yao when 'The birds and beasts
pressed upon men':[20] 'the waters, flowing out of their channels, inundated
the Middle Kingdom. Snakes and dragons occupied it, and the people had
no place where they could settle for themselves. In the low grounds they
made nests for themselves on the trees or raised platforms, and in the high
grounds they made caves.'[21] Oppen seems to align this reduced condition with

---

[18] Cf. UCSD 16, 17, 2: 'the occurrence, the treasure house: everything that is, happens'. A
possible source is E. R. Hughes's translation *The Art of Letters: Lu Chi's 'Wen Fu', AD 302. A
Translation and Comparative Study* (New York: Pantheon Books, 1951) to which Oppen alludes
on numerous occasions in his notes. There we read (96) that 'he roamed through the crowded
treasure-house of letters, admired the matching of matter and manner in its exquisitely traceried
works'.

[19] Cf. UCSD 16, 15, 8: 'to approach the metaphysical is to go toward ordinary reality, the
banal, with all one's force and with all one's courage.'

[20] Mencius, *The Works of Mencius*, trans. and ed. James Legge (New York: Dover, 1970), 250.

[21] Ibid. 279 (original in italics).

'small self interest' (another of the few remaining drafts of this poem speaks of 'Magic people   submen   subwomen | Subchildren in their small world among the plant roots' and of a 'small Religion of the Middle Things' (UCSD 16, 16, 1)).[22] Although these lines are rather densely encoded, they do seem to repeat the earlier motif of disaster and survival, perhaps implying, too, an element of self-criticism. The movement into the commonplace 'pierces or erodes || The mind's structure' but no 'miraculous' event actually takes place because it has already happened to someone else, 'the survivor'. That is clear in the final line of the second stanza, with its emphatic 'To him it happened', a line which seems to deny us any identification with the survivor. In an earlier essay,[23] I had proposed that this other person might represent a survivor of the Holocaust with whom Oppen would shy from too easy an identification, but a passage in his notes suggests something both more personal and more complicated: 'Nothing good or evil happens that one cannot credit. For one is someone else thereafter. It happened to this other, the survivor———in war' (UCSD 16, 31, 16). As the survivor, Oppen looks back upon a self he can no longer again become—'one is someone else thereafter'—though that self somehow lingers on in 'that other | The survivor', much as the child lives on in the adult ('the child still lives in him———the tragedy———and that he is someone else   But he remembers' (UCSD 16, 26, 8).

So, too, with the survivor of war. Oppen writes in his notes: 'The fox-hole: that *other* self, the self which is not suffering humiliation and terror and pain finally finally separates itself from the mortal self in the fox-hole, and all the guilts and pretences of that self sink deep into his soul and will never be obliterated wholly again' (UCSD 16, 13, 19). Surviving, then, means more than remembering the event which has dislocated a life: it is a reprieve, a stay of death, which by its nature forces the survivor to look at once to past and to future.[24] This might explain the designedly complex tense of Oppen's 'It

[22] Michael Heller also sees the elves and 'magic people' as 'subtly dangerous', as representative of 'superstitions and mystiques' (GOMP, 421), though we should also note that an earlier poem with the same title (NCP, 144) speaks of watching 'At the roots | Of the grass the creating | Now   that tremendous | plunge'. See too 'If it all went up in smoke' (NCP, 274: 'the small | selves haunting || us in the stones' and 'I am | of that people the grass || blades touch'.

[23] 'Of Being Ethical: Reflections on George Oppen', in Rachel Blau DuPlessis and Peter Quartermain (eds.), *The Objectivist Nexus: Essays in Cultural Poetics* (Tuscaloosa: University of Alabama Press, 1999) 249 ff.

[24] See Jean-François Lyotard, 'The Survivor', in *Toward the Postmodern*, ed. Robert Harvey and Martin S. Roberts (Atlantic Highlands, NJ and London: Humanities Press, 1993), 144: 'The word *survivor* implies that an entity that is dead or ought to be is still alive. The concept of this "still", a reprieve, a stay of death, brings with it a problematic of time—not just any problematic of time, but one of its relation to the question of the being and non-being of what is. More precisely, of a time in which the entity is in relation with its beginning and its end, in relation with the enigma in which the entity comes to its being as entity and then leaves this being.'

will have happened to that other | The survivor', the future anterior signalling an event completed in a future which has not yet taken place. This is, we might say, the harrowing temporality imposed upon the survivor, who may be afflicted by guilt through the very act of survival—'survival never a wholly admirable story', remarks Oppen (SL, 207)—but who lives also with the fear of outliving another disastrous event that *will have happened* in the future.[25] For Oppen, this will be not the luxurious 'loneliness' of his intimate life with Mary, but a loneliness in which he might survive her. Such thoughts are too private for critical commentary and they are frequently expressed by Oppen in notes which he did not expect anyone else to read. I shall not delve too deeply into them beyond invoking this doubled temporality, a kind of 'anticipated belatedness' (to borrow a phrase from Samuel Weber)[26] which creates the complex emotional tonality of Oppen's late poems.

At the same time, 'The Occurrences' also has a less personal and more 'metaphysical' dimension as the wartime experience of the survivor becomes a figure for some larger catastrophe. An early draft of the third stanza reads:

> Footed like Adam in basalt
> Night hums like the telephone dial tone blue gauze
> Of the forge flames all remaining
> Undone I dream the wind blowing out
> And out to sea tired
> Felt old felt guilty
>
> (UCSD 16, 23, 4)[27]

The association of the survivor with Adam and the reference to basalt, the product of volcanic eruption, brings into play ideas of disaster and (originary) guilt which are interwoven with Oppen's recurring sense of his own failure ('all remaining | Undone'). We will be reminded too of that 'tale of our wickedness' repudiated at the beginning of 'Of Being Numerous' (NCP, 163), for here the 'commonplace' seems to stand over against the 'small self interest' of 'superstition'. By way of contrast, the (Adamic) survivor 'rooted in basalt' is associated with the Blakean image of the forge which 'flames the pulse | of infant Sorrows' (a draft has 'Blue gauze of the forge flames, this I believe | Passions choose—No other choosing' (UCSD 16, 23, 4)). The 'infant sorrows' also seem to allude to Blake's poem 'Infant Sorrow' ('My mother groan'd! my father wept. | Into the dangerous world I leapt: | Helpless naked,

---

[25] Cf. UCSD 16, 26, 4: 'the major structure of event is this: that it will always have happened'.

[26] Samuel Weber, *Return to Freud: Jacques Lacan's Dislocation of Psychoanalysis*, trans. Michael Levine (Cambridge: Cambridge University Press, 1991), 9.

[27] Cf. the other draft variant (UCSD 16, 23, 4): 'Night hums like a telephone dial tone I am touched | By all zephyrs and feel myself footed like Adam | In basalt'.

piping loud: | Like a fiend hid in a cloud'[28]). Here and most notably in Oppen's next collection, *Myth of the Blaze*, Blake is drawn on for a wrathful imagery of power which acknowledges the resistant otherness of the world in a poetry which 'burns' with its own blazing flame (compare 'the obvious | Like a fire of straws' (NCP, 211)). As we shall see, though, the 'blaze' is both creative and destructive, just as the words of the poem shine out but with a force that can dazzle and blind. The world of Oppen's late poems is thus quite different from that of, say, *This in Which* where the sense of awe in face of the real produces a feeling of belonging ('we want to be here') and of 'something to stand on' ('World, World———' (NCP, 159)). In the poems after *Seascape*, Oppen's anxious fascination with his own mortality will make this world seem increasingly 'strange', at once dangerous and miraculous: 'too strange, all has become strange, the words not mine, nor am I in the words || too strange. all has become strange and I am sick with fear and sick with daring. I think it is daring. I know I am afraid' (UCSD 16, 14, 7).

* * * * *

Many of the concerns that surface in *Seascape* come clearly into focus in five unpublished leaves of typescript and autograph notations described by the Mandeville Special Collections as 'a draft of an unfinished and unpublished essay entitled "The Romantic Virtue" '[29] (the first of the five leaves is headed 'WORK—THE ROMANTIC VIRTUE, NOT THE PURITAN VIRTUE—THE RISK OF FAILURE', so the 'title' is actually not as clear as the catalogue entry suggests). The manuscript is, like much of Oppen's unpublished writings, a paste-up composition, the first leaf, for example, comprising as many as six typed cuttings attached to a handwritten draft of the typed comments (see Figs. 4 and 5). If it was intended to be an essay, 'The Romantic Virtue' is at a very preliminary stage indeed, but it is characteristic of Oppen's way of working in its use of a kind of dialogic form, directed at both others and himself, to unravel the intricacies of his own thought as it evolved. What the 'essay' might finally have looked like is impossible to say, but it merits some consideration partly for the ideas it brings together but also because it yields an intriguing glimpse of the rhythms of Oppen's thinking as he cancels passages, revisits them and revises them, often with cross-reference to lines and phrases from poems already written and to come. The untidiness of this thinking contrasts

[28] Blake, 'Infant Sorrow', *Complete Writings*, ed. Geoffrey Keynes (London: Oxford University Press, 1966), 217. Oppen's reference to the forge may also echo Blake's 'A Divine Image': 'The Human Dress is forged Iron, | The Human Form a fiery Forge' (ibid. 221).
[29] *Register of the George Oppen Papers, 1958–1984*. UCSD 16, 31, 16. The first page of the file is headed 'Essay | Interviews', probably in the hand of Rachel Blau DuPlessis.

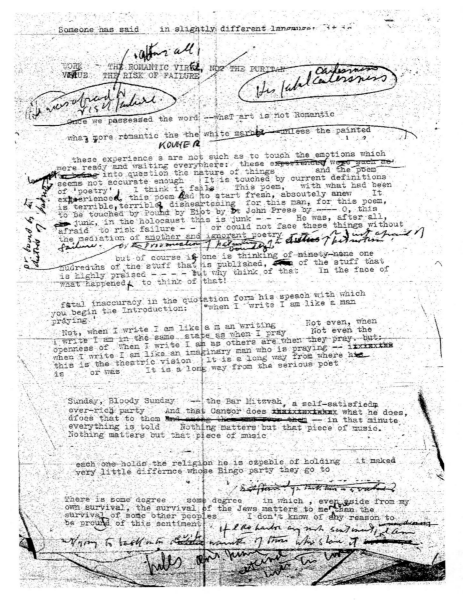

Figure 4. Typescript first page of 'The Romantic Virtue' (1972–3)

Figure 5. Manuscript page of 'The Romantic Virtue' to which first page is attached

helpfully, I think, with the published form of much of Oppen's originally unpublished writings, with 'daybooks' and notebooks seeming to represent their author more as an aphorist and master of the memorable phrase than the insistent and endlessly self-critical thinker that he actually was.[30] I also want to suggest that the ideas loosely assembled in these five pages offer a matrix of thoughts and allusions which underlie the poems subsequently assembled in *Myth of the Blaze* (1972–5) and *Primitive* (1978).

'The Romantic Virtue' was composed either in late 1972 or early 1973. Oppen begins with the following: 'Once we possessed the word—what art is not Romantic ||| what more romantic th[an] the white marble————unless

---

[30] Published selections from Oppen's notes are listed below, in the Bibliography.

the painted'. Then in handwritten capitals we read: 'KOVNER', a reference to
the Israeli poet Abba Kovner, whose work Oppen had come to know through
his friendship with fellow San Francisco poet, Shirley Kaufman. The two had
met in the late sixties and Kaufman recalls that she 'later gave George my first
collection when it was published in 1970. It was then that I began my visits to
George and Mary on Polk Street.'[31] Oppen responded enthusiastically to the
1970 volume, *The Floor Keeps Turning* ('Very, very beautiful poetry, Shirley'[32])
and shortly before or soon after Kaufman moved permanently to Israel in
1973 she sent him her translation of Abba Kovner's holocaust poem, *My Little
Sister*. The translation had first appeared in the volume *Abba Kovner and Nelly
Sachs*, edited and introduced by Stephen Spender and published in 1967.[33]
The source for Oppen's knowledge of the poem was, however, Kaufman's
1973 volume, *A Canopy in the Desert*, in which the translation was reprinted
alongside a selection of other works by Kovner.[34] In a letter almost certainly
written in 1972, Oppen refers to Kaufman's introduction to this text and asks
for a copy of the poem, thus indicating that he was using a proof or photocopy
of her prose text prior to its publication.[35]

The letter itself is curiously conflicted. Oppen recalls being taken by
Kaufman to hear the famous cantor Israel Reich, but while telling her how
much he enjoyed it he also wonders whether the performance wasn't 'too
consciously "pretty" at moments tho?' (SL, 235).[36] To which he adds: 'but

---

[31] Shirley Kaufman', 'Preface to some letters from George Oppen to Shirley Kaufman',
http://writing.upenn.edu/epc/authors/oppen/oppen_Kaufman_preface_to_letters.html.

[32] Oppen, Letter to Shirley Kaufman, Feb. 1970, *http://writing.upenn.edu/epc/authors/oppen/
oppen_letter_to_Kaufman_1.html.*

[33] First published by Farrar, Straus and Giroux, Inc., then in Britain by Jonathan Cape, 1968.
A Penguin paperback edition was issued in 1971.

[34] *A Canopy in the Desert: Selected Poems by Abba Kovner*, trans. Shirley Kaufman (Pittsburgh:
University of Pittsburgh Press, 1973). Kaufman's revised version of *My Little Sister* was later
published in Abba Kovner, *My Little Sister and Selected Poems*, trans. Shirley Kaufman (Ohio:
Oberlin College Press, 1986).

[35] See SL, 235: 'But also don't and could not understand the Introduction ||| without the
poem   Do send it please (do you have a Xerox?).' According to Rachel Blau DuPlessis, 'This
is a carbon draft (unsent?) of another somewhat less frank letter, dated 1972 by Kaufman.'
The letter in SL must have been written after the 25 June 1972 letter from Kaufman to Oppen
(UCSD 16, 6, 4) which tells him that 'the big Kovner book' (*Canopy in the Desert*) has gone
into production with the University of Pittsburgh Press and will be published in April 1973. An
abbreviated version of Kaufman's Introduction was later published in *European Judaism*, 8/1
(Winter 1973–4) under the title 'Who are the Living and Who are the Dead? (the poetry of Abba
Kovner)'. Oppen's 'The Book of Job and a Draft of a Poem to Praise the Paths of the Living'
was published in an early version in the same issue. At this time the editor of *European Judaism*,
Antony Rudolf, was hoping for an essay from Oppen for a subsequent issue (see UCSD 16, 9,
65); given the appearance of Kaufman's piece on Kovner, it is just possible that the manuscript I
am considering was an early shot at that essay.

[36] In the letter from Kaufman quoted in the previous note, Kaufman says she will be back in
San Francisco after 12 Aug., so the event described here took place in the latter part of 1972. An

I cannot overcome a claustrophobia finding myself (when Reich was not singing) as [at] a card-party, a soirée, an Old Grad's day among a collection of people who know the nature of god because their parents told them——as Eckhart rightly said of the Christians, that god would not be god enough for a flea———that room holds something less than a flea's world, a cozy half-of-a-flea——' (SL, 234). At the same time, though, while Oppen is scathing about religious practice ('card-party-bingo-church-picnic office parties Catholic Protestant or Jewish' (SL, 235)), he also declares: 'No escape; I come close to panic   Panic because unquestionably, consciously deep in my blood——— . . . deep in whatever I have is that story you tell again or speak of in the Introduction to Kovner's poem'.

This passage of the letter suggests that Oppen's dismissal of the assembly of worshippers is made in light of survivors' memories of the Holocaust; weighed in that balance, religious ritual seems unequal to Kovner's story of the Vilna ghetto which Oppen feels to be 'deep in my blood, and I know it. There is never any time when I do not know it'.[37] The 'incredible story', as Kaufman tells it, is this:

In November 1941 a young girl crawled up over the thousands of bodies in the pits at Ponar and made her way twenty miles through a frozen forest back to the Vilna ghetto. No one could believe her story, forty thousand Jews dead in a ditch. But Abba Kovner listened and believed. He was twenty-two years old. He wrote the first Jewish call to arms in the Vilna ghetto, a pathetic call since there was no way to get arms or ammunition.[38]

This story of survival exhibits a terrifying depth of experience which transcends any particular religious observance. Hence, perhaps, Oppen's reference in the letter to the thirteenth-century mystic Meister Eckhart, who had proclaimed 'the unity of God and man, a unity so intimate that there would be no need for kneeling and bowing, no room for a priest in between'.[39] Oppen's reference is

---

obituary for Reich, who died in 1999, published in the *Jewish News Weekly of Northern California* (Friday 19 Mar. 1999) notes that he served as cantor in the Bay Area for 25 years; 'Known nationally among colleagues as a "cantor's cantor", Reich helped train countless students, including his own three children, to become cantors.'

[37] John Taggart, 'Walk-Out: Rereading George Oppen', *Chicago Review*, 44/2 (1998), 48 recounts a story Oppen told him of a party he went to in Mexico where Holocaust survivors wept and sang the songs they had sung in the camps: 'Obviously, the experience moved him deeply', Taggart concludes. Oppen tells the same story in 'An Interview with George and Mary Oppen', conducted by Kevin Power, *Montemora*, 4 (1978), 192–3.

[38] *Canopy*, p. xiv. For a slightly revised version of this account, see Kovner, *My Little Sister and Selected Poems*, 17.

[39] Raymond Bernard Blakney, *Meister Eckhart: A Modern Translation* (New York: Harper & Brothers, 1957), 'Introduction', p. xxiii. Oppen's annotated copy of this volume is held in the Mandeville Special Collections.

to a passage from Eckhart's Sermons: 'And if a flea could have the intelligence by which to search the eternal abyss of divine being, out of which it came, we should say that god, together with all that god is, could not give fulfilment or satisfaction to the flea!'[40] It is Eckhart's way of aligning the divine principle with existence and stressing its continuity with humanity that Oppen remarks here. For those who listen to cantor Reich, however, 'God' has apparently degenerated into mere dogma, or what 'their parents told them'. In Oppen's handling of the passage from Eckhart the room in which the cantor sings thus embodies 'something less than a flea's world'.

My reason for pursuing the detail of Oppen's letter to Kaufman is that 'The Romantic Virtue' includes on its first page a later version of these remarks—later because Oppen has now read *My Little Sister* and is no longer dependent on Kaufman's synoptic account. The description of the party is now more abrupt: 'Sunday, Bloody Sunday ——the Bar Mitzvah, a self-satisfied, over-rich party   And that Cantor does what he does, does that to them ——in that minute everything is told   Nothing matters but that piece of music.'[41] In line with that, perhaps, Oppen is now openly critical of Kovner whose poem, he says, represents a loss of 'the Romantic Virtue' that Oppen here associates with the 'risk of failure'. In a note which clarifies the heading of these pages, he declares that 'I value work romantically, not puritanically: work as the risk of failure' (UCSD 16, 15, 10). In contrast, the 'Puritan Virtue' is elsewhere associated with the mechanics who appear in 'The Book of Job and a Draft of a Poem to Praise the Paths of the Living': 'the mechanical trades are monotheistic, the religion of the craftsman is monotheistic If the teeth engage, the gear will turn Always Monotheistic and therefore Puritan' (UCSD 16, 15, 12).[42] The Romantic, then, is speculative, unsure of where the work is headed, while the Puritan is wedded to his craft and confident of an appropriately finished product.[43]

This fragmentary first page is far from constituting even a draft of an essay, especially as in one place Oppen addresses Kaufman directly in what looks like a preliminary version of a letter to her: 'Fatal inaccuracy in the quotation from his speech with which you begin the Introduction: "when I write I am like a man praying".'[44] Having been moved initially by Kaufman's account of the 'story' of *My Little Sister*, Oppen on reading the poem itself reacts to it with

---

[40] *Meister Eckhart*, 229.

[41] Both versions of the letter refer to the scene with the Cantor in the 1971 film *Sunday, Bloody Sunday*.

[42] See below, pp 171–2.

[43] 'The Romantic Virtue' is transcribed in Appendix B, below. Further reference to these typescript pages will be given in the text to RV.

[44] *Canopy*, p. xiii: 'Reading his poems in Hebrew while on tour through the United States in January 1972, Abba Kovner told his audience: "When I write I am like a man praying." '

quite unexpected violence—'in the holocaust this is junk', he says, finding in the poem a damaging literariness which reflects Kovner's apparent failure to 'start fresh, absolutely new', outside of the frame of modernist precursors such as Pound, Eliot, and St-John Perse whose influence, it is implied, is unlikely to produce anything more than a merely aesthetic approach to the terrors of the Holocaust.

It's hardly surprising that Oppen abandoned this potentially upsetting letter to Kaufman, but the intensity of his reaction to Kovner's poem (or, more accurately, to Kaufman's translation of it) might explain the intermittent rejections of poetic language in the unpublished notes of this period.[45] For there is at this point in Oppen's thinking an intensification of the view that a poetry capable of engaging the 'actual' must abandon all pre-existing modes. He admires Basil Bunting's *Briggflats*, for example, but even there he is troubled by 'the echo of known music, known styles' (UCSD 16, 15, 11). He is even more suspicious of any taint of 'elegance' (Zukofsky's 'Mantis' is criticized for 'Taking refuge in elegance' (UCSD 16, 15, 9)) and the 'distinction between poetry and histrionics' which he had emphasized in 'The Mind's Own Place' now becomes a measure which he applies remorselessly to his own work and to that of others.[46] There must be, as he puts it in 'Two Romance Poems', 'No heroics, obviously' (NCP, 261) and no unearned identification with the plight of others—'I do not see how I can make "the Negro people" the subject of any declarative sentence', he writes (UCSD 16, 15, 10). Instead, poetry might offer a certain 'candor' which is in turn allied to a form of verbal opacity: 'The peculiar attribute of words is that they spring spontaneously in the mind, they flow continuously in the mind. They provide, if not hope, at least opacity' (UCSD 16, 15, 11).[47] The unexpected association of 'candor' with 'opacity' is indicative of Oppen's attempt to make a resistant verbal texture the register of the world's 'impenetrability'. To be 'candid' is to allow the words to speak for themselves with a minimum of authorial intrusion. Oppen's advice to young writer Paul Vangelisti about his first collection of poems was 'I wonder how

[45] There were several drafts of this letter, and ultimately Oppen seems to have decided to keep his criticism of Kovner to himself. He was, it seems, happy to meet with the poet when he visited Jerusalem in 1975. See SL, 306 and Shirley Kaufman, 'The Obvious and the Hidden: Some Thoughts about "Disasters"', *Ironwood*, 26 (Fall 1985) 152–8. The trip is discussed in Ch. 7, below.

[46] 'The Mind's Own Place', 176. Cf. Oppen, 'Three Poets', *Poetry*, 100/5 (Aug. 1962), 329: 'it is a question of the line between histrionics and the openness, the lack of preciousness which is at least a part of the value of this work and its impact'. As previously noted, Oppen often attacks Zukofsky for over-embellishment: 'I stripped myself while you, Louis, have hung on yourself every fancy rag you could find' (UCSD 16, 13, 20).

[47] For 'candor', see also UCSD 16, 15, 12: 'As against the histrionic, the candor of poetry, one could say.'

you would feel about omitting the stage directions. . . . would not the white space carry more—I should have said it this way—than the indication of "staging".'[48]

Oppen's recoil from the 'histrionic' is also evident in 'The Romantic Virtue', where Kovner's claim that 'when I write I am like a man praying' is dismissed with some disdain as 'the theatric vision' (RV, 1), a judgement which is clearer in the light of a terse comment elsewhere in his notes: 'Kovner's "Ladder" (symbolist)' (UCSD 16, 15, 2). In her introduction, Kaufman had commented on 'the wealth of associations which one word like "ladder" can evoke for the informed Hebrew reader' and it is this appeal to tradition in *My Little Sister* which leads Oppen to link it to the modernism of Pound, Eliot, and St-John Perse.[49] As he notes, 'The religious experience for me cannot lie in the ancient and sacred words, but in the me, the here, the now   the nouns: the fruits of the senses' (UCSD 16, 16, 7). As for religion, so for 'art': 'we need more faith in "it", the world, Being, than we have or can have in art' (UCSD 16, 15, 12). A chain of associations comes into play with Oppen's reiteration of this theme, with the language of 'art' once again damagingly equated with the theatrical and the avant-garde, and these in turn compared to the 'jet-set' culture represented by his own wealthy family.[50]

If it is the obligation of authentic art to 'risk failure', the poet must eschew anything that looks like embellishment or posturing, committing himself to 'the courageous mind' rather than to the easier route of 'fantasy, dream-world' that Oppen attributes to much contemporary art (RV, 4). In *Seascape: Needle's Eye*, 'Song, the Winds of Downhill' had already expressed this view:

> 'out of poverty
> to begin
>
> again'   impoverished
>
> of tone of pose that common
> wealth
>
> of parlance   Who
> so poor the words

---

[48] Oppen's letter is given as a preface to Paul Vangelisti, *Communion* (Fairfax, Calif.: The Red Hill Press, 1970), n.p. Vangelisti obviously took Oppen's advice though it hardly saved his poem.

[49] Kaufman, Introduction, p. xix. Oppen frequently dissociated himself from the Symbolist tendency, observing, for example, that 'my ego does not bear the peculiar symbolist affectation' (UCSD 16, 24, 15).

[50] See 'Guest Room' (NCP, 109): 'It is the courage of the rich || Who are an avant-garde || Near the limits of life . . .'. Compare UCSD 16, 15, 3: 'the upper classes live IN an art, their lives have been constructed by art, which is at all times a worn out art. One must get free of it.' Oppen also associates the Israelis with a kind of aristocracy: 'The Israeli: the dignity of an aristocracy as against the arab? The dignity of a nation? Or the dignity of Hebrew in place of Yiddish' (UCSD 16, 15, 2).

would with and take on substantial

meaning handholds footholds

to dig in one's heels   sliding

hands and heels beyond the residential
lots the plots it is a poem

which may be sung
may well be sung

(NCP, 220)

The opening quotation from Charles Simic's *White* (1972) leads into Oppen's evocation of a poetry which accepts a certain 'impoverishment' as its necessary condition, eschewing 'tone' and 'pose' in favour of a 'commonwealth | of parlance'.[51] That 'commonwealth', by analogy with Oppen's related celebrations of the 'commonplace', returns us to the 'little words' that give us purchase on a world that must be affirmed through the values of 'song' rather than those of 'residential lots'. The poem, in this sense, is written against 'those who confect, clothed and armoured in the words and phrases which first were made to tell one's nakedness' (RV, 5), attending to 'the voices of the common man, the common woman in other times' (RV, 2). The stripped-down style of Oppen's late work, with its eschewal of punctuation and visual imagery, constitutes, perhaps, a kind of 'poor' poetry (by analogy with Jerzy Grotowski's 'Poor Theatre') where all signs of a conventional literariness must be expunged in deference to 'actuality'.

Oppen's allusion to Blake on the last page of 'The Romantic Virtue'—'I must make *no* system, or I will be enslaved by another man's'[52]—reflects his late fascination with Blake's grasp of a vivid 'actuality' and his handling of the 'little words' in the *Songs of Innocence and Experience*: 'Blake's Tyger in the small words. They burn. The nouns are the visible universe, the night sky burning'.[53] This 'burning' is the force of disclosure and revelation—the

---

[51] Charles Simic, *White* (New York: New Rivers Press, 1972), 11: 'Out of poverty | to begin again: || With the color of the bride | And that of blindness, || Touch what I can | Of the quick, || Speak and then wait, | As if this light || Will continue to linger | On the threshold.' Kenner, *Homemade World*, 187 reads the poem similarly, though he underplays the relation Oppen implies to class. See also Peter Weltner, 'George Oppen's Last Poems: I would go out past the axioms of wandering', *Ironwood*, 26 (1985), 296–308 and Lyn Graham Barzilai, *George Oppen: A Critical Study* (Jefferson, NC and London: McFarland and Company, 2006), 121–4.

[52] See William Blake, *Jerusalem*, in *Complete Writings*, Keynes, 629: 'I must Create a System or be enslav'd by another Man's'.

[53] 'Selections from George Oppen's *Daybook*', ed. Dennis Young, *Iowa Review*, 18/3 (1988), 3. See also UCSD 16, 17, 9: 'Blake's Tyger: the visible universe. The myth of the blaze.' Oppen's *Collected Poems* was for a while to be entitled *Names of the Tyger* (see UCSD 16, 24, 1). In the BBC interview with Charles Tomlinson, Oppen observes similarly that 'the small words are Blake's

blazing forth of the 'actual'[54]—but it is also, for Oppen now as for Blake, a light which both illuminates and destroys, much as the divine creation gives birth to both the tiger and the lamb ('One had not thought | To be afraid || Not of shadow but of light' (NCP, 233)). It is this blazing light that confounds the 'solipsist position: that self-consciousness is unconditioned ((by any other actuality)) or is its own actuality' (RV, 3). In 'The Romantic Virtue', Oppen emphatically states and restates what he takes to be Hegel's argument against this position: 'Self consciousness in itself, of itself, carries the conviction of actuality. . . . it can be said that therefore we know of an actuality other than that, prior to that which is the consciousness' self-knowledge' (RV, 3). Only an 'impoverished' language, a language that withholds its descriptive riches, can approximate 'The primacy of the nominative, which Hegel spoke of, the primacy of subject. *Revelation of the nominative: there can be no predicate of revelation. It is never which is which'* (UCSD 16, 15, 9).

This, increasingly, is what Oppen means by 'the image': not an image *of* something, but 'the content of consciousness' (UCSD 16, 24, 2), or, to put it another way, the spatio-temporal 'world' which is the poem: 'The IMAGE THE SPATIAL DIMENSION, THE TEMPORAL DIMENSION: WITHOUT THIS THERE SEEMS NO PROOF, NO RECOGNITION, NO CONVICTION. ARGUMENT, CHATTER. . . . THE POEM MUST CONCEIVE THE WORLD OR IT IS ARGUMENT, CHATTER' (RV, 4). 'Image' in the late poems thus acquires a certain self-reflexiveness, which perhaps explains why Oppen repeatedly invokes it without exemplifying it (as, for example, in 'The Book of Job and a Draft of a Poem to Praise the Paths of the Living' 'image   the images' (NCP, 240) and in 'Semite', 'the proofs || are the images the images' (NCP, 251)).[55] It is at moments like these, when Oppen's language is at its most strategically 'impoverished', that 'the *conviction* of actuality' becomes, if anything, more important than the actuality itself. For it is 'conviction' which stands over against the traditionalism which Oppen detects in Kovner's poem, and it is 'conviction' which necessarily sustains the survivor whose world will never be as it once was. Perhaps that finally explains Oppen's irritable dismissal of *My Little Sister*, for literariness, 'symbolism', is part of the world before the disaster, offering thus a false reassurance that things might somehow continue

TYGER . . . "Burning bright", the visible universe, absolutely clear, absolutely impenetrable' (UCSD 16, 34, 4).

54 Compare 'From a Phrase of Simone Weil's and Some Words of Hegel's' (NCP, 211): 'the obvious | Like a fire of straws | Aflame in the world . . .'. The lines are quoted in RV, 4.

55 Oren Izenberg has also noted this tendency in the earlier 'Of Being Numerous'—see his 'Oppen's Silence, Crusoe's Silence, and the Silence of Other Minds', *Modernism/Modernity*, 13/1 (2006), 793–4.

as they were. Yet Oppen had himself had intimations of 'that *other* self' produced by traumatic experience, and in 'The Romantic Virtue' he notes that 'Nothing good or evil happens that one cannot credit For one is someone else thereafter' (RV, 4). To which he adds, in hand and as if reminding himself of those lines from 'The Occurrences': 'It happened to this other, the survivor. ——in war?'

* * * * *

While Oppen thus responded critically to Kovner's poem, there is little doubt that its powerful evocation of the Holocaust had a significant impact on him, provoking a series of questionings about his own Jewishness which would shape some of the late poems. Yet his reading of Kovner and perhaps, too, his dialogue with Shirley Kaufman, who had left San Francisco to take up permanent residence in Jerusalem, made him wary of what he called in 'The Romantic Virtue' 'the provincialism of patriotism' (RV, 1). Kovner was, he thought, either 'bound by the duties of patriotism or just afraid' (RV, 1); for his own part, 'I cannot see a place for myself, an identity, in Israel—and I cannot think at all of going thru a conversion, of going thru religious instruction—etc—I am a stiff-necked people———we————Mary and I, are a stiff-necked people' (UCSD 16, 15, 2).[56] He was sceptical, too, about the mission of Israel, speaking, in a passage already quoted, of 'The Israeli: the dignity of an aristocracy as against the arab? The dignity of a nation? or the dignity of Hebrew in place of Yiddish?' (UCSD 16, 15, 2). A 1972 letter to Donald Davie also registers his feelings of distance from Zionism:

Several million Zionists wish to tell me that, being Jewish, I am not quite American, and that being not quite Jewish——with two passionately assimilationist generations behind me——I am not quite either

about which I sometimes think that, being not quite American since I am a Jew, I am the MOST American. . . . (SL, 245)

As this passage indicates, Oppen found little promise of social identification in the Zionist project or, indeed, with any other form of political nationalism based in tradition.[57] This had much to do with his early break with his wealthy family which had entailed a deliberate distancing of himself from his Jewish

---

[56] The allusion is to Exodus 32: 9–10.

[57] The correspondence with Davie just quoted was partly about Oppen's problems in trying to write a blurb for Davie's forthcoming *Collected Poems* (1973). Again, he was troubled by Davie's apparent dependence on 'wit' and traditionalism, and in a note to himself described the volume as 'A work so strongly within a national, a racial tradition, a work of unfailing wit within that tradition——It is a poetry the most distant from me; in its distance, its brilliance, almost shattering to me' (UCSD 16, 4, 5).

background: as he wrote in one of his notes, 'I don't value my background, neither its wealth nor its Jewishness, I value only my rejection of it' (UCSD 16, 18, 5). If being Jewish remained important to him it was because it actually seemed to free him from prescriptive identifications based on race and religion: 'my jewishness means to me——our jewishness means to us ——being slightly different from the majority, and therefore partly free' (the identification here was partly figurative, of course, since Mary Oppen was not Jewish) (UCSD 16, 15, 2).[58] It was that difference which would provide one of the major themes of his later work, for, as he puts it in a passage quoted earlier, 'somewhere half-way between the fact of being singular and the fact of being numerous is the fact of being Jewish' (UCSD 16, 14, 15). That latter 'fact' and its 'half-way' positioning indicates at once Oppen's sense of removal from Jewish tradition—'my Yiddish is completely fake', he remarked in interview[59]—and his construal of his own Jewishness in terms of an essential foreignness: 'When I was about 16,' he says in the same interview, 'I read Israel Zangwill and came upon his phrase "walking-stick Jews", and I almost died and thought that is probably what I am. We were foreign in any country.'[60]

Until 1972, that sense of foreignness was something Oppen had tended to relish: 'My sense of the thing,' he recalled, 'was to be faintly foreign and, to tell the truth of it, rather aristocratic'.[61] Yet under the increasing pressure of feelings of anxiety and loneliness, the classic Jewish tropes of exile and nomadism began to acquire a new and troubling intensity in his writing. One contributory factor was perhaps the work of Edmond Jabès whose name appears in a list of writers from whom Oppen claims to have quoted in one of the most important poems in *Myth of the Blaze*, 'The Book of Job and a Draft of a Poem to Praise the Paths of the Living'.[62] Oppen published a first version of this serial poem in the *Grosseteste Review* in 1973,[63] and then contributed a revised copy to the London-based journal *European Judaism*, edited by Anthony Rudolf with whom he had been in correspondence for

---

[58] Linda Oppen adds (personal communication): 'She identified herself, the family, as Jewish but it is certainly true that she did not come from a Jewish family, felt keenly rejection by Jews.'

[59] 'Interview with George and Mary Oppen', conducted by Power, 194.

[60] Ibid.   [61] Ibid.

[62] See the 1973 letter to Michael Cuddihy (SL, 264):'I had not been thinking of Job as I wrote: thunderstruck to discover how closely the poem followed Job's argument—— | ——and so I named it. | (this the more startling in view of the number of quotes, so many, and none of them from Job   I'd made myself a list of the references, but seem to have lost it——includes Hölderlin, Jabès, Bobrowski, Luther, Montaigne (Florus' [*sic*] trans).' To date, only John Taggart has considered the importance of Jabès to Oppen. See his 'Walk-Out: Rereading George Oppen', 29–93.

[63] *Grosseteste Review*, 6/1–4 (1973), 250–6. In this version, the poem was entitled 'The Lever the Die the Cam' and subtitled '(from the Book of Job)'.

several years.[64] The two men were finally able to meet when Oppen visited England in May 1973 to give readings at a conference at the Polytechnic of Central London and at the University of East Anglia and Gonville and Caius College, Cambridge.[65] It was during this visit that Rudolf was able to secure Oppen's new poem for *European Judaism*.[66] It may at first sight seem a little out of character for Oppen to contribute to a publication so specifically aligned to the Jewish intellectual world, but this was a moment in which he was becoming increasingly preoccupied with religious questions, with the aftermath of the Holocaust, and with his own Jewish background (two years later, he and Mary would make an ultimately disappointing trip to Jerusalem). One imagines, too, that he must have been impressed by the stature of the work presented in *European Judaism* under Rudolf's enterprising editorship: writers published there included Nelly Sachs, Paul Celan, Maurice Blanchot, Paul Auster, Gabriel Josipovici, Franz Kafka, Charles Reznikoff, Carl Rakosi, Jerome Rothenberg, Larry Eigner, and Edmond Jabès.

In the summer 1973 issue of *European Judaism*, Rudolf presented Rosmarie Waldrop's translation of the whole of Jabès's 'The Book of the Absent: Third Part' alongside two short essays by, respectively, Emmanuel Levinas and Jean Starobinski under the joint title 'Jabès and the Difficulty of Being Jewish'.[67] It was this issue that fired Oppen's interest in Jabès and he obviously communicated his enthusiasm to Rudolf after his return to the United States, for the latter expressed himself 'overwhelmed by your letter' and went on to say that 'Donald Davie was so moved by the Jabès (and the two pieces on him) that he wrote a poem "His Themes", which has been published in

---

[64] Rudolf tells me that he was in touch with Oppen 'definitely before 1972' and 'I may have written to him as early as 1968' (personal communication). Rudolf was Managing Editor of *European Judaism* from 1970 to 1975.

[65] I was fortunate to attend the third of these events (organized by J. H. Prynne) at which Oppen read from *Seascape: Needle's Eye*. Oppen later wrote to Rudolf: 'The meeting with Michael Hamburger, and his translations, and the discovery of European Judaism have been incomparably the most important events of our stay in England' (see UCSD 16, 9, 65). The trip to England was particularly significant for Oppen because it allowed him to encounter Jewish intellectuals who were quite different from those, like Charles Reznikoff, who were closely aligned to the Yiddish tradition. See 'Interview with George and Mary Oppen', conducted by Power, 194: 'But in England I met Jews who are Jews in the sense I am and we thoroughly understood each other. It was really a considerable experience for me, a very moving experience.'

[66] It appeared in *European Judaism*, 8/1 (Winter 1973/4), 37–9. The same issue carried Kaufman's 'Who are the Living and who are the Dead?', 23–8.

[67] Jabès, 'The Book of the Absent: Third Part', trans. Rosmarie Waldrop, *European Judaism*, 7/2 (Summer 1973), 11–19; see Jabès, *The Book of Questions*, trans. Rosmarie Waldrop, 2 vols. (Hanover, and London: Wesleyan University Press, 1991), 121–41 (hereafter cited as BQ); Emmanuel Levinas and Jean Starobinski, 'Jabès and the Difficulty of Being Jewish', trans. Susan Knight, *European Judaism*, 7/2 (Summer 1973), 20–2. An excerpt from Jabès's *Book of Questions* had previously appeared in David Meltzer's *Tree*, 3 (Winter 1972), 149–57. Trans. Rosmarie Waldrop, this corresponds to BQ, i. 164–70.

Encounter' (UCSD 16, 9, 65).[68] Just how much of Jabès's voluminous works Oppen would read must remain an open question: while John Taggart, in the only discussion of the relationship so far, simply assumes an acquaintance with the whole of *The Book of Questions* (published in Rosmarie Waldrop's translation in 1976), there is, to my knowledge, no real evidence to confirm this.[69] Similarly, he might have read Jabès's *Elya*, which David Meltzer issued under his *Tree* imprint in 1973, but again we can't be sure. We do know that he had been in correspondence with the British poet and editor Anthony Barnett who had published a text by Jabès in his little magazine *Nothing Doing in London*. Barnett also included Jabès's 'Answer to a Letter' from *Aely* in the first issue of his *The Literary Supplement* (1973) which he sent to Oppen.[70] The traceable interest in Jabès's texts seems, then, to cover the period of *Myth of the Blaze*, 1972–5, though as Taggart's essay reminds us, Oppen was still sufficiently drawn to the French writer to attend a reading Jabès gave in San Francisco in March 1983 (by this time, Oppen was deep in the toils of Alzheimer's and would die in a nursing home the next year).[71]

What attracted Oppen to Jabès's writings? In the letter to Cuddihy he speaks of quoting Jabès in 'The Book of Job and a Draft of a Poem to Praise the Paths of the Living', though close perusal of the excerpt from *The Book of the Absent* published in the summer 1973 issue of *European Judaism* yields no obvious phrases or passages to support this contention (as he notes in the letter, Oppen was notoriously unreliable on this kind of question: 'Quotes from memory, which is my disreputable habit——' (SL, 264)). He did, however, jot down some passages from the excerpt in his notes: 'the wind of freedom blows as hard as the wind of madness', which may obliquely inform both the 'windy pines' of section 1 of 'The Book of Job' and, perhaps, 'the taste | of madness'

---

[68] Davie's poem was published in *Encounter*, 31 (Oct. 1973), 59–60. Oppen's letter to Rudolf appears not to have survived.

[69] Taggart, 'Walk-Out: Rereading George Oppen', 29–93.

[70] Edmond Jabès, 'Answer to a Letter', with J. H. Prynne, 'Es Lebe der König' and Paul Celan, 'Conversation in the Mountains', *The Literary Supplement, Writings*, i (London: The Literary Supplement, 1973), 4–8. Barnett thanks Oppen for his 'good words about the booklet' in a 1974 letter (UCSD 16, 2, 27). The copy is among Oppen's books at the Mandeville Special Collections.

[71] During the 1983 visit to the US, Jabès spoke at San Diego (invited by Michel de Certeau) and at San Francisco, Los Angeles and Stanford, where he met again with Robert Duncan. See Didier Cahen, *Edmond Jabès* (Paris: Pierre Belfond, 1991), 335. Cahen makes no mention of a meeting with Oppen, but Anthony Rudolf recalls seeing a photograph published in the newsletter of Berkeley's Cody's Bookshop in which the two men are pictured shaking hands. As the title of his essay suggests, Taggart makes a dramatic case about the Oppens leaving the reading halfway through. Linda Oppen writes, however (personal communication): 'At the time George was having extreme problems sitting and stayed put only briefly anywhere, movies, talks, visits. He got up abruptly and rushed away, absorbed in pain and escape. No meaning whatsoever to timing or the fact of walking out on anything.'

at the poem's end;[72] 'I DO NOT KNOW if a garden is heaven or Hell';[73] 'Water releases me from the word'.[74] More revealing, though, is another now famous sentence from Jabès's texts which Oppen wrote into his notes: ' "Do not ever forget that you are the kernel of a severance." ' Oppen muses: 'a severance from other people, or a severance from other things. Or is it the Jews who are the kernel of a severance. Consciousness which is a sev[erance]'.[75] Jabès's aphorism contains all these possibilities and perhaps more: severance is 'the truly vertiginous distance that separates the word from what it designates'[76] and which asserts itself, too, between one word and another, in those white spaces which connote the desert against which writing must always appear and which speak mutely of the absence of God.[77] This severance is also the gap which forever separates writing from an original divine language which was lost when the Tablets of the Law were broken. Maurice Blanchot, in an essay on Jabès published in an earlier issue of *European Judaism* which Oppen may well have seen, notes that the 'severance' concerns the relation of Judaism and writing, 'at once joined and separate'.[78] Blanchot also quotes another now familiar passage from 'The Book of the Absent: Third Part': 'I brought you my words. I talked to you about the difficulty of being Jewish, which is the difficulty of writing. Judaism and writing are but the same waiting, the same hope, the same wearing out.'[79] 'There is', writes Blanchot by way of gloss, 'the empty, desert-like waiting that holds back the writer who works at the threshold of the book, making him the guardian of the threshold, his writing

---

[72] UCSD 16, 17, 9. 'The Book of the Absent: Third Part', 13: 'The wind of freedom blows as hard as that of madness.'

[73] UCSD 16, 15, 5; 'The Book of the Absent: Third Part', 14: ' "*I do not know,*" says the disciple of Reb Simoni, "*if my garden is Heaven or Hell.*" ' (italics in original). The comment is followed by 'The Dialogue of the Two Roses' which concerns the inextricability of love and death.

[74] UCSD 16, 16, 8; 'The Book of the Absent: Third Part', 16

[75] UCSD 16, 13, 7; 'The Book of the Absent: Third Part', 13.

[76] Edmond Jabès, *From the Desert to the Book: Dialogues with Marcel Cohen*, trans. Pierre Joris (Barrytown, NY: Station Hill, 1990), 48–9.

[77] Cf. Paul Auster, 'An Interview with Edmond Jabès' (1979), repr. in Eric Gould (ed.), *The Sin of the Book: Edmond Jabès* (Lincoln, Nebr.: University of Nebraska Press, 1985), 19: 'What I mean by God in my work is something we come up against, an abyss, a void, something against which we know we are powerless. It's a distance . . . the distance that is always between things.'

[78] Maurice Blanchot, 'Edmond Jabès' *Book of Questions*', *European Judaism*, 6/2 (Summer 1972), 36. Jacques Derrida, 'Edmond Jabès and the Question of the Book', in *Writing and Difference*, trans. Alan Bass (London: Routledge & Kegan Paul, 1978), 67 comments on the same aphorism that 'God separated himself from himself in order to let us speak, in order to astonish and interrogate us. He did so not by speaking but by keeping still, by letting silence interrupt his voice and his signs, by letting the Tables be broken.' In 'Answer to a Letter' which Oppen knew (see above, n. 70), Jabès asks 'Is speaking, then, the attempt to fill the void left by the death of God?'

[79] 'The Book of the Absent: Third Part', 13–14; quoted in Blanchot, 'Edmond Jabès' *Book of Questions*', 35.

a desert, and from his very being the void and absence of a promise'.[80] On this 'threshold', a void opens in which belief and truth expire: we have only words which speak to us unceasingly of silence and emptiness, of the absence of any ground for meaning. Jabès posits 'Some basic incompatibility between man and his words, something that keeps them apart. Could it be that they are condemned to walk together, but have only the road in common? Exile within exile.'[81] In Jabès's texts, this incompatibility or distance is constantly exposed: the words that are spoken are, as it were, turned inside out so that what we read are meanings under erasure, the words rendered 'transparent' and denoting the empty event of language itself, what Giorgio Agamben calls 'the *outside* of language, the brute fact of its existence'.[82] It is in that taking place of language, in that 'severance' of words from things, that we also witness the absolute otherness of the world—for Jabès, the desert represents 'exemplary emptiness—but an emptiness with its own, very real dust'.[83]

While there is little to suggest that Oppen was persuaded by Jabès's absolute equation of Judaism and writing,[84] the mutually implicated ideas of severance and waiting obviously resonated with his own late sense of 'exile' and of an uncertain and fragile future. Jabès's talk of 'Judaism after God' may have spoken to Oppen's own unresolved sense of his Jewish identity;[85] and Jabès's impossible 'attempt to pull free of the yoke of words' clearly resonated with Oppen's own equally difficult pursuit of 'silence' and 'transparency'.[86] In the world after Auschwitz, we are doomed to that 'desert-like waiting' of which Blanchot speaks, a living-on in perpetual exile from any consolatory forms of traditionalism. 'Does surviving mean living *on* life,' asks Jabès, 'living on a dead life, living death all life long?'[87] It is easy to understand Oppen's interest in the gaps and silences that characterize the exilic language of Jabès's texts, literally and metaphorically. Here, to be sure, language and life have become

---

[80] 'Edmond Jabès' *Book of Questions*', 35.   [81] BQ, ii 373.

[82] Giorgio Agamben, *Remnants of Auschwitz: The Witness and the Archive*, trans. Daniel Heller-Roazen (New York: Zone Books, 1999), 139. Agamben draws on the linguistic theory of Émile Benveniste to describe a 'semantics of enunciation' (137).

[83] Jabès, *From the Desert to the Book*, 15.

[84] Taggart, 'Walk-Out', 78–9 claims rather dubiously that Oppen recast Jabès's equation of Judaism, writing, hoping and wearing out as 'difficulty | of writing the poem—the fact | confronts the Jew again and | again' (see Cynthia Anderson (ed.), '*Primitive*: An Archaeology of the Omega Point', *Ironwood*, 31/32 (Spring and Fall 1988), 318). At the same time, Taggart's main argument, that Jabès's Jewishness is rejected by Oppen (see 75), seems precisely to argue *against* any such equation of Judaism and writing.

[85] Edmond Jabès, 'The Question of Displacement into the Lawfulness of the Book', trans. Rosmarie Waldrop, in Gould (ed.), *Sin of the Book*, 232; BQ ii. 301; BQ ii. 142.

[86] BQ ii. 121. Jabès in translation also on occasion sounds curiously like Oppen, as in his determination to 'reject representation in order to stress the transparency of the word: seen and yet indistinguishable, heard and yet inaudible' (BQ ii. 188).

[87] BQ ii. 110 (his emphasis.)

radically 'impoverished'—'the white space of the paper becomes part of the poem' (UCSD 16, 34, 2)—and one can see how Oppen would have preferred that to what he thought of as Abba Kovner's dangerously 'theatric vision' ('when I write I am like a man praying'). At the same time, though, while Oppen's late poems would also opt for 'silence' rather than for 'talk', his own ideal of verbal 'transparency' was the means by which to *disclose* the real rather than to testify to the vacuity of the 'ruined world' of Jabès's texts.[88] In his 1973 interview with Charles Tomlinson, Oppen put it like this: 'Because the words are objects, the poem is an object, but the poem is ineluctably transparent also. It refers to those things' (UCSD 16, 34, 4). This 'transparency' is clearly different from that of Jabès, allowing us to see beyond language and to affirm a reality which is at once miraculous and terrifying in the absoluteness of its indifference.[89] As we shall see in the next chapter, Oppen was reading Jabès alongside Blake whose 'little words' spoke vividly of a material history that had all but been effaced in the desert landscape of *The Book of Questions*.[90]

[88] BQ ii. 301. See also the interview with Charles Tomlinson, p. 3: 'People descended from Williams have used this interest in the line as breath, as filling, filling the whole surroundings of the poem with noise, with sound, which is exactly what I didn't intend to do' (UCSD 16, 34, 4).

[89] A similar distinction, between Jabès and Celan, is made by William Franke, 'The Singular and the Other at the Limits of Language in the Apophatic Poetics of Edmond Jabès and Paul Celan', *New Literary History*, 36 (2005), 631: 'Jabès seems to acknowledge no outside of language; for him, rather, words themselves are already inhabited by singularity and alterity that nullify any positive content, every fixed territory or soil.' By way of contrast (633) 'Celan imagines the state before and beyond language through a maximum intensity of earthiness and massiveness'.

[90] Berel Lang, 'Writing-the-Holocaust: Jabès and the Measure of History', in Gould (ed.), *Sin of the Book*, 205 observes that 'the Holocaust turns out for Jabès not to be one event or set of events but a universal history'. Elsewhere in the essay, Lang observes that 'We know then why *The Book of Questions* moves so freely between events of the mid-twentieth century and the centuries of Jewish history before it: together they occupy a single, virtual present.'

7

'Out of the Whirl Wind': *Myth of the Blaze* and *Primitive*

The collection of poems written between 1972 and 1975 that Oppen called *Myth of the Blaze* was never published as a separate volume and first appeared as a sequence in the 1975 *Collected Poems*. One remarkable long poem from that collection—'The Book of Job and a Draft of a Poem in Praise of the Paths of the Living'—puts into play most of the principal themes of Oppen's late work. In doing so, it also develops the network of ideas provisionally assembled in 'The Romantic Virtue', pitting an 'impoverished' language against the 'theatric vision' of traditionalism and locating a certain promise of 'survival' in the image and its account of 'actuality'.

The poem is dedicated to Mickey Schwerner who was one of three Civil Rights workers killed by Klan members in Philadelphia, Mississippi in 1964 (the others were Andrew Goldman, like Schwerner a white New Yorker, and James Chaney, a black Mississippian). In 1967, eighteen men were tried for these murders; seven were convicted by an all-white jury but none served more than six years. As recently as June 2005, the alleged ringleader and head of the local Klan, 80-year-old Edgar Ray Killen, was tried and sentenced to sixty years (as I write, he has again been denied a release bond to appeal his conviction[1]). Oppen had known Mickey Schwerner who was the cousin of his friend, the poet Armand Schwerner, and who rented a room in the Oppens' apartment house while he studied at Columbia.[2] Section 1 of the poem, celebrates their memory, ending with almost apocalyptic images of 'a new sun, the flames | tremendous' (NCP, 241).

While the poem's opening section is reasonably clear, the title is at first sight puzzling. The poem's publication history gives us some clues since in its first printing in the *Grosseteste Review* in 1973 it bore the quite different

---

[1] See *New York Times*, 15 July 2006.
[2] McAleavey, 'The Oppens: Remarks towards Biography', 312. Oppen wrote an unpublished poem called 'Fame' about 'The young man | Who lived | In the basement' before he left New York City for San Francisco (UCSD 16, 27, 62).

title: 'The Lever the Die the Cam' and was then subtitled 'From the Book of Job'.³ That first title refers, no doubt, to Oppen's own time as a worker in a tool and die factory in Detroit and the phrase also appears in section 1 of the poem. But why call the final, collected version of the poem a 'draft'? To avoid the illusion of finish, perhaps, the 'too perfect' style he counselled Shirley Kaufman against? Certainly, as a serial poem 'The Book of Job' seems loosely articulated together in its various sections and the different published versions of the text suggest that Oppen was slow to arrive at its final form. In its first appearance in *Grosseteste Review* in 1973 it had a different opening from the version we now have, along with a different ordering of sections, some of which carried titles which were subsequently abandoned.⁴ When it appeared again with its final title later that year in *European Judaism*, the text was close to that of the version in the *Collected Poems* of 1975 but it now included the poem 'The Occurrences' as its seventh, concluding section.⁵ Subsequent printings in *Ironwood* and *Poetry Review* in 1975 gave the poem as we now have it, but when Oppen published it once more in the 1976 anthology *The New Naked Poetry* the order was different again, with 'The Occurrences' appearing as the poem's final section.⁶

The instability of the poem's text was bound up with the use of repetition and cross-reference which characterizes Oppen's late work, 'quoting, as is my wont, myself' (UCSD 16, 27, 13), with words and phrases echoing recurring preoccupations. As a result, the biblical reference in 'The Book of Job' is initially elusive. Indeed, Oppen's own comments suggest that the connection between the biblical story and the poem was actually quite fortuitous, something he discerned only after writing it. In the 1973 letter to Cuddihy, for example, he writes:

I had not been thinking of Job as I wrote: thunderstruck to discover how closely the poem followed Job's argument—

and so I named it. (SL, 264)

³ *Grosseteste Review*, 6/1–4 (1973), 250–6.
⁴ The poem has a brief section 1: 'wives | husbands | being killed   how write this and they had not found a way | to live I think during | this'. Section 2 begins: 'this fortune who dares say it this | bequest   winds | of our ignorance to the crowds | of our ignorance neither other | nor ours its least rags | stream among the planets. . . .' Section 3 (later section 5) has the title 'To Stand Still', while section 4 (later section 3) is headed 'Fancy Roam' [*sic*], section 5 (later section 2) 'Out of the Whirl Wind', section 6 (later section 4) 'Imagist, the Great Games', and section 7 (later section 6) 'This Fortune Who Dares'.
⁵ 'The Book of Job and a Draft of a Poem to Praise the Paths of the Living', *European Judaism*, 8/1 (Winter 1973/74), 37–9.
⁶ *Ironwood*, 5 (1975), 4–11; *Poetry Review*, 66/1 (1975), 2–5; Stephen Berg and Robert Mezey (eds.), *The New Naked Poetry: Recent American Poetry in Open Forms* (Indianapolis: Bobbs-Merrill Co., 1976), 310–15.

Whether or not the allusion was part of some subliminal process, Oppen clearly wanted the connection to function indirectly (in one early draft the title is 'Out of the Whirl Wind (demiurgos)' with the sub-heading '(from a series parallel to the Book of Job').[7] But why these emphatic pointers to the biblical story? It would seem that Oppen began to think about Job in the late sixties, probably at around the same time that he also became engrossed in Blake's poems (and Blake, of course, memorably illustrated the Book of Job). Interestingly, back in 1958 Oppen had seen Elia Kazan's Broadway production of Archibald MacLeish's play *J.B.*, a version of the story of Job which won the Tony award for Best Play and starred, amongst others, Raymond Massey and Christopher Plummer.[8] Perhaps it was this experience that first ignited his interest in the poem. Linda Oppen recalls that 'The Archibald MacLeish play was a high point earlier on, we all saw it. George taking it seriously for extended conversations. . . . A great production, with the cataclysmic power descending and swirling. The smaller and smaller lone Job bent and flattened by the heat and winds assailing him.'[9] Later, Oppen would also read Jung's *Answer to Job* and discuss it at length with his niece, Andy Meyer, who recalls that 'George was at the time interested in and irritated by Jung.'[10] The two also discussed the Old Testament and the Apocrypha; this influence on his thinking, he said, 'has amazed me' (UCSD 16, 18, 4) and he concluded that, by way of contrast, 'the New Testament is lacking in interest in that it raises no questions at all, it consists entirely of answers' (UCSD 16, 14, 1). Amongst the books of the Old Testament, Job came to occupy a special place for Oppen: 'Of the Old and New Testaments,' he writes, 'all but the poem Job [is] written by Job's comforters' (UCSD 16, 18, 4). The comforters of Job are those who counsel him to accept his fate and not to dispute with God; they are those who ask no questions, and Oppen notes that 'to Job's comforters nothing will answer and nothing speaks' (UCSD 16, 24, 2). They are the outwardly pious, the outwardly righteous, whom God will ultimately ignore in favour of the accursed and accused Job.

In the story, Job, a 'perfect and upright man' (1: 8) is handed over by God to Satan who wishes to test whether Job is loyal to God simply because God has shown him favour. Satan has Job's sons and daughters killed but even then 'Job sinned not, nor charged God foolishly' (1: 22). Satan is given another chance to break him down and this time smites him with boils 'from the sole of his foot unto his crown' (2: 7). Job's wife urges him to curse God and die,

---

[7] See SL, 410 n. 5 (I have not been able to consult this draft, though the lines quoted in SL suggests major differences from the final version).

[8] Archibald MacLeish, *J.B.* (Cambridge, Mass.: The Riverside Press, 1958).

[9] Linda Oppen, personal communication.

[10] Andy (Meyer) Levin, personal communication.

but Job refuses to do this.[11] The three friends come to visit him to comfort him in his suffering, but Job provides trenchant responses to their attempts to make him beg for mercy and to accept that suffering is proof of sin.[12] In his misery, Job decides that 'I will say unto God, do not condemn me; shew me wherefore thou contendest with me' (10: 2). As Job's trials continue, so this desire to have his question answered becomes more urgent. By chapter 13 he is saying, 'Surely I would speak to the Almighty, and I desire to reason with God' (13: 3). The very definition of divine justice is at issue here: 'Whereof do the wicked live, become old, yea, are mighty in power?' he asks (21: 7). After more counsel from the comforters, God finally answers Job 'out of the whirlwind' (38: 1) but, as one commentator puts it, 'The issue, as Job had posed it, is completely ignored. No explanation or excuse is offered for Job's suffering. As Job had expected, God refuses to submit to questioning. But, contrary to expectation, God does not crush him, or brush him away, or multiply his wounds. Rather he subjects Job to a series of questions which are ironical in the extreme, almost to the point of absurdity.'[13] Job, then, never has his question answered; in fact, God turns the tables and begins to question Job: 'Where was thou when I laid the foundations of the earth,' he asks, going on to overwhelm Job with a spectacular account of his creation of the awesome Behemoth and Leviathan. In face of this tirade, Job is humbled:

I know that thou canst do every thing and that no thought can be withholden from thee.

Who is he that hideth counsel without knowledge? Therefore have I uttered that I understood not; things too wonderful for me, which I knew not. (42: 2–3)

In recompense, God now gives Job new sons and daughters, along with twice-over reimbursement of his goods and cattle. 'After this lived Job an hundred and forty years', we are told, and the book comes to a close.

For generations of readers, this story has been seen variously as absurd, moving, ironic, alienating, terrible; either one is reconciled to God's actions by faith or one reels in horror at his sheer vindictiveness and moral inferiority. In the Gospel of James in The New Testament it is said: 'Ye have heard of the patience of Job, and have seen the end of the Lord; that the Lord

---

[11] Cf. UCSD 16, 16, 7: 'Job's wife: She did not perhaps concern herself with the nature of God. When everything that gave life value—when in fact her children had been destroyed—she said simply: curse God and die. That was the only thing she did say. It may not have been profound. But she knew at least when it was over.'

[12] Marvin H. Pope, (trans. and introd.), *The Anchor Bible: Job* (Garden City, NY: Doubleday & Company, 1965), p. lxxx. Cf. UCSD 16,15, 6: 'but perhaps the patients are comforted, as Job was not, by the "proof" that they suffer thru their own wickedness'.

[13] *The Anchor Bible: Job*, p. lxxx.

is very pitiful, and of tender mercy' (James 5: 11), but that seems to sit uneasily with both the cruel indifference shown by God and the vehement and sometimes blasphemous tones of Job's utterances. Our protagonist is profoundly *im*patient, in fact, and this is one of the most remarkable aspects of the book, though orthodox Christian readers have found that predictably hard to accept. Milton's *Paradise Regained*, for example, perpetuates James's version, referring to Job as 'Him whom thy wrongs with Saintly patience born. . . . Who names not now with honour patient *Job*?'[14] The 'wrongs' here are attributed to Satan, of course, but for modern readers the fault is more likely to rest with God for playing this murderous game in the first place. In Jung's *Answer to Job*, for example, the story is taken to represent 'the unvarnished spectacle of divine savagery and ruthlessness', and Jung concludes that 'Job stands morally higher than Jahweh'.[15]

In his largely unpublished notes and papers, Oppen in the late sixties and early seventies made many allusions to the Book of Job and it is clear from these that his understanding of the story was quite different from Jung's. For example, he writes: 'Job: the connection between divinity and a statement which is true The point of the parable is that god answered. <u>What</u> god said———they are of course the words of the man who wrote the parable, But <u>that</u> god answered: this is the fact that the poet reports' (UCSD 16, 16, 11); and, again: 'the important fact is: that God answered. Which means that there is a force, an inexplicable force, in a statement which is true' (UCSD 16, 14, 15); and yet again: 'I think as the writer of the book of Job thought: that if you say something which is true, the whirl-wind will answer'.[16] Oppen repeats variations of this construal of the Book many times in his notes and it is clear that his deep response to the story is motivated by this conjunction of truth and power. He has nothing to say about the content of God's answer (only on one occasion does he remark that 'The answer out of the whirl-wind was "no"' (UCSD 16, 17, 9)), nor does he concern himself with the question of Job's 'guilt', noting only that 'In the Book of Job there is no "confession"' (UCSD 16, 13, 19) and that Job makes no claims to knowledge ('the whirlwind will answer if you know that you do not know' (UCSD 16, 24, 2)).[17] Surprisingly, too, Oppen never comments on the terrifying grandeur of God's speech to Job, the first part of which has been described, uncontroversially, as 'a work of

---

[14] *The Poetical Works of John Milton*, ed. Helen Darbishire (London: Oxford University Press, 1963), 313.
[15] Carl Jung, *Answer to Job*, trans. R. F. C. Hull (London: Routledge & Kegan Paul, 1954), 4, 68.
[16] Oppen, 'Adequate Vision', ed. Davidson, 9.
[17] Cf. UCSD 16, 13, 5: 'I am as agnostic as Job. What I am told by the metaphysical presences (which are also the physical presences) is that I don't know.'

genius unequalled in world literature'.[18] Instead, Oppen's focus is consistently on the simple fact that God answered, which signifies that, as he puts it, 'a statement which is true is related, insofar as it is true to god. . . . only one point of honesty is required to find everything One moment of sincerity threatens to disclose everything' (UCSD 16, 15, 2).[19]

We can begin to see that Oppen is not looking for a moral answer to the fundamental question of why innocents like Job or, indeed, Mickey Schwerner have to suffer. This is surely why he would have felt Jung's reading to be inadequate, since Jung simply reverses the New Testament theodicy which shows God ultimately to be just. A reading closer to Oppen's is given by Northrop Frye in his study of Blake:

Job's comforters accuse him, or at least the Man he represents, of moral evil, and he defends himself in terms of moral virtue. But at the end God shows him that the question is not a moral one at all: that the source of his misery is simply the nature of the world he is in, symbolized in the irresistible power of Behemoth and Leviathan, with a vision of whom the poem concludes.[20]

Compare Oppen's view:

The Poem of Job: it is a great poem. But it is not, as the commentators say————Job's outcries are not, as the commentators say, a progress in the conception of god, and it is not the Godhead who answers. It is the demiurge, the god who made the world[.] There is nothing 'spiritual' in his speech, he has no concern with the spiritual values of good or of bad, he made the material world as the material world could be made[.] that god, as Eckhart said, is not god enough for a flea   he is the demiurge. A demonic god. (UCSD 16, 17, 2)

This distinction between Godhead and Demiurge, which Oppen probably took from Plato's *Timaeus*, grounds the story in a fallen material creation rather than in a world of ethical discriminations. It is of material truth rather than of morality that Oppen speaks, much as does Blake, to whom Oppen now frequently refers. As Frye puts it, 'Moral good and moral evil do not represent any genuine opposition. The one wages wars and executes criminals; the other murders. The one exploits labor; the other robs. The

---

[18] *The Anchor Bible: Job*, p. xxviii.

[19] Cf. UCSD 16, 16, 13: 'That a true statement possesses a power. A strength, the power of a natural storm.' Oppen may have been influenced in this aspect of his thinking by one of his favourite books, Simone Weil's *Waiting on God*, 113: 'That is what Job experienced. It was because he was so honest in his suffering, because he would not entertain any thought which might impair its truth, that God came down to reveal the beauty of the world to him.'

[20] Northrop Frye, *Fearful Symmetry: A Study of William Blake* (Princeton: Princeton University Press, 1969), 361–2. Jung similarly rejects a moral reading in *Answer to Job*, 33: 'it is the behaviour of an unconscious being who cannot be judged morally. Yahweh is a *phenomenon* and not a human being.'

one establishes marriage on the destruction of virginity; the other rapes. But they have a common enemy, the power of genius and prophecy.'[21] Truth, we might say, falls outside of the apparent contraries of 'moral virtue'—it is not about theodicy, the justification of God's ways to man, but about the material presence of the world, the creative force that speaks from out of the whirlwind, the force that, as Blake had said, creates both the tiger and the lamb and cannot be called to account for its actions. Truth is rather that 'moment of sincerity that discloses everything', a sincerity, that is, that equates not to an individual's intentions but to the actuality of the world itself.

Might this, then, help to explain the indirectness of the first section of Oppen's poem? Certainly, a perusal of the revised drafts of this shows him excising phrases like 'draft of a poem | to freedom' (UCSD 16, 24, 6) and 'how write of this' (UCSD 16, 24, 6), phrases which engage relatively clear political and emotional registers.[22] Such explanatory pointers disappear in the final version, shifting the emphasis from protest to the acknowledgement of some external force, the peculiar 'half-lit jailwinds' seen as a 'simulation' of the real force that is truth:

> Our
> lady of poverty the lever the fulcrum
> the cam and the ant
> hath her anger and the emmet
> his choler the exposed
> belly of the land
> under the sky
> at night and the windy pines unleash
> the morning's force what is the form
> to say it there is something
> to name Goodman   Schwerner   Chaney
>   (NCP, 240)

The killing of the three young men seems to take its place in an age-old chronicle of suffering innocents—it is the 'age || of the sea's surf'—and in a sequence of heavily stressed and compacted lines Oppen offers a 'prayer' to 'Our lady of poverty' which rises in a gradual crescendo of anger and is

---

[21] Frye, *Fearful Symmetry*, 197. Cf. Oppen's observation (UCSD 16, 28, 35) 'That God (the god of reward and punishment) said Meister Eckhart, would not be god enough for a flea[.]'

[22] See also the opening to the Grosseteste version: 'wives | husbands | being killed how write of this and they had not found a way | to live I think during | this'.

finally released in the wind's 'unleashing' of 'the morning's force'. [23] The implication is that something in the very frame of things will ensure that the poor and the weak exert some equivalent 'force' against their oppressors: 'the ant | hath her anger and the emmet | his choler'. The allusion is, rather unexpectedly, to a letter from Sir Francis Drake to Queen Elizabeth I in which Drake argues that although the odds are heavily ranged against them, the weak will ultimately secure the vengeance that is theirs by right:

As there is a general Vengeance which secretly pursueth the doers of wrong, and suffereth them not to prosper, albeit no man of purpose empeach them: so is there a particular Indignation, engraffed in the bosom of all that are wronged, which ceaseth not seeking, by all means possible, to redress or remedy the wrong received. . . . For as ESOP teacheth, *even the fly hath her spleen, and the emmet is not without her choler*; and both together many times find means whereby, though the eagle lays her eggs in JUPITER's lap, yet by one way or other, she escapeth not requital of her wrong done [to] the emmet.[24] (my emphases)

It is this 'general Vengeance' which blazes like 'a new sun' at the end of the first section of the poem. Oppen's poem is in no sense, then, a straightforward 'protest' against the crimes committed against Mickey Schwerner and his friends, but offers instead the more complicated proposition that the sincerity of these men's actions unleashes a 'force' that somehow illuminates reality and gives purpose to 'the paths of the living'. The connection to the Book of Job is here, in what Oppen calls in a draft of another poem 'the force | Of a statement thought true | the tremendous force' (UCSD 16, 23, 3), for the 'force', like the whirlwind in Job, comes from outside.[25] This may explain the emphatic dissociation in section 1: 'not we | who were beaten   children | not our | children'.[26] For the suffering of the three young men in Philadelphia, Mississippi is theirs alone and, as one commentator notes of Levinas's handling of this question, 'To ascribe meaning to the Other's suffering is always and necessarily to fall into theodicy, to justify it in the name of a higher order

---

[23] The reference to 'Our | lady of poverty' may be inspired by Jean Genet's *Our Lady of Flowers*. See UCSD 16, 15, 12 where Oppen remarks on Genet's 'transition from the Balcony to Our Lady'.

[24] 'Sir Francis Drake Revived', in Charles W. Eliot (ed.), *Voyages and Travels, Ancient and Modern* (New York: Collier & Son, 1910), 133. Oppen seems not to notice that ants and emmets are the same insect.

[25] Cf. these lines in 'The Tongues': the words | out of that whirlwind his | and not his strange | words surround him'. See below, 189.

[26] See the Grosseteste version: 'winds | of our ignorance to the crowds | of our ignorance neither other | nor ours'. In the draft of a letter (UCSD 16, 12, 5), Oppen speaks of 'a man writing of things that aren't his' and goes on to relate this to 'Goodman, Schwerner and Cheney'.

or purpose.'[27] The word 'ancestral' hovers here: what is the continuity that ties 'us' to these young men who were ready to risk everything (an early draft asks 'to whom | are we ancestral?' (UCSD 16, 26, 5))?[28] It is for this reason, perhaps, that Oppen says that 'there is something to name', for this is memorialization at its most minimal, a naming which refuses the consolations of simple identification. Yet it is from these names and their 'written' record in the poem that the 'vividness' bursts forth, disclosing 'a new sun', an '*island of light*' in which the repeated 'ourselves' proposes an elemental kinship with the murdered men.[29]

Oppen's act of commemoration is, then, a subtle and discriminating one, and while a sense of community is sought it has to be discovered on a different ground. Here his response to the Book of Job seems to accord with that of others who have read the story not as a vindication of God's moral law but as an exploration of the ambiguities of material power. This is the main argument of, for example, Philippe Nemo's *Job et l'excès du mal* which sees Job recognizing that 'this "God" to whom he addresses himself is quite other than the God of the three friends, distinct from the Law, subject to no necessity, capable of the darkest malice as well as the most unexpected benevolence'.[30] Nemo finds (like Jung, though for different reasons) a redemptive figuration of the Jesus narrative in the Book of Job, but other readings which place emphasis on creation rather than on law discern here a utopian, socialist promise which is closer to Oppen's poem. Ernst Bloch, for example, reads the Job story as the quintessential expression of 'the real Biblia pauperum' where the political 'murmuring of the children of Israel . . . reaches its high point'. Job's questioning of God is the ruin of any theodicy, according to Bloch, and allows a vision not of a 'Zeus-like' God, 'high up there', but of a realizable human future, 'the Before-us, of our true Moment'.[31] More recently, the

---

[27] Josh Cohen, *Interrupting Auschwitz: Art, Religion, Philosophy* (New York and London: Continuum Books, 2003), 88.

[28] It is possible that Oppen may have had in mind here his friend Jerome Rothenberg's 'ancestral poetry' book, *Poland/1931* (New York: New Directions, 1969) (Rothenberg described it thus to him in a letter of 1969—UCSD 16, 9, 60). Oppen received a copy of the 'first instalment' of the book in 1969. The difference between Rothenberg's sense of Jewish traditionalism and Oppen's own lack of relation to it might give an interesting inflection to the question of 'ancestry' here.

[29] With regard to the light here, compare SL, 92: 'I think of the truth as emerging not in the atmosphere of mystery, but in the brightest light that can be obtained or can be borne.' This idea is picked up on in the last of 'Some San Francisco Poems' (NCP 233): 'One had not thought | To be afraid || Not of shadow but of light'.

[30] Philippe Nemo, *Job et l'excès du mal* (Paris: Bernard Grasset, 1978), 169 (my trans.).

[31] Ernst Bloch, *Atheism and Christianity: The Religion of the Exodus and the Kingdom*, trans. J. T. Swann (1968; New York: Herder and Herder, 1972), 82, 106, 82. The translation was published just at the time Oppen was writing 'The Book of Job', though there is no direct evidence that he read it.

Italian Marxist Antonio Negri has construed Job's suffering as a form of active 'resistance' which succeeds in substituting material values for transcendental ones, ultimately restoring creative power to human labour. In terms that might recall the 'vividness' of Oppen's poem, Negri declares that when Job is finally able to 'see' God, 'it is like an explosion, a most intense light which illuminates existence, which removes from it even the obscurity on its edges, which makes life powerful again'.[32]

The second section of Oppen's poem seems to take us, albeit circuitously, into exactly this sort of territory. The poet scrutinizes first the windows of houses on California's coastal highway,[33] and then couples the world's 'self-evidence' with 'that fanatic glass from our own | homes our own | rooms we are fetched out' (NCP, 241–2), a rather obscure passage which he elsewhere glosses as 'the fanaticism of the desire to see out'.[34] This 'we' then suddenly acquires specificity:

> we
>
> *the greasers*
> says yesterday's
> slang in the path of tornado[35]

'Greasers' announces the mechanics who will be mentioned several lines later in the section; importantly, it is at once a word designating a particular type of labour and a term of abuse applied to Hispanics and Mexicans. The word is clearly an important 'key' to the poem which at one stage in its composition Oppen had titled 'The Slang Word out of [the] Whirl Wind' (UCSD 16, 24, 1).[36] In a slightly expanded version in one of the drafts he also writes: 'and there find the slang word, the argot out of the whirl-wind || It was awaiting us:—our heritage' (UCSD 16, 24, 2).[37] Rather than going 'feathery | and askew', the carpenter and mechanic are realists whose 'monotheism'—'our heritage'—is a religion anchored in a material world of 'scantlings' (small boat timbers) and navigation (the 'weather-side', or the side of the boat turned toward the wind). In a cancelled passage headed 'Out of the Whirl Wind', Oppen had

---

[32] Antonio Negri, *Il lavoro di Giobbe* (Rome: Manifestolibri, 2002), 51, 142–3 (my trans.).

[33] A draft has the note 'Southern Calif' beside it (UCSD 16, 24, 7).

[34] See 'Interview with George and Mary Oppen', conducted by Power, 201. On 'meaning's instant', see also UCSD 16, 13, 7: 'meaning is the instant of meaning, the image'.

[35] Cf. the early Grosseteste version: 'we the greasers | says the day's slang | in the path of tornado . . .'.

[36] See also UCSD 16, 27, 35: 'there the | slang word speaks | in the whirlwinds'.

[37] Another version of this piece called 'Statement' adds: 'I begin to be afraid of the clowning hoarded threatening rags of those who have refused this heritage' (UCSD 16, 24, 2). Rachel Blau DuPlessis (SL, 410 n. 5) quotes another (unspecified) draft where the use of 'argot' seems very differently weighted: 'argot | of the purchasers slang | of the buyers and "the commonplace || lost" '. See also UCSD 16, 23, 19 on 'the rough slum tongue'.

written: 'we live with iron with steel we move | like kings mechanics | in the path of tornado the wind' (UCSD 16, 24, 2). This 'slang' spoken in the force of the wind is the 'argot' by which an underclass is named and chooses then to name itself—it is 'our heritage', a 'common || wealth of parlance' (NCP, 220) which associates the speaking of 'truth' with a language which, as we saw in the last chapter, is in several senses 'impoverished'.

Here, in contrast to 'The Romantic Virtue', and its willingness to risk failure, 'the mechanical trades are monotheistic, the religion of the craftsman is monotheistic. If the teeth engage, the gear will turn. Always monotheistic and therefore Puritans' (UCSD 16, 15, 12).[38] It is 'The Puritan Virtue' that Oppen celebrates in this passage: while polytheism 'sees all in flux open to any intercession' (UCSD 16, 15, 6), monotheism finds its 'vividness' in the here and now (in interview, Oppen says—rather oddly but revealingly—'a rock is a rock. . . . It's a kind of monotheism, as a matter of fact. I don't think there are two worlds, and another world, this'[39]). 'Monotheism' thus seems to connote a world of material production and skilled labour, a world Oppen will continue to celebrate even though it may now appear anachronistic. In what looks like the draft of a letter, he writes to an unknown correspondent:

((Marx, by the way, was wrong about <u>absolute</u> impoverishment, almost entirely because, like other bourgeois, he was unable to believe that skilled labor involves, primarily——or most importantly——intellectual skills———everyone talking now, also, about the disappearance of skilled labor, the 'automatic' machines——— thousands of tool and die makers making said machines. (UCSD 16, 12, 7)

Yet as Oppen also notes here, 'it is true that the independence and dignity of the skilled worker is under attack——with the rationalization of that work to some extent: Lay-out photographed into the metal, etc——'. In the poem, the slang words ('yesterday's') that move with the 'dancing || valve stems' have accordingly become 'the last words', 'survivors' of another time but now gone 'feathery and askew'. We recall again those 'little words' of Blake's 'Tyger' which will resonate through Oppen's late poems, words whose 'blaze' is that of the factory forge which, in some early versions of the poem, would reappear in 'The Occurrences' 'blue gauze | of the forge' which closed the sequence. In an earlier draft of the 'valve stems' passage which, incidentally, seems to

---

[38] Cf. UCSD 16, 24, 2: 'the steering bar has been carried away, the helmsman swept overboard, the ship has [*illegible*] in the sea and the god appears on deck and the inevitable does not occur. But this is polytheism. The carpenter, the mechanic, thinks the inevitable will occur.' Cf. UCSD 16, 15, 6: 'I did not say the mechanics were Christian or Jewish either: I said they were monotheist——they accept good and evil as deriving from the same laws. . . .'

[39] 'Interview with George Oppen', conducted by Schiffer, 16.

contradict Oppen's claim that he had not been thinking about the biblical story when he composed the poem, the heading 'Job's Comforters' announces the following:

> The words
> Piled on each other, leaning
> Against each other
> Into vertigo: the words
>
> Out of square, have gone askew
> From the beginning. And here have been
> Job's comforters, no other voices
> Possible, the last
> Sound in the ears, the last
> Buzz of the last fly.
>
> (UCSD 16, 27, 23)[40]

In this draft, the association of the words 'Out of square' with Job's Comforters is clearer, but the evolution of the passage is somewhat hard to grasp since in other lines on the same sheet we read that 'The bird is tame | And stands near his feet. | It would be useless to speak to the bird, | And what could he say? | They have lived similar lives. Sometimes I | imagine that he speaks'. This 'Imaginary event', as the passage is titled, is somehow absorbed into the final version so that the birds become words, their tameness contrasting with the whirlwind slang that has preceded them.[41]

The difficulties here are characteristic of Oppen's last two collections of poems and accord surprisingly closely with what Edward Said characterized in his own final book as 'late style'. Prominent features of such a style include 'intransigence, difficulty, and unresolved contradiction', responses to an existential condition in which a sense of ending is bound up with a powerful awareness of the present.[42] Said's particular sense of 'lateness' is indebted to Adorno who writes:

The power of subjectivity in the late works of art is the irascible gesture with which it takes leave of the works themselves. It breaks their bonds, not in order to express itself,

---

[40] The 'Buzz of the last fly' probably alludes to Emily Dickinson's 'I heard a fly buzz—when I died'.

[41] It is clear from the draft that the 'last words' of the final version derived from 'The last bird will be tame'. As for the curious resulting image of the words 'stand[ing] near our feet', Oppen had recently read Celan's 'Conversation in the Mountains' (see above, p. 158 n. 70) where 'you see all the syllables stand around, waiting' (Celan, *Collected Prose*, trans. Rosmarie Waldrop (Manchester: Carcanet Press, 1986), 19). Celan's play here with a 'babbling', deliberately 'impure' Jewish speech might have resonated with Oppen's idea of 'slang'. See John Felstiner, *Paul Celan: Poet, Survivor, Jew* (New Haven: Yale University Press, 1995), 144–5.

[42] Edward Said, *On Late Style: Music and Literature Against the Grain*, introd. Michael Wood (New York: Pantheon Books, 2006), 7.

but in order, expressionless, to cast off the appearance of art. Of the works themselves it leaves only fragments behind, and communicates itself like a cipher, only through the blank spaces from which it has disengaged itself. Touched by death, the hand of the master sets free the masses of material that he used to form; its tears and fissures, witnesses to the finite powerlessness of the I confronted with Being, are its final work.[43]

This conjunction of 'irascible' productive energy with the recognition of an ultimate 'powerlessness' in the face of Being is an ever-present feature of Oppen's late poems and in works like 'The Book of Job' it is crucial that the contradiction between them be left open and unresolved. The style itself is thus infected with what Oppen now begins to call 'strangeness': 'One approaches the nearness of death,' he writes, 'and all becomes strange'; and, again: 'Too strange, all has become strange, the words not mine, nor am I in the words.'[44] The resulting style registers the strangeness of ageing in a world which is at the same time constantly renewing itself; it is, in Said's words, '*in*, but oddly *apart* from the present', coloured by figures of exile and anachronism and caught up in the double temporality of 'ending *and* surviving together'.[45] Here once more Oppen's ideal of 'transparency' will be equated with 'cast[ing] off the appearance of art', in Adorno's words. So, after the wrathful 'vividness' of our poem's opening, the third section sets art aside so as to confront that curious condition of survival:

> luxury, all
> said Bill, the fancy things   always
>
> second hand, but in extreme
> minutes guilt
>
> at the heart
> of the unthinkable hunger fear enemy
> world
>
>   (NCP, 242–3)

In William Carlos Williams's poem, 'All the Fancy Things' of the title refers to 'music and painting and all that', the 'second hand' things which are apparently of no help to us when we face the extremes of fear and guilt.[46] Once again

43 Adorno, quoted from his *Essays on Music* in Said, *On Late Style*, 9.

44 Oppen in '*Primitive*: An Archaeology of the Omega Point', ed. Cynthia Anderson, *Ironwood*, 31–2 (Spring and Fall 1988), 321; UCSD 16, 14, 7. As Alan Golding also notes in 'Place, Space, and Syntax in *Seascape: Needle's Eye*', *Sagetrieb* (forthcoming), the word 'strange' figures prominently in Oppen's late poems.

45 Said, *On Late Style*, 24, 136.

46 William Carlos Williams, *The Collected Poems 1909–1939*, ed. A. Walton Litz and Christopher MacGowan (Manchester: Carcanet Press, 1986), 268–9. The poem is about Williams's mother who 'doesn't know what to do | with herself alone | and growing old up here . . .'.

we enter the time of the survivor: 'all that has touched | the man || touches him | again arms and dis- || arms him', lines that echo the passage in Oppen's notes where 'all the guilts and pretences of that self sink deep into his soul and will never be obliterated wholly again' (UCSD 16, 13, 19). Even the image, 'meaning in the instant', now loses its lyric association with 'the cherry | tree blossoms' of section 2 and becomes something almost ominous: 'tho we forget || the light', lines which recall the last of 'Some San Francisco Poems': 'One had not thought | To be afraid || Not of shadow but of light' (NCP, 233).[47]

The 'shame of loneliness' which here recalls the guilty 'ur-scene' of the fox-hole will return in section 5, but the focus of the sequence suddenly shifts again, this time to the Oppens' 1972 sailing holiday in Maine (part of the passage is drawn from a letter to Oppen's niece in which he records that 'we are ecstatically happy flopping about this rocky coast like a bird gone nuts in the wind' (SL, 242–3)). Here 'we suffer | loneliness painlessly' because it is shared, and while the wind that 'blows thru my head' has lost none of the force it had in the poem's opening sections, in these lines its power occasions 'marvellous games'. 'Inshore', however, it is different, as the fifth section makes clear. Instead of the movements of the 'hurrying sea', the only option now is 'to stand still || like the bell buoy telling || tragedy so wide | spread so || shabby'. These last two lines refer to a painting by Bernard Buffet, *Pietà* (1946), which Oppen saw on a visit to Paris in 1961 and described in these terms in a letter to Linda (see Figure 6).[48] The sombre, muted colours of Buffet's crucifixion scene complement a starkness of composition which emphasizes the harsh angularity of the crosses in the background and the ladders that stand by them. The figures wear contemporary greatcoats and headscarves, and one, who is comforting a very modern-looking schoolboy, carries a shopping-bag. This is the mundane 'shabbiness' that so impressed Oppen—another version of tragedy 'impoverished' and grounded in the social realities of the commonplace.[49] For there is actually no need of eloquence when we speak of mortality: 'the bones of my hands' tell the whole story of ageing, of this 'travelling' through 'always || undiscovered | country'.

In the next section, that motif of journeying finds us 'mid continent', as Oppen recalls the rail journey he and his family made when they moved

---

[47] The light here is both revealing and threatening, a complication of a much earlier (1963) expression of a similar thought: 'the tremendous pull of truth, the tremendous desire to know and to say I think is, as someone said——I forget who——because the truth is all there is; on the other hand, the truth is everything that there is——most terrible, most wonderful, most to be loved in the blazing daylight' (SL, 92–3).

[48] See SL, 53: 'that style of his creates a picture of tragedy so wide spread that it has become mere shabbiness. And it is an immensely effective and sincere picture.'

[49] During this visit to Paris, Oppen explored the working-class district of Ménilmont and concluded in the same letter that 'One could live there perfectly happily'.

Figure 6. Bernard Buffet, *Pietà* (1946)

from New York to San Francisco in 1918.[50] Here again there is tremendous movement, the luxury ('crack') train speeding along with its 'galloping carpets' and 'the highlights | of the varnished tables' (fittingly, perhaps, because the poet was one of Oppen's early enthusiasms, the lines allude to Carl Sandburg's 'Limited': 'I am riding on a limited express, one of the crack trains of the nation'[51]). But this movement also 'sounds':

> we ring
>   in the continual bell
>   the undoubtable bell found music   in itself
>   of itself speaks the word
>   actual heart breaking
>   tone row it is not ended
>   not ended the intervals
>   blurred ring

[50] As Rachel Blau DuPlessis notes (SL, 234), after their 1972 holiday in Maine, the Oppens 'returned to San Francisco via Canada, taking a rail trip across the continent', a trip that may have revived memories of 1918.

[51] Carl Sandburg, *Complete Poems* (New York: Harcourt, Brace, 1950), 20. The poem also has its macabre aspect which Oppen may have recalled here: '(All the coaches shall be scrap and rust and all the men | and women laughing in the diners and sleepers shall | pass to ashes)'.

like walls
between floor
and ceiling

(NCP, 245)

A draft of this passage had at one stage been titled 'The Hegelian Bell' (UCSD 16, 24, 11) and the 'in itself| of itself' that 'speaks the word | actual' recalls, of course, that allusion to Hegel's 'Preface' that Oppen had so frequently cited and had repeatedly worked over in 'The Romantic Virtue' ('consciousness in itself,   of itself carries the principle of actuality' (SL, 290)).[52] Here his memory of that boyhood journey to the West Coast modulates into an idea of humanity 'ringing' in the music of 'the continual bell' that, like the bell buoy of section 5, encloses the self in the ceaseless sounding of the 'actual'.[53] Yet that ringing is at the same time 'heart breaking': 'it is not ended', but the poet knows that it will soon have ceased for him. It is, though, the 'paths of the living' that must be 'praised' here, since the various sufferings of Schwerner and his friends, of the ancient patriarch Job, and of the impoverished 'hired hands' together express a sincerity which 'threatens to disclose everything' (UCSD 16, 15, 2). The enigma of creativity remains, but now seen as the force of 'actuality' itself, it opens at the poem's very end a perspective on the future, on the world of the living:

Pave
the world o pave
the world carve
thereon..[54]

We might seem now to have travelled far from the story of Job. There, God does indeed answer Job, as Oppen stresses, but he does so only to affirm the distance that separates him from humanity. In the King James version of the parable, this distance is that between slave and master. Job replies to God: 'I have heard of thee by the hearing of the ear; but now mine eye seeth thee. Wherefore I abhor myself, and repent in dust and ashes' (42: 5–6). This self-effacement strikes a tone very different from the strong imperatives of Oppen's closing lines. Interestingly, though, a new translator of the Book,

[52] See 'Who Shall Doubt' (NCP, 259) which also uses the phrase for its opening lines.

[53] As my phrasing suggests, this 'ringing' may also have a Heideggerian aspect, as e.g. in *Poetry, Language, Thought*, 72: 'the Open brings beings to shine and ring out', and *On the Way to Language*, 98: 'It is just as much a property of language to sound and ring and vibrate, to hover and to tremble, as it is for the spoken words of language to carry a meaning.'

[54] An earlier draft of this passage is as follows: 'Insects | in the pathless | Forests live their lives | Under the bark Pave | the earth . . . .'. The final words may derive from the Earl of Rochester's 'Upon a drinking Bowle': 'But carve thereon a spreading Vine'. If this is indeed the source, then it gives a hedonistic spin to Oppen's final lines.

Stephen Mitchell, has recently argued that the familiar version of the lines in Job rests on 'the shakiest of philological foundations' and that Job's final words 'issue from surrender; not from submission'.[55] Mitchell's own translation of the lines in question reads as follows: 'I had heard of you with my ears; | but now my eyes have seen you. | Therefore I will be quiet, | comforted that I am dust' (p. 88). There is an enormous difference between these versions, with Mitchell's refusing the orthodox gesture of self-abasement and opting instead for Job's final acceptance of his mortality.[56] As in some of the other 'unorthodox' readings of Job cited in this chapter and, I think, in Oppen's own, it is precisely the troubling relation of personal finitude to the infinite creativity of the real that the biblical story is taken to express.[57] Said's sense of 'ending *and* surviving' is very much to the point here, since this doubleness refuses the reconciliation of contradiction which conventional theodicy would provide. At the same time, that very lack of reconciliation also dramatizes lateness as, to recall a passage from Jabès, 'the same waiting, the same hope, the same wearing out'. Rather similarly, Oppen finds his own late work 'written from the edge of despair, the edge of the void, a paean of praise to the world' (UCSD 16, 15, 3). That second comma abridges a complex movement of thought as it discovers at the Jabèsian 'edge' of nothingness the sheer force of the real. But it is in that moment of pause or transition which no discursive logic can adequately fill that contradiction powerfully inscribes itself in the form of Oppen's writing. In these late poems we find accordingly a recurring rhythmical shape which gives the last stress of each line a kind of finality which is immediately undermined by the enjambement, the sense carrying across into the next line:

> his choler the exposed
> belly of the land
> under the sky
> at night and the windy pines unleash
> the morning's force what is the form
> to say it there is something
> to name . . . .

---

[55] Stephen Mitchell (trans. and introd.), *The Book of Job* (San Francisco: North Point Press, 1987), pp. xxv, xxvii. Further references will be given in the text.

[56] As Bloch notes (118), there is no conception of the afterlife in Job. According to Susan Schreiner, *Where Shall Wisdom Be Found? Calvin's Exegesis of Job from Medieval and Modern Perspectives* (Chicago: Chicago University Press, 1994), 159, 'the idea of a life after death was emerging in Job's day but was ultimately rejected by Job'.

[57] See e.g. Nemo, *Job et l'excès du mal*, 39–40 (my trans.): 'the process that invisibly guides all living things to their death suddenly becomes visible. . . . It is merely a reprieve. Because the end is henceforth *envisaged*, it is already *present*, even if it is far off in the future.' Compare Oppen's note (UCSD 16, 14, 10): 'If we are able to imagine the world from outside, we see that it was our home.'

The lines tend to break in the middle, with an emphatic caesura, while the final syllables seem to halt—almost turning back—and are then propelled over into the next line. Not elegance, then, or a suavity of movement, but an almost ungainly progress which seems to hesitate and sometimes almost to break down altogether. What I'm describing here has much in common with Maurice Blanchot's conception of an 'interrupted' writing: it is, he says,

as though, having renounced the uninterrupted force of a coherent discourse, it were a matter of drawing out a level of language where one might gain the power not only to express oneself in an intermittent manner, but also to allow intermittence itself to speak: a speech that, non-unifying, is no longer content with being a passage or a bridge—a non-pontificating speech capable of clearing the two shores separated by the abyss, but without filling in the abyss or reuniting its shores: a speech without reference to unity.[58]

In the essay on Jabès which Oppen may have read in *European Judaism*, Blanchot described this 'intermittence' as 'a rupture which is the skill of rhythm',[59] and this is exactly what we find in Oppen's late poems where the caesural pause inhibits any rhetorical 'smoothness' and situates the subject on both sides of the 'abyss' at once (as in Jabès's 'kernel of a severance', perhaps). If Jabès's equation of Jew and writer speaks to Oppen's concerns it is in the kind of indeterminacy or 'betweenness' they might seem to share (Jewishness as both singularity *and* numerousness, for example).[60] Oppen's 'non-pontificating speech' becomes 'strange' to the poet himself, and as an uncollected poem called 'To Find a Way' suggests, there is one word spoken in the whirl wind which epitomizes this:

> the turn the cadence the verse and the music,
> clarity, plain glass and the slang word
>
> speaks in the whirl wind the insulted
>
> the challenged

---

[58] *The Infinite Conversation*, trans. Susan Hanson (Minneapolis: University of Minnesota Press, 1993), 77–8. Drawing on Blanchot's essay, Derrida observes in *Writing and Difference*, 71 that 'the caesura makes meaning emerge. It does not do so alone, of course; but without interruption—between letters, words, sentences, books—no signification could be awakened.'

[59] Maurice Blanchot, 'Edmond Jabès' *Book of Questions*', *European Judaism*, 6/2 (Summer 1972), 36.

[60] Cf. Steven Jaron, *Edmond Jabès: The Hazard of Exile* (Oxford: Legenda, 2003), 161–2: 'It is thus that Jabès denied himself the false comfort of the widely used designation *écrivain juif*, and stubbornly insisted on bifurcating it into the separate terms, *écrivain* and *juif*.' On forms of American Jewish 'betweenness', see Stephen Fredman, *A Menorah for Athena: Charles Reznikoff and the Jewish Dilemmas of Objectivist Poetry* (Chicago: University of Chicago Press, 2001), ch. 3.

> blood of childhood now patriarchal
> Jew most strange
>
> to myself neither Roman
>
> nor barbarian the words
>
> and their strangeness saving
>
> ray of strangeness ray
> of exile
>
> ray of light
>
>   (NCP, 302)

The slang word ('yid'?) loses none of its force for remaining unspoken here, and in passing from the insults suffered as a child to his status now as 'patriarchal | Jew' the poet is able to discover a 'saving' self-irony and sense of difference in his 'challenged || blood'.

'To Find a Way' seems to have been developed from an unpublished poem called 'The Powers':

> strange as luck
> and its guilts strange
>
> strange and the slang word speaks
> in the whirl-winds   Semite
>
> to find a way
>
> for myself now
>
>   (NCP, 344)

Here, too, the slang word in the wind is left unspoken and is replaced by 'Semite', though the oddness of this designation points once again not to some sort of collective identification but rather to the speaker's heightened, 'saving' sense of his capacity for self-determination. Yet perhaps even the word 'Semite' might echo as 'slang', not only because of its association with the 'greasers' or the underclass whose name this wind has already spoken, but also because of the now automatic echo of '*anti*-Semite' which the word voices in the wake of the Holocaust. For, as we see in the poem which takes the word 'Semite' as its title, Oppen's late work begins to place his personal 'guilts | of the foxhole' (NCP, 251–2) in the context of larger 'guilts' about living on in the wake of the Nazi genocide. 'Semite' sees Oppen describing himself again as 'neither Roman || nor barbarian', but here he also questions his own motives for enlisting:

> Think
>
> think also of the children
> the guards laughing

> the one pride the pride
> of the warrior laughing so the hangman
> comes to all dinners . . .

> (NCP, 252)

Guilt here arises from Oppen's sense that he enlisted out of arrogance ('the pride | Of the warrior') rather than for the sake of his own family or of those suffering in the camps (we recall the 'jewel' of 'From a Phrase of Simone Weil's'). Interestingly, an early draft of the poem had been more direct:

> . . . shamed degraded

> stripped naked   herded into the gas ovens   Think
> Think also of the children   the guards laughing

> (UCSD 16, 24, 14)

Perhaps mistrusting the dramatic tone here, Oppen later removes the reference to the 'gas ovens', and the final version is designedly elliptical, with the words 'shamed | degraded || stripped naked' referring also to 'my loves' which had 'deceived themselves'.

'Semite' was written around the time of the 1973 Yom Kippur war and various letters show that Oppen was shocked by the invasion of Israel by Egyptian and Syrian troops ('Incredible, incredible history of the Jews, our history, people cannot bear our presence', he wrote to Shirley Kaufman (SL, 271)).[61] At the same time, though, while he was very conscious of 'the Judaism of the poems' he was now writing ('a very strange thing to happen' (SL, 271)), he was, as ever, cautious about any form of political identification.[62] 'I feel a bit like the late Romans in Gaul,' he wrote to Allan Planz, 'Ausonious [*sic*], was it, writing to a friend in Spain———(odd to be neither Roman nor Barbarian as the walls are breached)' (SL, 271). The phrase 'neither Roman nor Barbarian' also appears in 'The Lighthouses' which is dedicated to Louis Zukofsky '*in time of the breaking of nations*', a clear reference to the conflict in the Middle East. Here again the concluding 'ray | of darkness ray of light' is the 'saving | ray of exile' from 'The Powers', the ray that sets Oppen apart, while 'Semite' ends with an even more emphatic separateness:

---

[61] Kaufman was now living in Jerusalem and her letters to Oppen gave him an insider's view of the conflict. 'They still want to eliminate us,' she wrote, 'how can we not believe that—how can we believe anything else?' (UCSD 16, 6, 4).

[62] Cf. UCSD 16, 15, 8: 'Jewish themes increasing in my poems'. In the 1978 interview with Kevin Power, 193, Mary Oppen observes that 'George has also been writing Jewish poems', a reference, presumably to *Primitive*.

> . . . the instant
>
> in the open the moving
> edge and one
> is I
>
> (NCP, 253)

This is the 'meaning's instant' of the image which Oppen now links to Rilke's concept of 'the open' and to the 'moving edge' of *Seascape*. An untitled poem published in 1975 but not subsequently included in *Myth of the Blaze* quotes Rilke's 'the animals and the insects stare at the open' (NCP, 301), but it is notable that the allusion in 'Semite' excludes these inhabitants of the scene. In a progressive narrowing down and purging of the particular, these closing lines literally enact the poem's earlier call for

> a poetry
>
> of the narrow
> end of the funnel proximity's salt gales in the narrow
>
> end of the funnel the proofs
>
> are the images the images
>
> (NCP, 251)

This is what Oppen calls 'a negative metaphysics' which he then goes on to say is 'Not arcane, not metaphysical: except that it is, vividly, the narrow end of the funnel——the "place" where one stands   Space, in that sense: where you stand' (UCSD 16, 16, 8). This is, we might say, a kind of negative theology in the sense that it establishes truth as pre-predicative, as something we can't talk about rather than as a successful assertion ('the proofs | are the images' which are presented 'vividly', as full of life, like the vividness of 'The Book of Job'). The aim must then be 'To hold in our minds the subject: not to allow the comment, the predicate, to destroy it' (UCSD 16, 17, 1). There are indications that Oppen was reading Heidegger's 'On the Origin of the Work of Art' while he was at work on the poems of *Myth of the Blaze*, and passages like the following from 'Semite' certainly echo parts of that essay:[63]

> the proofs
>
> are the images the images
> overwhelming earth

---

[63] The essay was published in Heidegger's *Poetry, Language, Thought*, trans. Albert Hofstadter (New York: Harper & Row, 1971). See e.g. UCSD 16, 24, 11 where amongst drafts of *Myth of the Blaze* poems there are notes on Heidegger's concept of the 'rift [*Riss*]' in *Poetry, Language, Thought*, 63–4. These notes are discussed below, pp. 191–2.

rises up

in its light

(NCP, 251)

As Heidegger puts it, 'as a world opens itself the earth comes to rise up'.[64] Oppen's 'images' are now frequently generic ones which do not evoke particular objects but which point toward a 'world' ('The poem must conceive the world or it is "a thought" a remark' (UCSD 16, 14, 7)). The emphatic reference to 'the images' in this poem and in a number of others takes us to what is now Oppen's primary concern: 'Words cannot be wholly transparent' ('Route', NCP, 194) and thus give us unmediated access to 'actuality' but in privileging subject over predicate they can yield an 'impoverished' language which derives ethical probity from the acknowledgement of art's illusoriness in face of reality's superior creative power. How, then, to weigh 'Semite's' 'one | is I' against 'the seed sprouting | green at my feet among a distant || people' ('The Lighthouses', NCP, 257)? Reflecting on those closing lines from 'Semite', Oppen noted 'Only one is I   only one is the jews——only one is this————this bag' (UCSD 16, 14, 1).[65] Singularity, 'thisness': a persistent concern of Oppen's, as we have seen throughout this book, but here the aporetic space between 'I' and 'the jews' gestures silently toward a dilemma that would continue to trouble him. In the last poems, published as *Primitive* in 1978, many of the themes and figures of *Myth of the Blaze* would reappear, illuminated once again by a light both dazzling and revelatory. As Oppen began his descent into the illness that would soon make writing impossible, so the very fact of creativity became the object of a persistent fascination for him. At this late hour, with his sense of 'ending *and* surviving', Oppen sought finally to transfigure lateness into something 'primitive': 'the name for it,' he wrote, 'is something like the first light imagined' (UCSD 16, 15, 5).[66]

* * * * *

Oppen's unresolved thoughts about Judaism were to meet a more direct challenge when in 1975 his friend Shirley Kaufman secured the couple a place

---

[64] Heidegger, *Poetry, Language, Thought*, 63.

[65] As Oppen notes here, 'Semite' had originally been titled 'Reznikoff's Reading: The Quiet Earth Rises', a reference to the reading on 21 Mar. 1974 at San Francisco State University when Oppen introduced Reznikoff.

[66] See also UCSD 16, 15, 5: '<u>Primitive</u>. First things in that humanity is the light of the world   The <u>Primitive fact: the existence of the world</u> and that the light of the world is our humanity (our humanity is the light of the world . . . "Primitive" i.e: first things.'

at Mishkenot Sha'ananim, an artist's retreat in Jerusalem. Receiving this news from Kaufman, Oppen wrote back to her:

As for us, we think it will be marvellous. Marvelous. Almost literally. For, no, I don't think I could become an Israeli: my sense of Jewishness is a vague sense of being foreign and therefore, in an american way, or rather one of the american ways, faintly aristocratic———the word may not be the exact word, and the feeling may be hard to define, but it's mine, and I'm stuck with it.[67]

Oppen is keen to make his position clear at the outset, and his tone suggests that he already knew that the trip to Israel would be, as he later put it, no 'vacation in Maine' (SL, 307) and that it would likely bring to a head the troubled thoughts he had been having since 1972 about his own Jewishness. In his notes, he wrote with perhaps a sense of foreboding: 'In Israel: will we discuss only our Jewishness? I can understand, in the circumstances that we may be able to discuss nothing else. It is one of the terrible consequences of the attack on the Jews———about the most terrible perhaps' (UCSD 16, 13, 17). To his niece Andy, Oppen confided that 'I also don't know how we can be buying a ticket to the Middle East, but we are. I feel adrift' (UCSD 16, 7, 28). Might Jerusalem be, he wondered, 'the way away from home' (UCSD 16, 16, 7)?[68] He remained sceptical, however: 'we'll soon be embraced, enwrapped, argued with,' he wrote to Andy, ' "It's home" (as our friend Julian [Zimet] wrote), "and I'd leave it again" ' (UCSD 16, 7, 28).

The Oppens arrived in Jerusalem at the beginning of September and stayed until 13 October. During that time, as Mary records in her unpublished *Jerusalem Journal*, they explored the old city of Jerusalem and visited several kibbutzim—Degania, the first of these communities to be founded, and Ein Hahoresh, where Abba Kovner lived.[69] They went to the Mosque and the Wailing Wall, with its stones from Solomon's Temple (29), to 'the man-made mountain' Herodian (12), the Dead Sea (3–4) and Lake Kinneret (12), wondering at the harsh but beautiful landscape and 'the relentless desert' (27) which frequently seemed 'enchanted, unreal, a back-drop, not three dimensional' (10). They watched the 1972 film *Pourquoi Israel?* made by Claude Lanzmann, a visitor to the Mishkenot (26–7), and they made the most of opportunities to meet Israeli writers. Evenings were spent in discussion with

---

[67] Oppen, Letter to Shirley Kaufman, July 1975, *http://writing.upenn.edu/epc/authors/oppen/oppen_letter_to_Kaufman_5.html*

[68] The passage in full reads 'Jerusalem as the way away from home—of what has been home for too long. And a depth of time so great that I feel I will never be at home again—if I ever was.' The phrase is used in the later poem 'To Make Much' (NCP, 271–2) to recall the Oppens' youthful 'escape' from their family backgrounds.

[69] *Jerusalem Journal*, Mary Oppen Papers, UCSD 125, 1, 28. The *Journal* comprises forty pages of typescript with autograph corrections. Page numbers will be given in the text.

the Tel Aviv poet Meir Weisltier (18), novelist David Shahar (20), poet Yehuda Amichai (SL, 306), and, of course, 'our friend' Abba Kovner (26). Writing from Israel to his publisher, James Laughlin, Oppen spoke of 'Wonderful conversations—Amichai, Abba Kovner, and others, all treating us as if we had known each other for ever' (SL, 306) and he seems to have kept to himself his earlier doubts about *My Little Sister*. Indeed, Kaufman recalls that 'George and Abba spoke about the War in Europe and the early Communist ideology of Kovner's kibbutz. They communicated with long, warm silences, Abba's halting English, and my husband as interpreter.'[70] At the same time, predictably, there were tensions.[71] Oppen was concerned, for example, that there was little evidence of 'accommodation to the Arabs to heal the breach, to understand the Arab viewpoint' (he debated this issue with David Shahar (20)), and there was the disturbing presence of armed guards everywhere which, as he wrote to James Laughlin, suggested that 'there is no possibility of anything but war forever' (SL, 306). For her part, Mary found the religious commitments of socialist kibbutz members 'difficult to understand and very difficult to tolerate' and it was a relief to her that 'Abba himself is not religious or is probably agnostic' (23).

The most pressing problem, though, as Oppen had reckoned in advance, was that 'everyone wants to ask us why we don't immigrate, and we are ashamed to answer . . . and they're too polite to force us to answer————, and we are heartsick' (SL, 306). In her *Journal*, Mary was characteristically direct on this issue: 'Even though there is anti-semitism and although it may be increasing—still our lives in the U.S. are flourishing lives even though the question of identity does plague many, increasingly in the U.S and is hard to solve' (12). 'George and I have a sense of identity with the U.S.', she concluded, 'I have tasted exile and I know the desolation of the soul of being expatriate and I am not a Jew' (14). Perhaps for Oppen, too, the ever-present dilemma of immigration and exile could not but recall the difficult years in Mexico: 'I think of the nine years we spent in Mexico as refugees,' wrote Mary, 'and I remind myself that no matter how one has been treated in one's own country it is still the country of one's birth and of one's earliest and most

---

[70] Kaufman, 'The Obvious and the Hidden: Some Thoughts about "Disasters"', *Ironwood*, 26 (Fall 1985), 153. Kaufman notes that 'We spent a day with the Kovners at their kibbutz; there were other visits in Jerusalem.'

[71] According to John Taggart, 'Walk-Out', 31 Oppen told friends Frances Jaffer and Mark Linenthal that the visit was 'frustrating' and 'disappointing'. 'The reasons', says Taggart, 'ranged from the expensiveness of living in Jerusalem to the relative lack of interest in Oppen's work among Israeli writers.' Neither 'reason' is given much prominence in Mary's *Journal*; indeed she enjoyed 'conversation that is understood like poetry' (16) and noted that 'The professor in Comparative Literature at the Hebrew University is going to teach George's poetry and the Objectivists at the University this fall' (19).

integrated memories and there is a love that cannot be entirely foresworn' (35). For all the friendliness encountered during their visit, Israel was in a 'state of embattlement' (5), 'The life, the dangers giving every moment a poignant heightened immanence, a shining forth' (16), and while there was much natural beauty to admire, the legacy of the Holocaust was everywhere in evidence: 'The expressions on the faces of the older people are harried, worried, sad, closed; the bitterly closed mouth does not smile easily nor do the eyes light up at a chance encounter—some of these have been through the Holocaust. People at extremity are not preoccupied with harmony' (15). Israel seemed 'part of the disturbed world with problems no one knows how to solve', Mary thought (21), while at the same time its historical density made it seem alien and intractable, the villages 'little changed since Bible times' (30). Mary's journal is a valiant attempt to make sense of all this and to acknowledge vitality and generosity where she finds it, but ultimately Jerusalem left them both at a loss, throwing them back upon themselves in face of a history which was not theirs and a present which was so tangled by different strands of immigration that exile seemed almost a generic condition. By the end of their first month, Mary concluded: 'Two—a unity of two, G. and I came to this ancient land a unity of two. We go everywhere with our lives wrapped around us, puzzling over history. What is history? I make out our history and our lives by two, but the past? But the people round us? What do I make of them?' (26). On their last day, the Oppens 'sat and talked about Israel, about ourselves, about what we would say on our return to the U.S., about what we want of our lives now that we are sixty-seven years old'. They concluded that 'war with the Arabs is a fact, continuing into a far distant future' and that 'after the Holocaust our resolve joins that of Israel—the Holocaust must never be forgotten—Jews must fight for their lives—for our lives—' (38). Their lives, our lives: certain distances would remain.

On 14 October the couple flew on to Athens where they spent five days before returning to the US. Only two pages of Mary's *Journal* record their time in Greece, but visits to the Parthenon and to the temples of Poseidon at Sounion and Aphaea at Aegina left her with a strong impression of harmony: 'A monument of respect and love has been found and preserved in a triumph of the human spirit among the forces of wind and wave, mountain and storm' (39). In contrast to Jerusalem, there was 'good eating' here (39), and the overall impression recorded in her notes is one of beauty and peace. '[W]e had five precious Greek days': so Mary ends her *Journal*, tacitly contrasting this with the intellectual and emotional turmoil of their six weeks in Israel.

* * * * *

It would nonetheless be the harsh desert landscape of Israel and not the vivid harmonies of Greece that would set the tone for some of the key poems in *Primitive*, a volume whose very title evoked for Oppen ' "that other antiquity", the Northern, the non-classic' (SL, 18), a 'monotheism' of labour and of 'sharp corners' and 'rocky edges' (UCSD 16, 17, 8) rather than the sensual delights of Mediterranean polytheism.[72] The difference here may recall the contrast Emmanuel Levinas draws between 'the myth of Ulysses returning to Ithaca' and 'the story of Abraham who leaves his fatherland forever for a yet unknown land, and forbids his servant to even bring back his son to the point of departure'.[73] The Hebraic story is, in Levinas's view, the more 'radical' since it exemplifies '*a movement of the same unto the other which never returns to the same*'. Ironically it was Oppen's visit to Israel that convinced him that the only 'way away from home' would remain the one that he and Mary had already taken in their youth. Certainly, the severity of not returning and the unremitting openness to the other that Levinas values resonate with the mood of Oppen's last volume. In notes for *Primitive*, he declared that 'The Law and the prophets is not that we are united, that we are brothers, but that we are here' (UCSD 16, 26, 4), and this simple recognition yields an all-embracing paradox whereby, as the earth turns and we assume the full weight of 'that great loneliness', 'all or nothing confronts us' ('A Political Poem', NCP, 265):

> the day
>
> dawns on the doorsteps its sharpness
> dazes and nearly blinds us

Once again, the whirlwind which announces the miracle of creation blows through these poems: there is 'this wind that || rises like a gift | in the disorder' ('Disasters', NCP, 267), 'a wind | utterly outside ourselves' ('The Poem', NCP, 270), 'the words | out of that whirlwind' ('The Tongues', NCP, 275), 'the wind's || squall' ('Populist', NCP, 277), 'winds as you pass' ('*Gold on Oak Leaves*', NCP, 280), and 'a wind destroyed || shelter' in 'The Whirl Wind Must' (published in 1978, but not included in *Primitive*, NCP, 308). In these last poems, that wind from 'The Book of Job' often stirs a landscape which derives, as Taggart notes, partly from Jabès's texts and partly from the visit to Israel: in

---

[72] As we saw earlier, 'primitive' was used by Oppen in a special sense to mean 'first light', 'first things'. He had no time for 'primitivism': see e.g. UCSD 16, 5, 3: 'The wisdom of primitive man—though it was wisdom—is the wisdom from which I most wish to free myself.'

[73] Emmanuel Levinas, 'The Trace of the Other', trans. Alfonso Lingis, in Mark C. Taylor (ed.), *Deconstruction in Context: Literature and Philosophy* (Chicago: University of Chicago Press, 1986), 348 (emphases in original).

'Disasters', for example, written in Jerusalem,[74] 'the wind has blown the sand about | and we are alone' (NCP, 267), the sands are 'dazzling' (NCP, 268), there is the 'tent in the desert', and the 'dance || of the wasp wings' that evokes the belly-dance (NCP, 268).[75] The figures of loss in this poem, of Sarah, of a sister, of an imaginary brother, are echoed in the 'salt || and terrible hills' and 'the caves | of the hidden people' (NCP, 269). The motif of travelling ('journey immense | journey' (NCP, 275))[76] through 'the forever | savage country' (NCP, 274) is coupled with an imagery of heat and movement that runs through *Primitive*: 'burning burning for we are not | still nor is this place a wind | utterly outside ourselves' (NCP, 270).

What is most remarkable about these late poems, though, is not finally a Jabèsian negativity but actually its reverse: here 'the marvel || of the obvious' (NCP, 268) which lies 'outside ourselves' is so intense that it behoves the poet to say as little as possible *about* it ('comment, the predicate', will 'destroy it'). Like any negative theology, this poetics seeks to protect the absolute otherness of what it venerates, but where, for Jabès, this is figured by absence and vacuity, for Oppen the spectacle of the earth as it 'rises up in its light' ('Semite', NCP, 251) is, like Job's vision of creation, of such material force that language is almost speechless before it. Yet it is not just that the fragmented and elliptical mode of these late poems enacts an unequal confrontation of poetry with the real, but that in the act of enunciation which brings a world into being the poet is somehow effaced, his voice become empty and indeterminate. This is perhaps what Oppen had always meant when he invoked 'silence' and 'transparency' as his poetic ideals, but it is only in his late style that the temporally divided self of the survivor comes also to define the poet's relation to language. In 'The Tongues', for example:

> the words
> out of that whirlwind his
> and not his strange
> words surround him

> (NCP, 275)

Again, the poet's words are 'strange' to him, at once familiar and unfamiliar, detached from him and utterly remote from anything he might think of as 'speech', as the 'interrupted' rhythm of the lines emphasizes. This is not,

---

[74] See Shirley Kaufman, 'The Obvious and the Hidden: Some Thoughts about "Disasters"', 153.

[75] In the ancient practice of belly-dancing, a wasp was apparently hidden in the woman's veils.

[76] Cf. the epigraph to 'The Little Pin: Fragment' (NCP, 254): '*The journey fortunately [said the traveller] is truly immense*' (italics in original). The quotation is from Kafka's parable 'My Destination': 'No provisions can save me. For it is, fortunately, a truly immense journey.'

of course, a mere poetic fancy, and Oppen's increasingly anxious condition during these last years made this kind of uncanniness terrifyingly real for him ('The Tongues' appeared in 1977, the year in which his illness became clear).[77] At the same time, though, it is easy to see how this sense of a fading linguistic agency was, for Oppen, at once symptomatic of a frightening and all-pervading 'strangeness' *and* a fulfilment of his poetic of 'impoverishment', with its tacit critique of modernism's 'theatric vision'.

In the poems of *Primitive*, the poet as survivor is adrift in time, speaking of himself in the third person, the words 'his | and not his', and seeing himself as 'another' who is lost:

> *O I see my love I see her go*
> *over the ice alone* I see
> myself   Sarah   Sarah   I see the tent
> in the desert my life
> narrows my life
> is another I see
> him in the desert I watch
> him he is clumsy
> and alone my young
> brother he is my lost
> sister her small
> voice among the people the salt
> and terrible hills whose armies
> have marched and the caves
> of the hidden
> people.

('Disasters', NCP, 268–9)

As John Taggart has noted, Sarah is a composite figure here: as Abraham's half-sister she doubles as wife and sister (Oppen's Mary and Libby) and the story that is told of her in Genesis is clearly located in 'the salt || and terrible hills' of Israel, where Oppen wrote the poem.[78] These figures of loss seem to fold back into the poet's own sense of himself as another, a projection which is clearer in one of the drafts of this section where Oppen writes 'I see that I approach my life's | end my life | and my life | narrows I | is another I see him go | in the streets . . . ' (UCSD 16, 26, 5).[79] The sense of temporal disjunction here—the

---

[77] Cf. UCSD 16, 14, 7: 'Too strange, all has become strange, the words not mine, nor am I in the words.'

[78] See Taggart, 'Walk-Out', 65–70. Taggart suggests that Oppen's address to Sarah may recall Kovner's *My Little Sister*, though there is no direct textual reference. Kaufman makes a similar suggestion, in 'The Obvious and the Hidden'.

[79] Taggart, 'Walk-Out', 67 notes the probable allusion to Rimbaud's 'I is another'.

remembered childhood ('the child still lives in him——the tragedy——and that he is someone else' (UCSD 16, 26, 8), the experience of 'that other | The survivor' (NCP, 212))—these disjunctions destroy the familiar bond between the poet and his words, making them seem to come to him from outside. In 'The Poem', for example, 'language || lives and wakes us together | out of sleep', its advent signalled by

> . . . burning burning for we are not
> still nor is this place a wind
> utterly outside ourselves and yet it is
> unknown and all the sails full to the last
>
> rag of the topgallant, royal
> tops'l, the least rags
> at the mast-heads
>
> to save the commonplace save myself Tyger
> Tyger still burning in me . . . .
>
> (NCP 270)

The wind is once again the corrosive force of the real, the inflated sails recalling the world's 'least rags' which, in 'The Book of Job' poem, 'stream among the planets' (NCP, 240). Yet this wind is also 'unknown' and there is frequently the sense in these poems that poetry is hard pressed to meet the challenge of the world which in its sheer material reality is 'Too strange for poetry—to strange for writing or for signature'.[80] In notes written at this time, Oppen goes back to Heidegger, and specifically to the recently translated essay on 'The Origin of the Work of Art', to try to get some purchase on this dilemma. For writing can no longer be thought of as self-expression—'Truth', he observes, 'Not statement: an open clearing' and this 'clearing' is linked directly to a quotation from Heidegger's essay, 'the saying of the unconcealedness of what is' (UCSD 16, 24, 11).[81] Poetry, Heidegger claims here, is 'the saying of world and earth', it is a holding together of the artwork, which 'set[s] up a world' (44), and the earth which resists it and withdraws from it ('Earth juts through the world and world grounds itself on the earth only so far as truth happens as the primal conflict between clearing and concealing' (55)).

It is here that Heidegger introduces the concept of the 'rift [*Riss*]' between world and earth, a 'cleft' in which 'figure, shape, Gestalt' (64) disclose

---

[80] Oppen in '*Primitive*: An Archaeology of the Omega Point', ed. Anderson, 321.
[81] See Heidegger, *Poetry, Language, Thought*, 74: 'Poetry is the saying of the unconcealedness of what is.' Further references will be given in the text.

truth as the simultaneous expression of revelation and concealment. As one commentator puts it:

Together they disclose the rift which separates language and reality. Just as the material presence of the object prevents language from fully penetrating and subjecting it so that some opacity always remains, so by forcing what is to be known into our linguistic molds we prevent what is from showing itself to us as it is. Heidegger's term 'earth' points towards the irreducible opacity which attends like a shadow all our knowledge of the real.[82]

In his notes, it is precisely this 'rift' which now draws Oppen's attention: ' "what unites opposites is the <u>rift</u>" ', he writes (UCSD 16, 24, 11),[83] and where Heidegger finds in 'figure' 'the structure in whose shape the rift composes and submits itself' (64), Oppen now defines the image in this way: 'images: the world unified by the cleft, the gap: "the world" extant in the gap' (UCSD 16, 24, 11). Just as the prosodic 'gap' induced by Oppen's emphatic use of the caesura had banished the speaking voice, so now the author is effaced in the 'blaze' of the world's disclosure. As Heidegger puts it, 'It is not the "N. N. fecit" that is to be made known. Rather, the simple "factum est" is to be held forth into the Open by the work: namely this, that unconcealedness of what is has happened here, and that as this happening it happens here for the first time; or that such a work *is* at all rather than is not' (65).

The poem called 'Myth of the Blaze' had already produced an exemplary image of the rift as revelation *and* concealment, as transparency *and* opacity:

> . . . to speak
> to the eyes
>
> of the Tiger   blaze
> of the tiger   who moves in the forest leaving
>
> no scent
>
> but the pine needles' his eyes blink
>
> quick
> in   the shack
> in the knife-cut
> and the opaque

---

[82] Karsten Harries, 'Language and Silence: Heidegger's Dialogue with Georg Trakl', in William Spanos (ed.), *Martin Heidegger and the Question of Literature: Toward a Postmodern Literary Hermeneutics* (Bloomington: Indiana University Press, 1976), 166.

[83] There is no direct source in Heidegger's essay for Oppen's quotation, but it is said there that 'This rift carries the opponents [earth and world] into the source of their unity by virtue of their common ground' (63).

white

bread each side of the knife

(NCP, 249)

Here the 'gap', literalized again in the 'cut' of the caesura and in the poem's spatial layout, 'unites opposites'—and 'opposites are not contraries' (UCSD 16, 24, 11)—evoking the tiger as both stealthy predator and disembodied presence ('leaving || no scent'), while the incisive 'knife-cut' is bounded at its edge by the 'opaque' masses of the white bread. '[T]he Open brings beings to shine and ring out,' writes Heidegger (72), and that sense of exultant revelation is there in the brilliance of Oppen's commonplace image. It is all finally very simple, as Oppen observes in his notes: 'the white bread: the Tyger is material existence——matter. The bread too is the Tyger, tho the image of the bread is also disclosure, an image of disclosure' (UCSD 16, 24, 1). But this is simplicity in its most potent form, and in the lines that precede my quotation Oppen has referred again to 'the narrow || end of the funnel', 'the "place" where one stands' (UCSD 16, 16, 8), the point at which 'world' and 'earth' converge. Amidst the brooding 'strangeness' of his last, ailing years, it is as if the sure knowledge of an end in sight is coupled with the conviction that what happens in the poem 'happens here for the first time', as Heidegger puts it, offering thus yet another beginning, another 'first light', and a final recognition that 'the light | in the rear-view mirror is not | death but the light || of other lives' ('Populist', NCP, 276). This is truly to find poetry at 'the edge of despair, the edge of the void, a paean of praise to the world' (UCSD 16, 15, 3) and no amount of explanatory 'grammar' can quite explain how poem and poet can inhabit both at once. It is fitting, perhaps, that *Primitive* should end with a minute adjustment of a line from Eliot's 'The Love Song of J. Alfred Prufrock', 'Till human voices wake us, and we drown'. Attentive, as ever, to the 'little words', Oppen substitutes 'or' for 'and' so that his version, as he notes elsewhere, says 'contrary to Eliot, other voices | than those we have heard must wake | us, or we will drown'.[84] Not, then, even now, the false consolations of sleep and separateness, but rather an awakening to new and as yet unheard voices: this final poem concludes with a generosity of attention which is the more impressive for having to consort with Oppen's recognition of his own fearfulness. As an ending, 'Till Other Voices Wake Us' expresses the full force of Oppen's poetics which, as we have seen in so many different ways, constantly commits itself to new beginnings. So in this late moment there are 'no heroics, obviously'

---

[84] Oppen in '*Primitive*: An Archaeology of the Omega Point', ed. Anderson, 323.

('Two Romance Poems', NCP, 261), only the more impressive discovery in that 'first light' of *Primitive* of another genuine beginning in 'the light || of other lives':

> . . . the myriad
> lights have entered
> us it is a music more powerful
> than music

> (NCP, 286)

Oppen's Reading of Heidegger

'I was startled on encountering Heidegger some time ago, 1950', remarked Oppen in his 1973 interview with Charles Tomlinson. So began an interest which would colour Oppen's thinking throughout the sixties and on into the early seventies. In the interview he is referring to his discovery of the first English translation of Heidegger's work, *Existence and Being*, which contained four important essays: 'Remembrance of the Poet', 'Hölderlin and the Essence of Poetry', 'On the Essence of Truth', and 'What is Metaphysics' (the essay which includes Heidegger's account of 'boredom'). The collection was edited by Werner Brock who also supplied a long and detailed account of *Being and Time* and of the four essays. Oppen never seems to quote from *Being and Time* in his notes, and his copy (held in the Mandeville Special Collections) is unmarked and shows little indication of extensive use. When asked in an interview in 1980 whether it was this work in particular which had influenced him, Oppen replied 'Yes, in particular',[1] but it is likely that his knowledge of the text came in fact mainly from Brock's essay.[2] Perhaps for this reason, *Existence and Being* remained an important collection for him and there is some evidence that he returned to it in the early sixties.[3] Rachel Blau DuPlessis has suggested that it is this volume along with *Being and Time* that Oppen loaned to Robert Duncan in 1969.[4]

During the sixties and into the seventies, Oppen seems to have kept up with translations of Heidegger as they appeared. As noted above (Ch. 2 and Ch. 3), Oppen was familiar with *Introduction to Metaphysics* which exerted a formative influence on *This in Which*, and a passage in a 1963 Daybook (UCSD 16, 19, 6), shows his

---

[1] 'Poetry and Politics: A Conversation with George and Mary Oppen', conducted by Burton Hatlen and Tom Mandel, GOMP, 34.

[2] Martin Heidegger, *Existence and Being*, introd. Werner Brock (Chicago: Henry Regnery, 1949). This paperback edition owned by Oppen is paginated differently from the hardback published at the same time. Brock's 'An Account of "Being and Time"' occupies pp. 11–116. Most of Oppen's markings are of passages in Brock's Introduction. In a letter to John Crawford (UCSD 16, 3, 44), Oppen refers to a passage 'from Heidegger— —or, for brevity, Werner Brock commenting on and partly quoting from Heidegger'. The volume is referred to in David McAleavey's interview 'Oppen on Literature and Literary Figures and Issues', 120 where Mary also confesses 'I got nowhere with *Being and Time*, I had to give it up.'

[3] A marginal annotation in Oppen's copy compares a passage from Heidegger to a view held by William Bronk, whose manuscript of *The World, Worldless* Oppen was reading in Jan 1963. Heidegger's quotation of Holderlin's line 'Foolish is my speech' (260) provokes the marginal comment: 'cf. Bronk: The center of things as "To not know".'

[4] See SL, 182: 'lending you a selection of Heidegger "early" and "Late" periods, if it matters'. Oppen had also loaned Charles Tomlinson a work by Heidegger in 1964—see SL, 386 n. 8.

familiarity with *What Is Philosophy?* (translation 1958).[5] As is shown in Chapter 3, above, he also read the 1960 translation *Essays in Metaphysics: Identity and Difference* (SL, 136), one passage of which became the object of a particular fascination for him (see above, pp. 77–82). Additionally, in his 1978 interview with David McAleavey, Oppen recalled reading Heidegger's 'Conversation on a Country Path', one of two short pieces that comprise *Discourse on Thinking* (translation 1966).[6] It is likely that his reference to 'indwelling' in a letter to John Crawford was a result of his reading this text.[7]

A quotation from Heidegger's *The Question of Being* (translation 1958) in Oppen's notes indicates his acquaintance with that text,[8] and according to Alexander Mourelatos Oppen also owned a copy of *Kant and the Problem of Metaphysics* (translation 1962).[9] This almost systematic interest in Heidegger's writing persisted into the seventies and had some impact on Oppen's late poems. He read the essays in *On the Way to Language* (1971), a line from which—Stefan George's 'No thing may be where words break off'—apparently concludes an uncollected poem called 'Words',[10] and in the McAleavey interview, he recalled his enthusiasm for 'A Dialogue on Language' included in that volume.[11] As unpublished notes on Heidegger's concept of the 'rift [*Riis*]' indicate, he also read *Poetry, Language, Thought* quite soon after the translation appeared in 1971.[12]

---

[5] In a passage from the *Daybook*, Oppen quotes from Heidegger's *What is Philosophy?*, trans. William Kluback and Jean T. Wilde (London: Vision Press, 1958) 29: 'We have uttered the word "philosophy" often enough. If, however, we use the word "philosophy" no longer like a wornout title, if, instead, we hear the word "philosophy" coming from its source, then it sounds thus: *philosophia*. Now the word "philosophy" is speaking Greek. The word, as a Greek word, is a path' (UCSD 16, 19, 6).

[6] McAleavey, 'Oppen on Literature', 118.

[7] SL, 115: 'That which exists of itself cannot be explained   it cannot be analysed. It is the object of contemplative thought, it is known by "indwelling".' The letter is dated June 1965 in SL, but the original carries no date. It is therefore tempting to think that Oppen's sudden use of 'indwelling', a word not found elsewhere in the Heidegger texts he was reading, makes the date of this letter some time in 1966. Heidegger develops the term in *Discourse on Thinking*, trans. John M. Anderson and E. Hans Freund (New York: Harper, 1966), 82 ff. The German *In-Sein* is rendered 'Being-in' in the translation of *Being and Time* (see, e.g. 79). See also Laszlo Versényi, *Heidegger, Being, and Truth* (New Haven: Yale University Press, 1965), 11 on 'Being-in' or 'in-dwelling': 'In Heidegger's use the term (*In-Sein*) refers to Dasein's intentionality, its interest in, awareness of, openness toward, familiarity and involvement with the beings in its world.' As noted above, Ch. 3, Oppen owned a copy of this work.

[8] See UCSD 16, 17, 6 where Oppen quotes the following from *The Question of Being* (1959; London: Vision Press, 1974), 43: 'For it is a part of the essence of the will to power not to permit the reality which it has power over to appear in that reality in which it itself exists.'

[9] Alexander Mourelatos, personal communication.

[10] See Burt Kimmelman, *The 'Winter Mind'*, 90. The line is apparently quoted in a 1971 letter from Cid Corman to William Bronk (Columbia University Archives). This poem, which differs from an unpublished one with the same title in the UCSD archive, was, says Kimmelman, 'published at the time in a magazine'. I have not so far been able to locate it.

[11] McAleavey, 'Oppen on Literature', 117.

[12] For the notes on *Poetry, Language, Thought*, trans. Albert Hofstadt (New York: Harper & Row, 1971), 63–4, see UCSD 16, 24, 11, discussed in Ch. 7, above. A reference in a letter of 1973 to 'the predominance of objects' (SL, 254) may recall Heidegger's talk of 'the predominance of objectness' in his account of Rilke there (130).

This brief outline should give some sense of the intensity and persistence of Oppen's interest in Heidegger. Indeed, an interview with him in 1980 intimates that he was still reading the philosopher in his final years, though Mary carefully corrects this by remarking that 'those were ideas that were digested. . . . Heidegger somehow isn't there any more. We seem to have taken it. We look at it again and somehow it doesn't have that freshness or that discovery that it did have'.[13] By 1980, Oppen was almost certainly too ill to wrestle with the intricacies of Heidegger's works, though when one of the interviewers remarks 'I've seen—within the last 6 or 8 months—I've seen Heidegger open on your table, so you must still be reading Heidegger', Oppen's simple rejoinder 'Yes' testifies, perhaps, to the symbolic significance the philosopher's works still held for him.

[13] 'Poetry and Politics: A Conversation with George and Mary Oppen', conducted by Burton Hatlen and Tom Mandel, GOMP, 34, 35.

'The Romantic Virtue' (UCSD 16, 31, 16)

The following is a transcript of the typescript pages gathered together under the heading 'The Romantic Virtue'. Insignificant typographical errors have been silently corrected. Italic is used to indicate handwritten material and strikethrough to show deletions. Insertion arrows signal text placed above the line. Horizontal lines show separate, pasted strips of text.

[p.1]

WORK   THE ROMANTIC VIRTUE, NOT THE PURITAN
VIRTUE   THE RISK OF FAILURE

was afraid ˆafter allˆ to
    risk failure   *His fatal carelessness*

Once we possessed the word— —what art is not Romantic
What more romantic than white marble— —unless the painted

KOVNER

These experiences are not such as to touch the emotions which were ready and waiting everywhere: these ~~experiences were such as to bring~~ into question the nature of things   and the poem seems not accurate enough   It is touched by current definitions of 'poetry'   I think it fails   This poem, with what had been experienced, this poem had to start fresh, absolutely anew   It is terrible, terrible, disheartening for this man, for this poem, to be touched by Pound by Eliot by St John Perse by— — — —O, this ~~is~~ junk, in the holocaust this is junk— — —He was, after all, afraid to risk failure— —or could not face these things without the mediation of another and ignorant poetry— — —
failure. or the provincialism of patriotism   *bound by the duties of patriotism or just*
afraid

        But of course if one is thinking of ninety-nine one hundredths of the stuff that is published, ~~even~~ of the stuff that is highly praised— — — —but why think of that   In the face of what happened to think of that!

Fatal inaccuracy in the quotation from his speech with which you begin the introduction: "when I write I am like a man praying"

Not, when I write I am like a man writing   Not even, when I write I am in the
same state as when I pray   Not even the openness of   When I write I am
as others are when they pray. but: when I write I am like an imaginary man who
is praying— —this is the theatric vision It is a long way from where he is   or
was   It is a long way from the serious poet

Sunday, Bloody Sunday— —the Bar Mitzvah, a self-satisfied, over-rich party   And
that Cantor does what he does does that to them ~~and among them and over them~~— —
in that minute everything is told   Nothing matters but that piece of music.
Nothing matters but that piece of music

---

each one holds the religion he is capable of holding   it makes very little difference
whose Bingo party they go to

There is some degree   some degree   in which, even aside from my own survival,
the survival of the Jews matters to me ˆ*more*ˆ than the survival of some other peoples I
don't know of any reason to be proud of this sentiment

        If I do harbour any such sentiment, I am not going to bask in the
warmth of those who share it

[p.2]

Someone has said   in a slightly different language: it is
nonsense to say that the square root of 456 = You

    Why?

ie why is nonsense? ~~Which is~~ A basic question
That haunts ~~idealism and the thematics~~ *philosophy*
The obverse of the epistemological question

[illegible] and in the ~~shapeless~~ desert would we have the oppressed, the suppressed
not pay with their lives for this order, these rules these laws, this rightness and wrong
~~ness~~, these judgements

Rather turn them loose, rather turn ourselves loose?

the old become orphans, perhaps they are glad of it, they seem to speak less often than
the young of Mother Nature— — —

---

        as the Greeks could not think of the slaves to do so would have ended
everything—the Gods, the stone statues the vows the oaths the honor the philosophy
the poetry—

Romantic egotism   without the power of observation, of precise observation:
without, one could say, intelligence.

[illegible]
What we have discovered is that the extreme point that can be reached by reason is an intolerable ~~nightmare~~ dream   or seem to have discovered

A romantic egotism operates largely among the young none of the intellectual systems now assuage our fears who are not young very young— — —

we feel that the bourgeois order has created a sterile and therefore intolerable life ~~but~~, *because* we have not heard the voices of the common man the common woman in other times—

Paz: solitude appears as 'a promise that our exile will end'
        a promise that one's exile will end[1]

the presence of a crowd— —I do not know why— —has the contrary meaning

[Note: this page is partially glued over another, half of which is visible and contains an autograph draft of paragraph 2 of p.1]

[p.3]
        The problem of personality and of the identity, the 'who am I?' or what am I/— —is it actually the future in question which puts everything in question?
        Man standing on a spring-board. He can make any number of accurate statements about himself   Including this: that he is standing on a spring board, and including also this, that he is not sure whether or not he is going to dive— —and whether, therefore, he will be in the air—will be in the water— — —

It is also true that   [illegible deletion]   all men who have lost a leg are one-legged men
— — —Is this what the question is?

A poem—still more the work of a new poet can have the effect of a light turned on which turns out as in a Dylan Thomas, the Alexandria Quartet, and such work, to have been not light but at ~~best~~ a new color

The solipsist position: that self-consciousness is unconditioned ((by any other actuality)) or is its ~~only~~ actuality.
Self consciousness in itself, of itself, carries the conviction of actuality   therefore the solipsist position perhaps is not important to dispute or to argue ~~over~~— — — — —
But it can be said that therefore we know of an actuality other than that, prior to that which is the consciousness' self-knowledge

---

(consciousness in any case is actual? [illegible] *we have our concept of actuality.*

[1] See Octavio Paz, *The Labyrinth of Solitude: Life and Thought in Mexico*, trans. Lysander Kemp (New York and London: Grove Press, 1961), 196: 'Solitude is both a sentence and an expiation. It is a punishment but it is also a promise that our exile will end. All human life is pervaded by this dialectic.'

The empty consciousness is not consciousness   'the skull spins/empty of sub-ject— —² ~~also~~ a pun, or rather the ~~inherent~~ incorrigible contradiction in the word 'subject'

The comparison between the subject and the object <u>is</u> consciousness

---

Science and poetry again—that poetry is more basic. It deals with more basic questions, it speaks of the self it must speak of the self   each self   *'science' is trying to avoid this.*

Since it carries the conviction of actuality, the solipsist position would be important only to technology—but it is not important precisely to technology—that is what we do know

---

But solipsism would say: self consciousness is absolutely unconditioned   One would derive from that simply the statement that anything is possible— — — —one can easily accept this without the extreme idealist ~~argument~~ position

---

The absolutely ~~unconditioned~~ knowledge [illegible] is consciousness' knowledge of itself

---

Say 'idealism' if you mean something having to do with ~~general~~ ideas   Use the word as a term of approval if you approve of a concern with ~~general~~ ideas

---

If you say eternal, it must HAVE BEEN in the poem   The hills don't become eternal with the word

[**Note:** this page is partially glued to another, part of which is visible and comprises largely illegible handwritten notes including:

(actuality other than that   <u>prior</u> to has ~~*which can*~~
be known   ~~*or proven to be*~~   ~~*has what the mind holds*~~]

[p.4]
The Poem (Imitating ^*or partly imitating*^ Hegel's words here) must descend into the depths of the subject matter itself

---

The words must descend into the ^*depth of the*^ subject matter itself

                    and how can they?   They cannot   But must
<u>Must</u> and <u>can't</u> are not contradictories   ~~Unfortunately~~

— — ~~or~~ *but* maybe we can?
Nothing good or evil happens that one cannot credit ~~In that~~ *For* one is someone else thereafter. *It happened to this other, the survivor.*

---

² See 'Some San Francisco Poems', NCP, 225: 'The skull spins | Empty of subject || The hollow ego || Flinching from the war's huge air . . .'.

— —in war?

One tires, tires and credits
Finally death   [illegible]
Ob via   the obvious
Like a fire of straws

The seriousness of the idea ^*must*^ descend s
Into the depth of the subject matter
it cannot/and MUST

We speak of emotion as all one has ~~It is obvious, isn't it? One has emotion or one has nothing~~

THE ACTUAL IS THE ESSENTIAL

THE ACTUAL IS THE MYSTERY

THe IMAGE THE SPATIAL DIMENSION, THE TEMPORAL DIMENSION: WITHOUT THIS THERE SEEMS NO PROOF, NO RECOGNITION, NO CONVICTION. ARGUMENT, CHATTER

Absence of the image, THE ABSENCE OF THE WORLD IN WHICH THE STATEMENT IS TRUE OR NOT — — — —   ~~THE POEM MUST CONCEIVE THE WORLD OR IT IS ARGUMENT, CHATTER~~

absence of the memory of truth. Chatter.

HOW ELSE BUT THE IMAGE CAN THE WORDS DESCEND IN TO THE SUBJECT MATTER ITSELF' (or rather, this ((from Hegel)) is what is meant by 'image'

'Those of feeble or weak minds are people who know the truth but only affirm it so far as is consistent with their own interest. But, apart from that, they renounce it' (Pascal)[3]   Pill-head philosophers

[**Note**: the following passage is glued as a flap at the top of p.4]

self-consciousness [illegible] of itself, ~~and~~ in itself carries the conviction of actuality

         useless to talk of this at the moment: there is such absolute acceptance of fantasy, dream-world as equivalent to the word 'art'—it is the now current form of the attack on art' on spirit, mind, [illegible deletion]. ~~Above all,~~ *First of all,* on the courageous mind— —

[**p. 5**]
         the makers of poem as object, those who confect, clothed and armoured in the words and phrases which first were made to tell one's nakedness   'The word

---

[3] Oppen's annotated copy of *Pensées: The Provincial Letters* by Blaise Pascal (New York: Random House, 1941) is held at the Mandeville Special Collections, University of California at San Diego.

comes to existence
and for the last time
as language'[4]

[Letter head] GEORGE OPPEN   2811 POLK STREET SAN FRANCISCO CALIFORNIA 94109

The work of art — —

a work of the intellect in that it marks the extreme outer limits of the ego but is not separate from the ego[5]

If separate from the ego it presents a false ego, which is charlatanism

If coterminous with the ego it ^*includes*^ ~~contains a strong touch of~~ [illegible] the charlatan

---

'The crutches'   Pride pleasure thought?
Whereas Doing what is approved in a group is a crutch sufficient to shore up an old barn

---

I must make <u>no</u> system, or I will be enslaved by another man's[6]

The division of the line: the cadence of disclosure ~~at the same time that it is everything else — —~~ a music, a comment on the syntax, a modification of the syntax, and form, which makes meaning possible to <u>grasp</u>

Say only what is obvious   And all else ~~which~~ that cannot be understood   But do not pontificate

---

Do not talk of the intelligible ~~The mathematicians can take care of that~~

Talk of what one cannot NOT see

I believe there must have been ^*early*^ in one's life, some dominant

---

The 'NY poets': rock-bottom frivolity, game-playing, achieves extremes of viciousness

---

⁴ This quotation, which Oppen uses many times in his notes in different forms, is unattributed and so far I have been unable to find a source. One possibility is the following passage in Wittgenstein's 'A Lecture on Ethics', *Philosophical Review*, 74/1 (Jan. 1965), 11: 'And I will now describe the experience of wondering at the existence of the world by saying: it is the experience of seeing the world as a miracle. Now I am tempted to say that the right expression in language for the miracle of the existence of the world, though it is not any proposition *in* language, is the existence of language itself.' Oppen knew the essay (see UCSD 16, 15, 4).
⁵ Oppen is quoting Plotinus. See above, p. 137.
⁶ See William Blake, *Jerusalem*, in *Complete Writings*, ed. Geoffrey Keynes (London: Oxford University Press, 1966), 629: 'I must Create a System or be enslav'd by another Man's'.

Bibliography

The Bibliography gives details of works referred to in the text; it is not intended to provide an exhaustive listing of relevant materials.

Works by George Oppen

Books

Collected Poems (London: Fulcrum Press, 1972).
Collected Poems (New York: New Directions, 1975).
The Daybooks and Essays of George Oppen, ed. Stephen Cope (Berkeley and Los Angeles: University of California Press, 2008).
Discrete Series (New York: Objectivist Press, 1934).
The Materials (New York: New Directions and San Francisco Review, 1962).
New Collected Poems of George Oppen, ed. Michael Davidson (New York: New Directions, 2002).
Of Being Numerous (New York: New Directions, 1968).
Primitive (Santa Barbara, Calif.: Black Sparrow Press, 1978).
Seascape: Needle's Eye (Fremont, Mich: The Sumac Press, 1972)
Selected Letters of George Oppen, ed. Rachel Blau DuPlessis (Durham, NC: Duke University Press, 1990).
Selected Poems of George Oppen, ed. and introd. Robert Creeley (New York: New Directions, 2003).
This In Which (New York: New Directions and San Francisco Review, 1965).

Essays, Interviews, and Working Papers

'An Adequate Vision: A George Oppen Daybook', ed. Michael Davidson, *Ironwood*, 26 (Fall 1985), 5–31.
'Anthropologist of Myself: A Selection from Working Papers of George Oppen', ed. Rachel Blau DuPlessis, *Sulfur*, 26 (Spring 1990), 135–64.
'"The Circumstances": Selections from Unpublished Poems and Working Papers of George Oppen', ed. Rachel Blau DuPlessis, *Sulfur*, 25 (Fall 1989), 10–43.
'A Conversation with George Oppen', conducted by Charles Amirkhanian and David Gitin, *Ironwood*, 5 (1975), 21–4.
'From Pipe-Stem Daybook Two', ed. Stephen Cope, *Jubilat*, 4 (2002), 40–55.
'An Interview with George and Mary Oppen', conducted by Kevin Power on 25 May 1975, *Montemora*, 4 (1978), 186–203.
'Interview with George Oppen', conducted by L. S. Dembo, *Contemporary Literature*, 10/2 (Spring 1969), 159–77.
'Interview with George Oppen', conducted by Reinhold Schiffer on 11 May 1975, *Sagetrieb*, 3/3 (Winter 1984), 9–23.

'Letters to Andy Meyer', *Ironwood*, 26 (Fall 1985), 104–12.

'Letters to June Oppen Degnan', *Ironwood*, 26 (Fall 1985), 215–36.

'Meaning to be Here: A Selection from the Daybook', ed. Cynthia Anderson, *Conjunctions*, 10 (1987), 186–208.

'The Mind's Own Place', *Kulchur*, 3/10 (Summer 1963), 2–8; repr. in *Selected Poems*, ed. Creeley, 173-82.

'Non-Resistance, etc. Or: Of the Guiltless', *West End*, 3/1 (1974), 5.

' "The Philosophy of the Astonished": Selections from the Working Papers of George Oppen', ed. Rachel Blau DuPlessis, *Sulfur*, 27 (Fall 1990), 202–20.

'Poetry and Politics: A Conversation with George and Mary Oppen', conducted by Burton Hatlen and Tom Mandel, in Hatlen (ed.), *George Oppen: Man and Poet*, 23–47.

'Pound in the U.S.A, 1969', *Sagetrieb*, 1/1 (1982), 119.

'*Primitive*: An Archaeology of the Omega Point', ed. Cynthia Anderson, *Ironwood*, 31/32 (Spring and Fall 1988), 306–23.

'A Selection from "Daybook One", "Daybook Two" and "Daybook Three" ', ed. Stephen Cope, *The Germ*, 2 (1999), 192–253.

'Selections from George Oppen's *Daybook*', ed. Dennis Young, *Iowa Review*, 18/3 (1988), 1–17.

'Statement on Poetics', *Sagetrieb*, 3/3 (1984), 25–7.

'Three Poets', *Poetry*, 100/5 (Aug. 1962), 329–32.

Works Cited

Adorno, T. W., *Essays on Music*, ed. Richard Leppert (Berkeley and Los Angeles: University of California Press, 2002).

—— *Hegel: Three Studies*, trans. Shierry Weber Nicholsen (Cambridge, Mass.: MIT Press, 1993).

—— *Negative Dialectics*, trans. E. B. Ashton (New York: Continuum Books, 1973).

—— *Notes to Literature*, 2 vols., trans. Shierry Weber Nicholsen (New York: Columbia University Press, 1992).

—— *Prisms*, trans. Samuel and Shierry Weber (Cambridge, Mass.: MIT Press, 1983).

Agamben, Giorgio, *Language and Death: The Place of Negativity*, trans. Karen E. Pinkus with Michael Hardt (Minneapolis: University of Minnesota Press, 1991).

—— *Remnants of Auschwitz: The Witness and the Archive*, trans. Daniel Heller-Roazen (New York: Zone Books, 1999).

Anhalt, Diana, *A Gathering of Fugitives: American Political Expatriates in Mexico, 1948–1965* (Santa Maria, Calif.: Archer Books, 2001).

Aquila, Richard E., 'Predication and Hegel's Metaphysics', *Kant-Studien*, 64 (1973), 231–45.

Auerbach, Eric, *Mimesis: The Representation of Reality in Western Literature*, trans. Willard R. Trask (Princeton: Princeton University Press, 1953).

Auster, Paul, 'An Interview with Edmond Jabès' (1979), repr. in Gould (ed.), *Sin of the Book*, 3–25.

Belgrad, Daniel, *The Culture of Spontaneity: Improvisation and the Arts in Postwar America* (Chicago: University of Chicago Press, 1998).

Bell, Daniel, 'The Background and Development of Marxian Socialism in the United States', in Donald Drew Egbert and Stow Persons (eds.), *Socialism and American Life*, 2 vols. (Princeton: Princeton University Press, 1952), i. 213–405.

Bennington, Geoffrey, *Legislations: The Politics of Deconstruction* (London: Verso, 1994).

Berg, Stephen, and Mezey, Robert (eds.), *The New Naked Poetry: Recent American Poetry in Open Forms* (Indianapolis: Bobbs-Merrill Co., 1976).

Berry, Eleanor, 'Language made Fluid: The Grammetrics of George Oppen's Recent Poetry', *Contemporary Literature*, 25/3 (1984), 305–22.

Blake, William, *Complete Writings*, ed. Geoffrey Keynes (London: Oxford University Press, 1966).

Blanchot, Maurice, 'Edmond Jabès' *Book of Questions*', *European Judaism*, 6/2 (Summer 1972), 34–7.

—— *The Infinite Conversation*, trans. Susan Hanson (Minneapolis: University of Minnesota Press, 1993).

Bloch, Eric, *Atheism and Christianity: The Religion of the Exodus and the Kingdom*, trans. J. T. Swann (1968; New York: Herder and Herder, 1972).

Blumenberg, Hans, *Shipwreck with Spectator: Paradigm of a Metaphor for Existence* (Cambridge, Mass.: MIT Press, 1997).

Bonnefoy, Yves, *The Act and the Place of Poetry: Selected Essays*, trans. John T. Naughton (Chicago: University of Chicago Press, 1989).

—— *Hier régnant désert* (Paris: Mercure de France, 1964).

—— *On the Motion and Immobility of Douve*, trans. Galway Kinnell (Newcastle upon Tyne: Bloodaxe Books, 1992).

Bowie, Andrew, *Aesthetics and Subjectivity: From Kant to Nietzsche* (Manchester: Manchester University Press, 1990).

Barzilai, Lyn Graham, *George Oppen: A Critical Study* (Jefferson, NC and London: McFarland and Company, 2006).

Bronk, William, *Life Supports: New and Collected Poems* (Jersey City, NJ: Talisman House, 1997).

Browder, Earl, *The Popular Front* (New York: International Publishers, 1938).

Brumbaugh, Robert S., *Plato for the Modern Age* (New York: Crowell-Collier, 1962).

Brustein, Robert, *The Culture Watch: Essays on Theatre and Society, 1969–1974* (New York: Alfred A. Knopf, 1975).

Buhle, Paul, *Radical Hollywood: The Untold Story behind Hollywood's Favorite Movies* (New York: New Press, 2002).

Bürger, Peter, *Theory of the Avant-Garde*, trans. Michael Shaw (Minneapolis: University of Minnesota Press, 1984).

Butler, Judith, *Subjects of Desire: Hegelian Reflexions in Twentieth-Century France* (New York: Columbia University Press, 1987).

Cahen, Didier, *Edmond Jabès* (Paris: Pierre Belfond, 1991).

Caputo, John D., *The Mystical Element in Heidegger's Thought* (Athens, Ohio: Ohio University Press, 1978).

Carlyle, Thomas, *Critical and Miscellanous Essays*, 7 vols. (London: Chapman & Hall, 1888).

Celan, Paul, *Collected Prose*, trans. Rosmarie Waldrop (Manchester: Carcanet Press, 1986).

Chilton, Randolph, 'The Place of Being in the Poetry of George Oppen', in Hatlen (ed.), *George Oppen: Man and Poet*, 89–112.

Chisholm, Lawrence W., *Fenollosa: The Far East and American Culture* (New Haven: Yale University Press, 1963).

Clark, Timothy, *The Poetics of Singularity* (Edinburgh: Edinburgh University Press, 2005).

Cohen, Josh, *Interrupting Auschwitz: Art, Religion, Philosophy* (New York and London: Continuum Books, 2003).

Connolly, William E., *Identity/Difference: Democratic Negotiations of Political Paradox* (Minneapolis: University of Minnesota Press, 2002).

Cotkin, George, *Existential America* (Baltimore: Johns Hopkins, 2003).

Crozier, Andrew, 'Inaugural and Valedictory: the Early Poetry of George Oppen', in R. W. Butterfield (ed.), *Modern American Poetry* (New York: Barnes & Noble, 1984), 142–57.

Cuddihy, Michael, *Try Ironwood: An Editor Remembers* (Boston: Rowan Tree Press, 1990).

Davidson, Michael, 'Dismantling "Mantis": Reification and Objectivist Poetics', *American Literary History*, 3/3 (Fall 1991), 521–41.

Davie, Donald, 'His Themes', *Encounter*, 31 (Oct. 1973), 59–60.

Dembo, L. S., *The Monological Jew: A Literary Study* (Madison: University of Wisconsin Press, 1988).

—— 'The "Objectivist" Poet: Four Interviews', *Contemporary Literature*, 10/2 (Spring 1969), 155–219.

Demske, James M., *Being, Man, and Death: A Key to Heidegger* (Lexington: Kentucky University Press, 1970).

Derrida, Jacques, *Aporias*, trans. Thomas Dutoit (Stanford, Calif.: Stanford University Press, 1993).

—— *Resistances of Psychoanalysis*, trans. Peggy Kamuf et al. (Stanford, Calif.: Stanford University Press, 1998).

—— *Writing and Difference*, trans. Alan Bass (London: Routledge & Kegan Paul, 1978).

Dimitroff, G., *The United Front* (New York: International Publishers, 1938).

Duncan, Robert, and Levertov, Denise, *The Letters of Robert Duncan and Denise Levertov*, ed. Robert J. Bertholf and Albert Gelpi (Stanford, Calif.: Stanford University Press, 2004).

DuPlessis, Rachel Blau, *Blue Studios: Poetry and its Cultural Work* (Tuscaloosa: University of Alabama Press, 2006).

—— 'Objectivist Poetics and Political Vision: A Study of Oppen and Pound', in Hatlen (ed.), *George Oppen: Man and Poet*, 123–48.

—— 'An Oppen Chronology', in *Selected Poems of George Oppen*, ed. and introd. Creeley, 191–8.

Eckhart, Meister, *Meister Eckhart: A Modern Translation*, trans. Raymond Bernard Blakney (New York: Harper and Brothers, 1941).

Eliot, Charles W. (ed.), *Voyages and Travels, Ancient and Modern* (New York: Collier & Son, 1910).

Enzensberger, Hans, *The Consciousness Industry*, ed. Michael Roloff (New York: Seabury Press, 1974).

Faucherau, Serge, 'Three Oppen Letters with a Note', *Ironwood*, 5 (1975), 78–85.

Felstiner, John, *Paul Celan: Poet, Survivor, Jew* (New Haven: Yale University Press, 1995).

Fenollosa, Ernest, *The Chinese Written Character as a Medium for Poetry*, ed. Ezra Pound (San Francisco: City Lights Books, 1969).

Field, Frederick Vanderbilt, *From Right to Left: An Autobiography* (Westport, Conn.: Lawrence Hill and Co., 1983).

Forrester, John, *The Seductions of Psychoanalysis: Freud, Lacan, and Derrida* (Cambridge: Cambridge University Press, 1990).

Franke, William, 'The Singular and the Other at the Limits of Language in the Apophatic Poetics of Edmond Jabès and Paul Celan', *New Literary History*, 36 (2005), 621–38.

Fredman, Stephen, *A Menorah for Athena: Charles Reznikoff and the Jewish Dilemmas of Objectivist Poetry* (Chicago: University of Chicago Press, 2001).

Freud, Sigmund, *Pelican Freud Library*, ix. *Case Histories II*, ed. Angela Richards, trans. James Strachey (Harmondsworth: Penguin Books, 1981).

Froment-Meurice, Marc, *That Is To Say: Heidegger's Poetics* (Stanford, Calif.: Stanford University Press, 1998).

Frye, Northrop, *Fearful Symmetry: A Study of William Blake* (Princeton: Princeton University Press, 1969).

Gann, Kyle, *The Music of Conlon Nancarrow* (Cambridge: Cambridge University Press, 1995).

Giorcelli, Cristina (ed.), *The Idea and the Thing in Modernist American Poetry* (Palermo: Ila Palma, 2001).

Godzich, Wlad, and Kittany, Jeffrey, *The Emergence of Prose: An Essay in Poetics* (Minneapolis: University of Minnesota Press, 1987).

Goldberg, Chad Alan, 'Haunted by the Specter of Communism: Collective Identity and Resource Mobilization in the Demise of the Workers Alliance of America', *Theory and Society*, 32 (2003), 725–73.

Gould, Eric (ed.), *The Sin of the Book: Edmond Jabès* (Lincoln, Nebr.: University of Nebraska Press, 1985).

Groth, Miles, *Translating Heidegger* (New York: Humanity Books, 2004).

Geuss, Raymond, *Morality, Culture, and History: Essays on German Philosophy* (Cambridge: Cambridge University Press, 1999).

Gunn, Drewey Wayne, *American and British Writers in Mexico, 1556–1973* (Austin: University of Texas Press, 1974).

Halliburton, David, *Poetic Thinking: An Approach to Heidegger* (Chicago: Chicago University Press, 1981).

Hamalian, Linda, *A Life of Kenneth Rexroth* (New York: W. W. Norton, 1991).

Harries, Karsten, 'Language and Silence: Heidegger's Dialogue with Georg Trakl', in William Spanos (ed.), *Martin Heidegger and the Question of Literature: Toward a Postmodern Literary Hermeneutics* (Bloomington: Indiana University Press, 1976), 155–71.

Hatlen, Burton, 'Feminine Technologies: George Oppen talks at Denise Levertov', *American Poetry Review*, 22/3 (1993), 9–14.

—— (ed.), *George Oppen: Man and Poet* (Orono, Me.: National Poetry Foundation, 1981).

—— ' "Not Altogether Lone in a Lone Universe": George Oppen's *The Materials*', in Hatlen (ed.), *George Oppen: Man and Poet*, 325–57.

—— 'Opening Up the Text: George Oppen's "Of Being Numerous" ', *Ironwood*, 26 (Fall 1985), 263–95.

Heale, Michael, *The Sixties in America: History, Politics and Protest* (Edinburgh: Edinburgh University Press, 2001).

Hegel, Georg Wilhelm Friedrich, *The Phenomenology of Spirit*, trans. A. V. Miller (Oxford: Oxford University Press, 1977).

Heidegger, Martin, 'The Age of the World View', trans. Marjorie Green, in William V. Spanos (ed.), *Martin Heidegger and the Question of Literature: Toward a Postmodern Literary Hermeneutics* (Bloomington: Indiana University Press, 1976), 1–15.

—— *Being and Time*, trans. John Macquarrie and Edward Robinson (Oxford: Blackwell, 1962).

—— *Discourse on Thinking*, trans. John M. Anderson and E. Hans Freund (New York: Harper & Row, 1966).

—— *Essays in Metaphysics: Identity and Difference*, trans. Kurt F. Leidecker (New York: Philosophical Library Inc., 1960).

—— *Existence and Being*, ed. and introd. Werner Brock (Chicago: Henry Regnery Company, 1949).

—— *Identity and Difference*, trans. Joan Stambaugh (New York: Harper & Row, 1969).

—— *An Introduction to Metaphysics*, trans. Ralph Manheim (New Haven: Yale University Press, 1959; New York: Anchor Books, 1961).

—— *Kant and the Problem of Metaphysics* (Bloomington: Indiana University Press, 1962).

—— *On the Way to Language*, trans. Peter D. Hertz (New York: Harper & Row, 1971).

—— *Poetry, Language, Thought*, trans. Albert Hofstadter (New York: Harper & Row, 1971).

—— *The Question of Being* (1958; London: Vision Press, 1959).

—— *What is Philosophy?*, trans. William Kluback and Jean T. Wilde (London: Vision Press, 1958).

Heller, Michael, 'Conviction's Net of Branches', in Hatlen (ed.), *George Oppen: Man and Poet*, 417–28.

—— ' "Knowledge is Loneliness Turning": Oppen Going Down Middle-Voice', *Ironwood*, 26 (Fall 1985), 51–61.

Hesse, Herman, *Magister Ludi (The Glass Bead Game)*, trans. Richard and Clara Winston (1943; New York: Bantam Books, 1970).

Hewitt, Andrew, *Fascist Modernism: Aesthetics, Politics, and the Avant-Garde* (Stanford, Calif.: Stanford University Press, 1993).

Hittinger, John P., *Liberty, Wisdom, and Grace: Thomism and Democratic Political Theory* (Lanham, Md.: Lexington Books, 2002).

Hughes, E. R. (trans.), *The Art of Letters: Lu Chi's 'Wen Fu', AD 302: A Translation and Comparative Study* (New York: Pantheon Books, 1951).

Izenberg, Oren, 'Oppen's Silence, Crusoe's Silence, and the Silence of Other Minds', *Modernism/Modernity*, 13/1 (2006), 787–811.

Jabès, Edmond, 'Answer to a Letter', with J. H. Prynne, 'Es Lebe der König' and Paul Celan, 'Conversation in the Mountains', *The Literary Supplement, Writings*, i (London: The Literary Supplement, 1973), 4–8.

—— *The Book of Questions*, trans. Rosmarie Waldrop, 2 vols. (Hanover and London: Wesleyan University Press, 1991).

—— 'The Book of the Absent: Third Part', trans. Rosmarie Waldrop, *European Judaism*, 7/2 (Summer 1973), 11–19.

—— 'From *The Book of Questions*', *Tree*, 3 (Winter 1972), 149–57.

—— *From the Desert to the Book: Dialogues with Marcel Cohen*, trans. Pierre Joris (Barrytown, NY: Station Hill, 1990)

—— 'The Question of Displacement into the Lawfulness of the Book', trans. Rosmarie Waldrop, in Gould (ed.), *Sin of the Book*, 227–44.

James, Henry, *The Complete Tales of Henry James*, ed. and introd. Leon Edel, vol. xi (London: Rupert Hart-Davis, 1964).

Jameson, Fredric, *Marxism and Form: Twentieth-Century Dialectical Theories of Literature* (Princeton: Princeton University Press, 1971).

Jaron, Steven, *Edmond Jabès: The Hazard of Exile* (Oxford: Legenda, 2003).

Jenkins, G. Matthew, 'Saying Obligation: George Oppen's Poetry and Levinasian Ethics', *Journal of American Studies*, 37/3 (2003), 407–33.

Josephson, Matthew, *Infidel in the Temple: A Memoir of the Nineteen-Thirties* (New York: Knopf, 1967).

Jung, Carl, *Answer to Job*, trans. R. F. C. Hull (London: Routledge & Kegan Paul, 1954).

—— *Memories, Dreams, Reflections*, trans. Richard and Clara Winston (London: Collins, and Routledge and Kegan Paul, 1963).

Kaufman, Shirley, 'The Obvious and the Hidden: Some Thoughts about "Disasters"', *Ironwood*, 26 (Fall 1985), 152–8.

—— 'Preface to Some letters from George Oppen to Shirley Kaufman', *http://writing.upenn.edu/epc/authors/oppen/oppen_Kaufman_preface_to_letters. html*.

—— 'Who are the Living and Who are the Dead? (the Poetry of Abba Kovner)', *European Judaism*, 8/1 (Winter 1973/4), 23–8.

Kaufmann, Walter, *From Dostoevsky to Sartre* (1956; New York: Meridian Books, 1958).

—— *Hegel: Reinterpretation, Texts, and Commentary* (New York: Doubleday and Company, 1965).

Kenner, Hugh, *A Homemade World: The American Modernist Writers* (London: Marion Boyars, 1977).

Kerouac, Jack, *On the Road* (New York: Viking, 1957).

Kimmelman, Burt, *The 'Winter Mind': William Bronk and American Letters* (Madison: Farleigh Dickinson, 1998).

King, Magda, *A Guide to Heidegger's* Being and Time (Albany, NY: SUNY, 2001).

Kolb, David, *The Critique of Pure Modernity: Hegel, Heidegger, and After* (Chicago: University of Chicago Press, 1986).

Kovner, Abba, *A Canopy in the Desert: Selected Poems*, trans. Shirley Kaufman (Pittsburgh: University of Pittsburgh Press, 1973).

—— *My Little Sister and Selected Poems*, trans. Shirley Kaufman (Ohio: Oberlin College Press, 1986).

—— and Sachs, Nelly, *Selected Poems*, trans. Shirley Kaufman et al. (Harmondsworth: Penguin Books, 1971).

Lacoue-Labarthe, Philippe, and Nancy, Jean-Luc, *Retreating the Political*, trans. Simon Sparks (London: Routledge, 1997).

Lang, Berel, 'Writing-the-Holocaust: Jabès and the Measure of History', in Gould (ed.), *Sin of the Book*, 191–206.

Lauer, Quentin, *A Reading of Hegel's* Phenomenology of Spirit (New York: Fordham University Press, 1976).

Levertov, Denise, *Poems 1960–1967* (New York: New Directions, 1968).

—— *The Poet in the World* (New York: New Directions, 1973).

Levinas, Emmanuel, 'The Trace of the Other', trans. Alfonso Lingis, in Mark C. Taylor (ed.), *Deconstruction in Context: Literature and Philosophy* (Chicago: University of Chicago Press, 1986).

—— and Starobinski, Jean, 'Jabès and the Difficulty of Being Jewish', trans. Susan Knight, *European Judaism*, 7/2 (Summer 1973), 20–2.

Lorence, James J., *Organizing the Unemployed: Community and Union Activists in the Industrial Heartland* (Albany, NY: SUNY Press, 1996).

Lyotard, Jean-François, *The Differend: Phrases in Dispute*, trans. Georges Van Den Abbeele (Manchester: Manchester University Press, 1998).

—— 'The Survivor', in *Toward the Postmodern*, ed. Robert Harvey and Martin S. Roberts (Atlantic Highlands, NJ and London: Humanities Press, 1993), 144–63.

McAleavey, David, 'Oppen on Literature, Literary Figures and Issues', *Sagetrieb*, 6 (1987), 109–35.

—— 'The Oppens: Remarks towards Biography', *Ironwood*, 26 (Fall 1985), 309–18.

McGilligan, Patrick, and Buhle, Paul, *Tender Comrades: A Backstory of the Hollywood Blacklist* (New York: St Martin's Griffin, 1999).

MacLeish, Archibald, *J.B.* (Cambridge, Mass.: The Riverside Press, 1958).

Mailer, Norman, *Advertisements for Myself* (1959: Cambridge, Mass.: Harvard University Press, 1992).

—— *Barbary Shore* (1952; St Albans: Panther Books, 1972).

—— *The Bullfight: A Photographic Narrative with Text by Norman Mailer* (New York: Macmillan, 1967).

Marcuse, Herbert, *Reason and Revolution: Hegel and the Rise of Social Theory*, 2nd edn. (London: Routledge and Kegan Paul, 1968).

Marinaccio, Rocco, 'George Oppen's "I've Seen America" Book: *Discrete Series* and the Thirties Road Narrative', *American Literature*, 74/3 (2002), 539–69.

Maritain, Jacques, *Creative Intuition in Art and Poetry* (New York: Meridian Books, 1955).

—— *Existence and the Existent: An Essay on Christian Existentialism*, trans. Lewis Galantiere and Gerald B. Phelan (1948; Garden City, NY: Image Books, 1956).

Marriott, D. S., 'Aspects of *Ousia* and Transitive Verb Form in Fenollosa's *The Chinese Written Character* and Pound's *Cantos*', in Karl Simms (ed.), *Language and the Subject* (Amsterdam and Atlanta, Ga.: Rodopi, 1997), 65–73.

—— 'An Introduction to the Poetry of J. H. Prynne, 1962–1977', D.Phil. diss., University of Sussex, 1993.

Marx, Werner, *Hegel's* Phenomenology of Spirit: *Its Point and Purpose—A Commentary on the Preface and Introduction* (New York and London: Harper & Row, 1975).

Mencius, *The Works of Mencius*, trans. and ed. James Legge (New York: Dover, 1970).

Miller, Tyrus, *Late Modernism: Politics, Fiction, and the Arts between the World Wars* (Berkeley and Los Angeles: University of California Press, 1999).

Milton, John, *The Poetical Works of John Milton*, ed. Helen Darbishire (London: Oxford University Press, 1963).

Mitchell, Stephen (trans. and introd), *The Book of Job* (San Francisco, Calif.: North Point Press, 1987).

Mulhall, Stephen, *Heidegger and* Being and Time (London: Routledge, 1996).

Nancy, Jean-Luc, *Hegel: The Restlessness of the Negative*, trans. Jason Smith and Steven Miller (Minneapolis: University of Minnesota Press, 2002).

Naughton, John T., *The Poetics of Yves Bonnefoy* (Chicago: University of Chicago Press, 1984).

Naylor, Paul, 'The Pre-Position of Being, Seeing, and Knowing in George Oppen's Poetry', *Contemporary Literature*, 32/1 (1991), 100–15.

Negri, Antonio, *Il lavoro di Giobbe* (Rome: Manifestolibri, 2002).

Nemo, Philippe, *Job et l'excès du mal* (Paris: Bernard Grasset, 1978).

Nicholls, Peter, ' "2 doits to a boodle": Reckoning with *Thrones*', *Textual Practice*, 18/2 (June 2004), 233–49.

—— 'Divergences: Modernism, Postmodernism, Jameson and Lyotard', *Critical Quarterly*, 33/3 (1991), 1–18.

—— *Ezra Pound: Politics, Economics and Writing* (Basingstoke: Macmillan, 1984).

—— 'Lorine Niedecker: Rural Surreal', in Jenny Penberthy (ed.), *Lorine Niedecker: Woman and Poet* (Orono, Me.: National Poetry Foundation, 1996), 193–217.

—— 'Modernising Modernism: From Pound to Oppen', *Critical Quarterly*, 44/2 (Summer 2002), 41–58.

—— *Modernisms: A Literary Guide* (Basingstoke: Palgrave Macmillan, 1995).

—— 'Of Being Ethical: Reflections on George Oppen', in Rachel Blau DuPlessis and Peter Quartermain (eds.), *The Objectivist Nexus: Essays in Cultural Poetics* (Tuscaloosa: University of Alabama Press, 1999), 240–53.

Nietzsche, Friedrich, *On the Genealogy of Morals, Ecce Homo*, trans. Walter Kaufmann (New York: Vintage Books, 1969).

Nietzsche, Friedrich, *Daybreak: Thoughts on the Prejudices of Morality*, trans. R. J. Hollingdale (Cambridge: Cambridge University Press, 1997).

O'Gorman, Farrell, 'The Angelic Artist in the Fiction of Flannery O'Connor and Walker Percy', *Renascence*, 53/1 (Fall 2000), 61–81.

Olson, Charles, *Human Universe and Other Essays*, ed. Donald Allen (New York: Grove Press, 1967).

Oppen, Mary, *Meaning a Life: An Autobiography* (Santa Barbara, Calif.: Black Sparrow Press, 1978).

Peck, John, 'George Oppen and the World in Common: A Descriptive Polemic', in Hatlen (ed.), *George Oppen: Man and Poet*, 63–87.

Perloff, Marjorie, *Radical Artifice: Writing Poetry in the Age of Media* (Chicago: University of Chicago Press, 1991).

Peterson, Jeffrey, 'George Oppen', in *Dictionary of Literary Biography: American Poets since World War II, 4th Ser.*, ed. Joseph Conte et al. (Farmington Mills, Mich.: Gale Research Inc., 1996), 188–206.

Piven, Francis Fox, and Cloward, Richard A, *Poor People's Movements: Why They Succeed, How They Fail* (New York: Pantheon Books, 1977).

Plato, *The Republic*, trans. Benjamin Jowett (Oxford: Clarendon Press, 1888).

Plotinus, *Plotinus*, trans. A. H. Armstrong (New York: Collier Books, 1962).

Pope, Marvin H. (trans. and introd.), *The Anchor Bible: Job* (Garden City, NY: Doubleday & Company, 1965).

Pound, Ezra, *ABC of Reading* (London: Faber and Faber, 1961).

—— 'The Approach to Paris . . . V', *New Age*, 13/23 (2 Oct. 1913), 662–4.

—— *The Cantos* (London: Faber and Faber, 1994).

—— *Gaudier-Brzeska: A Memoir* (1916; Hessle: Marvel Press, 1960).

—— *Literary Essays*, ed. T. S. Eliot (London: Faber and Faber Ltd, 1968).

—— *Selected Letters of Ezra Pound 1907–1941*, ed. D. D. Paige (London: Faber and Faber, 1971).

Preda, Roxana, *Ezra Pound's (Post)Modern Poetics and Politics: Logocentrism, Language and Truth* (New York: Peter Lang, 2001).

Ricoeur, Paul, *Time and Narrative*, 3 vols., trans. Kathleen Blamey and David Pellauer (Chicago: University of Chicago Press, 1988).

Riddel, Joseph, 'Decentering the Image: The "Project" of "American" Poetics', in Josué Harrari (ed.), *Textual Strategies: Perpectives in Post-Structuralist Criticism* (London: Methuen, 1980).

Riley, Denise, *The Words of Selves: Identification, Solidarity, Irony* (Stanford, Calif.: Stanford University Press, 2000).

Rilke, Rainer Maria, *Selected Works*, ii. *Poetry*, trans. J. B. Leishman (London: Hogarth Press, 1960).

Rosenzweig, Roy, ' "Socialism in Our Time": The Socialist Party and the Unemployed, 1929–1936', *Labor History*, 20 (Fall 1979), 485–509.

Rothenberg, Jerome (ed.), *Technicians of the Sacred: A Range of Poetries from Africa, America, Asia & Oceania* (1968; New York: Anchor Books, 1969).

—— *Poland/1931* (New York: New Directions, 1974).

Rouverol, Jean, *Refugees from Hollywood: A Journal of the Blacklist Years* (Albuquerque: University of New Mexico Press, 2000).

Safranski, Rudiger, *Martin Heidegger: Between Good and Evil* (Cambridge, Mass.: Harvard University Press, 1998).

Said, Edward W., *On Late Style: Music and Literature Against the Grain*, introd. Michael Wood (New York: Pantheon Books, 2006).

Sandburg, Carl, *Complete Poems* (New York: Harcourt, Brace, 1950).

Santner, Eric L., *On the Psychotheology of Everyday Life: Reflections on Freud and Rosenzweig* (Chicago: University of Chicago Press, 2001).

Sartre, Jean-Paul, *Being and Nothingness: An Essay on Phenomenological Ontology*, trans. Hazel E. Barnes (1957; London and New York, Routledge, 2003).

—— *Critique of Dialectical Reason*, trans. Alan Sheridan-Smith, ed. Jonathan Reé (London: NLB, 1976).

—— *Nausea*, trans. Lloyd Alexander (1949; London: Hamish Hamilton, 1962).

—— *Nausea*, trans. Robert Baldick (Harmondsworth: Penguin Books, 1965).

—— *Search for a Method*, trans. Hazel E. Barnes (1963; New York: Vintage Books, 1968).

Schneidau, Herbert N., *Ezra Pound: The Image and the Real* (Baton Rouge: Louisiana State University Press, 1969).

Schreiner, Susan, *Where Shall Wisdom Be Found? Calvin's Exegesis of Job from Medieval and Modern Perspectives* (Chicago: University of Chicago Press, 1994).

Schutz, Alfred, *The Phenomenology of the Social World*, trans. George Walsh and Frederick Lehnert (London: Heinemann, 1972).

Schwartz, Stephen, *From West to East: California and the Making of the American Mind* (New York: The Free Press, 1998).

Sharp, Tom, 'The Objectivists' Publications', *Sagetrieb*, 3/3 (Winter 1984), 41–7.

Simic, Charles, *White* (New York: New Rivers Press, 1972).

Stevens, Wallace, *Collected Poetry and Prose* (New York: The Library of America, 1997).

Taggart, John, 'Walk-Out: Rereading George Oppen', *Chicago Review*, 44/2 (1998), 29–93.

Taylor, Charles, *Hegel* (Cambridge: Cambridge University Press, 1975).

Thackrey, Susan, *George Oppen: A Radical Practice* (San Francisco, Calif.: O Books, 2001).

Tytell, John, *The Living Theatre: Art, Exile and Outrage* (London: Methuen, 1997).

Vangelisti, Paul, *Communion* (Fairfax, Calif.: The Red Hill Press, 1970).

Versényi, Laszlo, *Heidegger, Being and Truth* (New Haven: Yale University Press, 1965).

Vescia, Monique Claire, *Depresssion Glass: Documentary Photography and the Medium of the Camera Eye in Charles Reznikoff, George Oppen, and William Carlos Williams* (New York and London: Routledge, 2006).

Wardi, Eynel, *Once below a Time: Dylan Thomas, Julia Kristeva, and Other Speaking Subjects* (Albany, NY: SUNY, 2000).

Weber, Samuel, *Return to Freud: Jacques Lacan's Dislocation of Psychoanalysis*, trans. Michael Levine (Cambridge: Cambridge University Press, 1991).

Weil, Simone, *Waiting on God*, trans. Emma Craufurd (London: Routledge and Kegan Paul, 1951).

Weltner, Peter, 'George Oppen's Last Poems: I would go out past the axioms of wandering', *Ironwood*, 26 (Fall 1985), 296–308.

White, David A., *Heidegger and the Language of Poetry* (Lincoln, Nebr.: University of Nebraska Press, 1978).

Whitman, Walt, *The Portable Walt Whitman*, ed. Mark Van Doren (New York: Viking Press, 1969).

Will, Frederic, *Literature Inside Out: Ten Speculative Essays* (Cleveland, Ohio: Press of Western Reserve University, 1966).

Williams, William Carlos, *The Autobiography* (New York: Random House, 1951).

—— *The Collected Poems 1909–1939*, ed. A. Walton Litz and Christopher MacGowan (Manchester: Carcanet Press, 1986).

—— *The Selected Letters*, ed. John C. Thirlwall (New York: New Directions, 1957).

Woodcock, George, *To the City of the Dead: An Account of Travels in Mexico* (London: Faber and Faber, 1957).

Woods, Tim, *The Poetics of the Limit: Ethics and Politics in Modern and Contemporary American Poetry* (Basingstoke: Palgrave, 2003).

Yeats, W. B., *The Poems*, ed. Daniel Albright (London: Dent & Sons, Ltd., 1990).

Young, Dennis, 'Conversation with Mary Oppen', *Iowa Review*, 18/3 (1987), 18–47.

Young, Julian, *Heidegger's Later Philosophy* (Cambridge: Cambridge University Press, 2002).

Ziarek, Krzystof, *The Historicity of Experience: Modernity, the Avant-Garde, and the Event* (Evanston, Ill.: Northwestern University Press, 2001).

—— 'The Reception of Heidegger's Thought in American Literary Criticism', *diacritics*, 19/3–4 (1989), 114–27.

Zukofsky, Louis, *All: The Collected Shorter Poems* (New York: Norton, 1971).

—— (ed.), *An 'Objectivists' Anthology* (Le Beausset and New York: To Publishers, 1932).

—— 'Sincerity and Objectification', *Poetry*, 37/5 (Feb. 1931), 272–85.

Index